IMAGES OF THE HUMAN BODY

SHAMBHALA AGILE RABBIT EDITIONS

BOSTON

1999

IMAGES OF THE HUMAN BODY

Shambhala Publications, Inc.
Horticultural Hall
300 Massachusetts Avenue
Boston, Massachusetts 02115
http://www.shambhala.com

9 8 7 6 5 4 3 2 1
Printed in Singapore
∞ This edition is printed on acid-free paper that meets the American National Standards Institute z39.48 Standard.
Distributed in the United States by Random House, Inc., and in Canada by Random House of Canada Ltd

See page 8 for Library of Congress Cataloging-in-Publication data

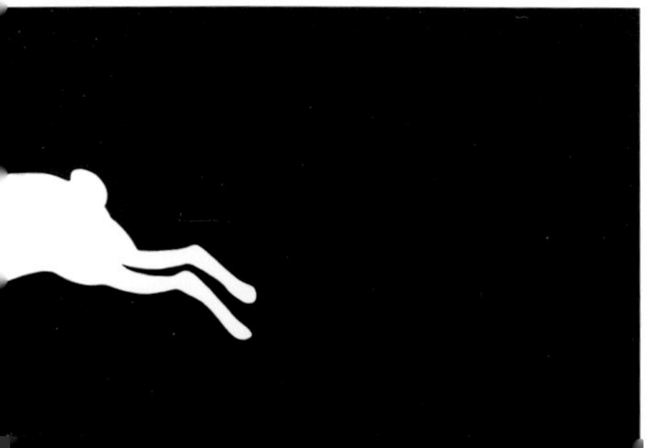

Other books with CD-ROM by Shambhala Agile Rabbit Editions:

ISBN 1-57062-477-1 Batik Patterns
ISBN 1-57062-480-1 Chinese Patterns
ISBN 1-57062-483-6 Decorated Initials
ISBN 1-57062-478-x Floral Patterns
ISBN 1-57062-484-4 Graphic Frames
ISBN 1-57062-482-8 Sports Pictures
ISBN 1-57062-481-x Transport Pictures

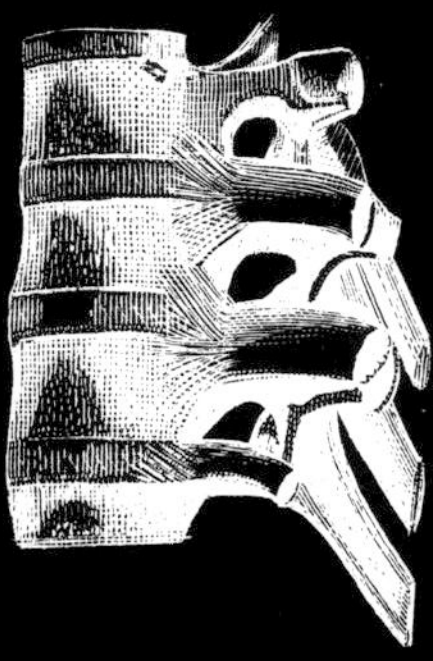

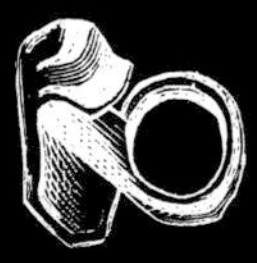

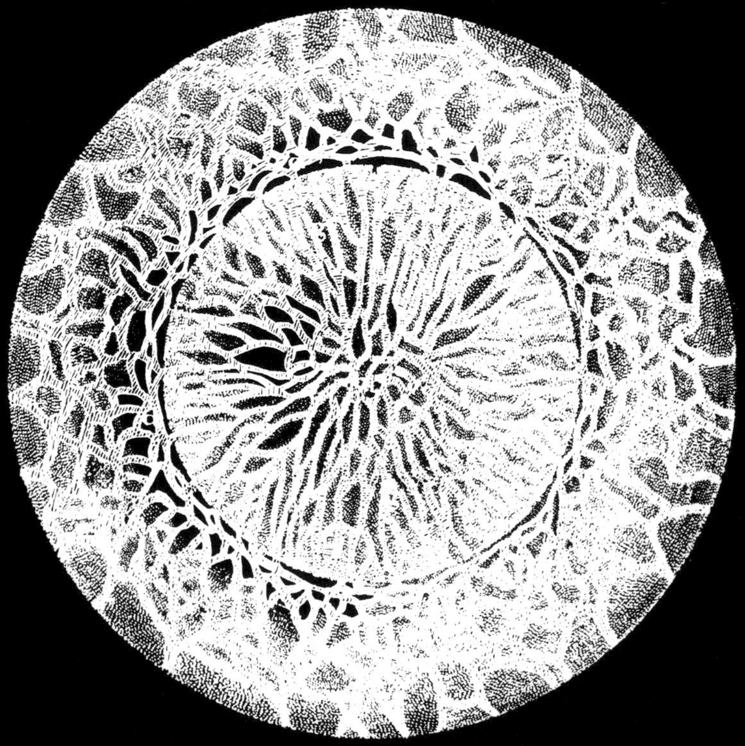

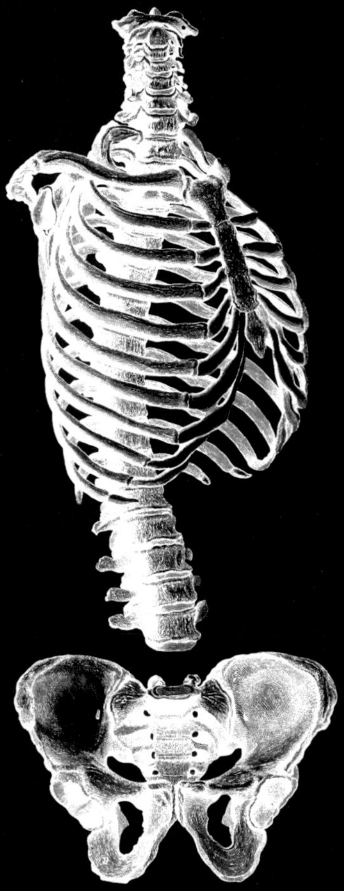

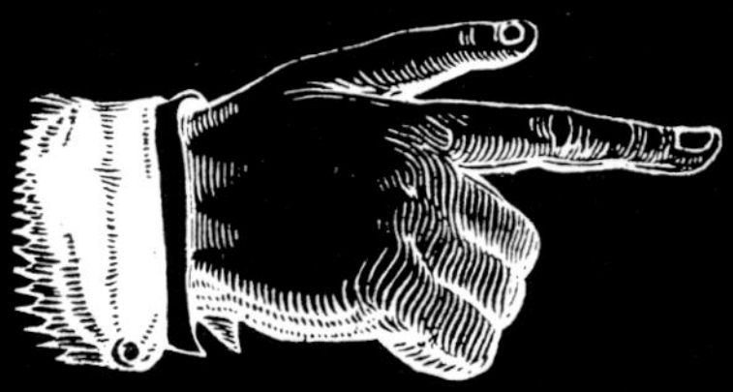

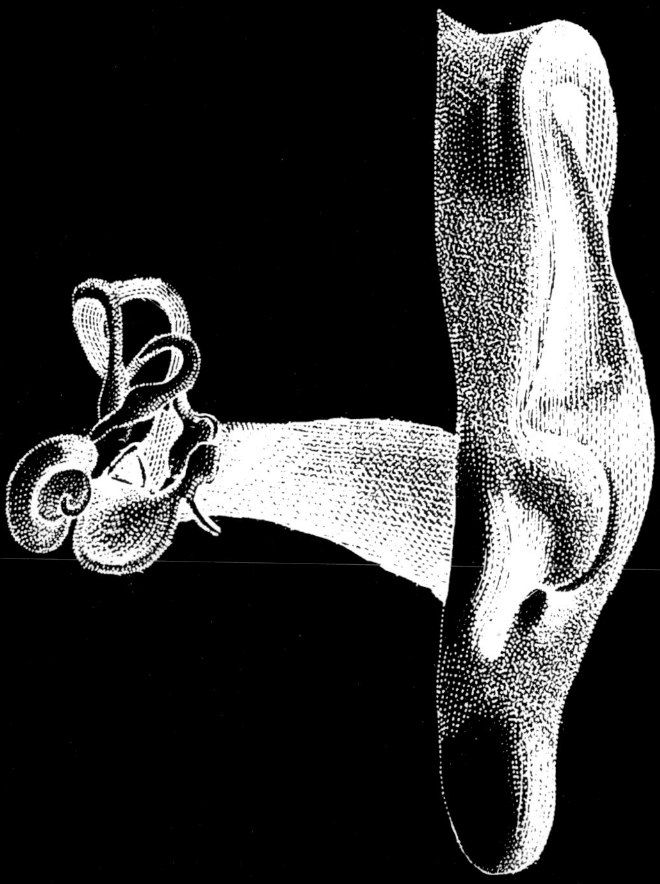

Library of Congress Cataloging-in-Publication Data

Roojen, Pepin van.
Images of the human body / Pepin van Roojen. – 1st ed.
p. cm.
ISBN 1-57062-479-8 (alk. paper)
1. Body, Human–Atlases I. Title.
QM25.R585 1999
611'.022'2–dc21 98-52470
CIP

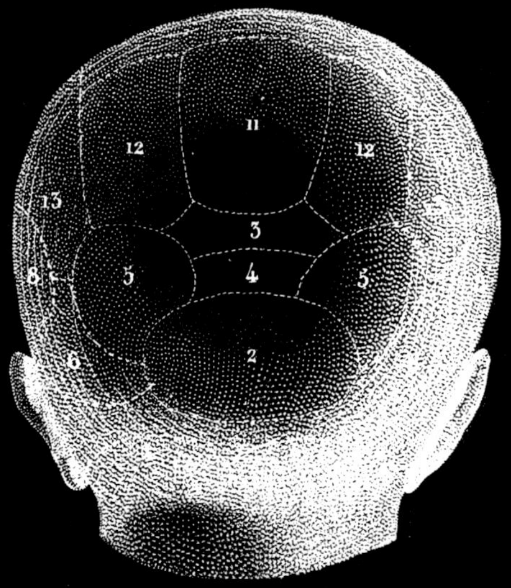

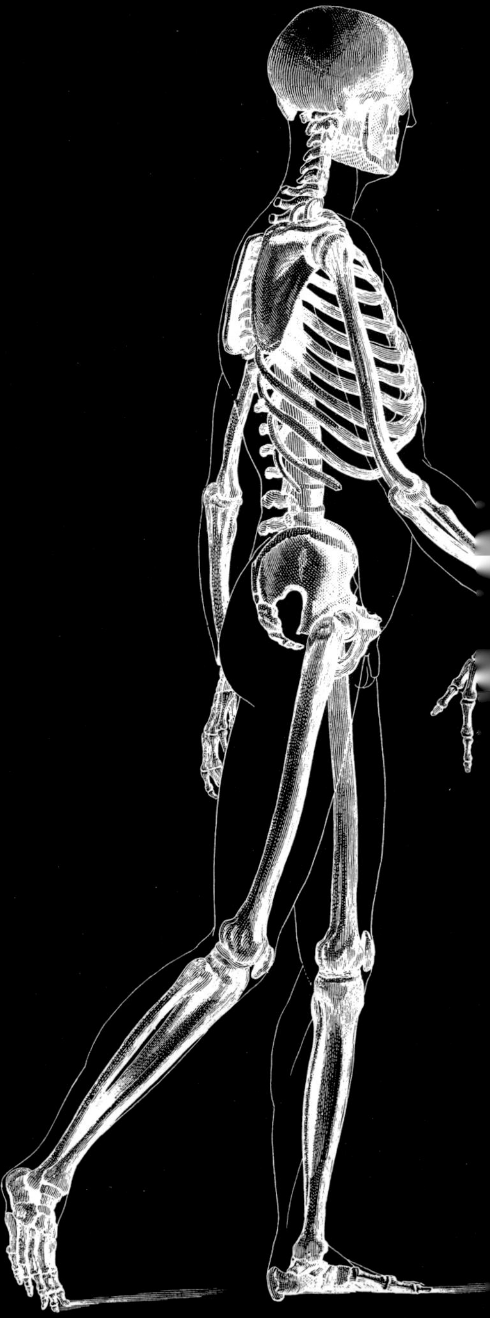

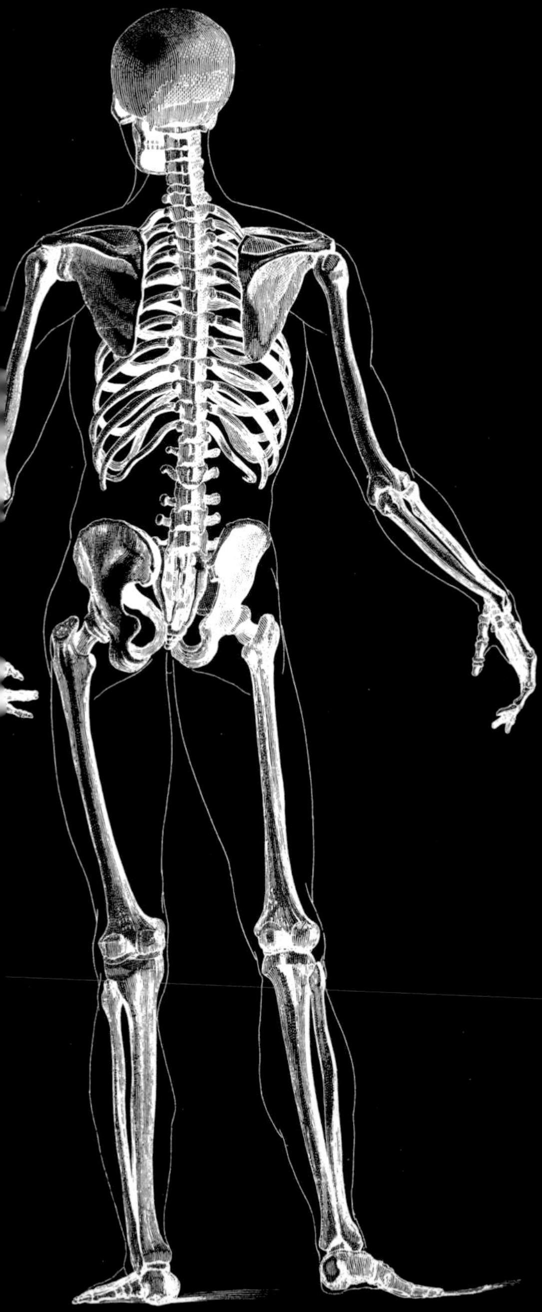
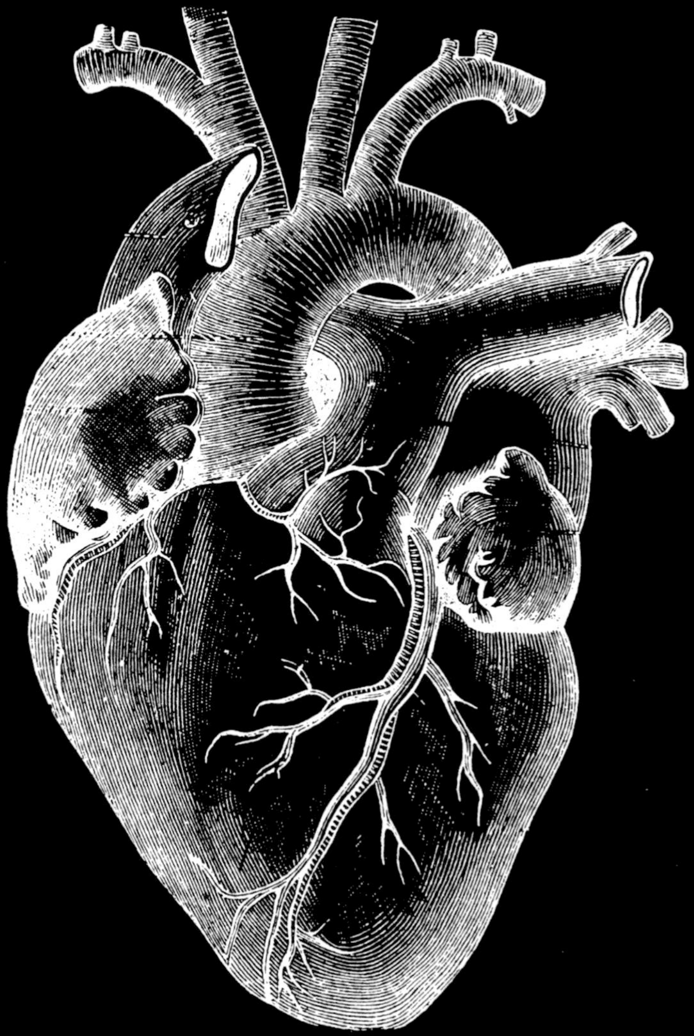

This book contains high-quality images for use as a graphic resource or inspiration. All the images are stored on the accompanying CD-ROM in professional-quality, high-resolution format and can be used on either Windows or Mac platforms. The images can be used free of charge.

The documents can be imported directly from the CD-ROM into a wide range of layout, image-manipulation, illustration, and word-processing programs; no installation is required. Many programs allow you to manipulate the images. Please consult your software manual for further instructions.

The names of the files on the CD-ROM correspond with the page numbers in this book. Where applicable, the position on the pages is indicated: T = top, B = bottom, C = center, L = left, and R = right.

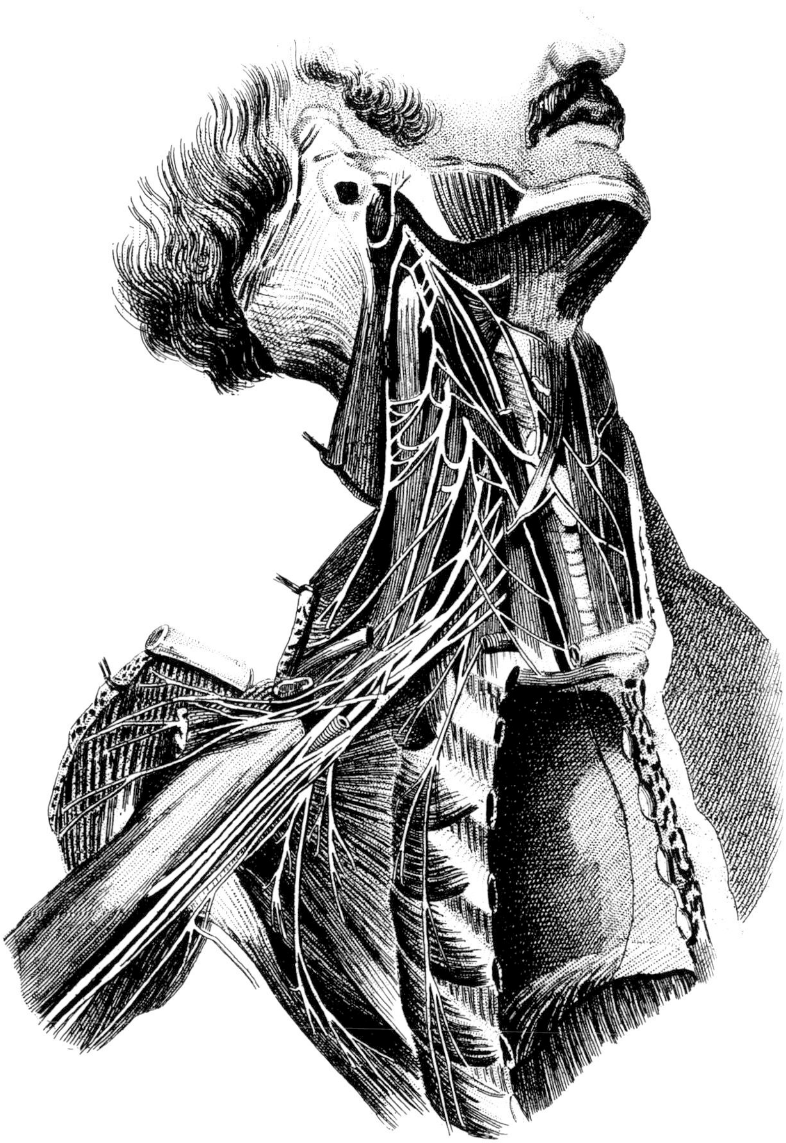

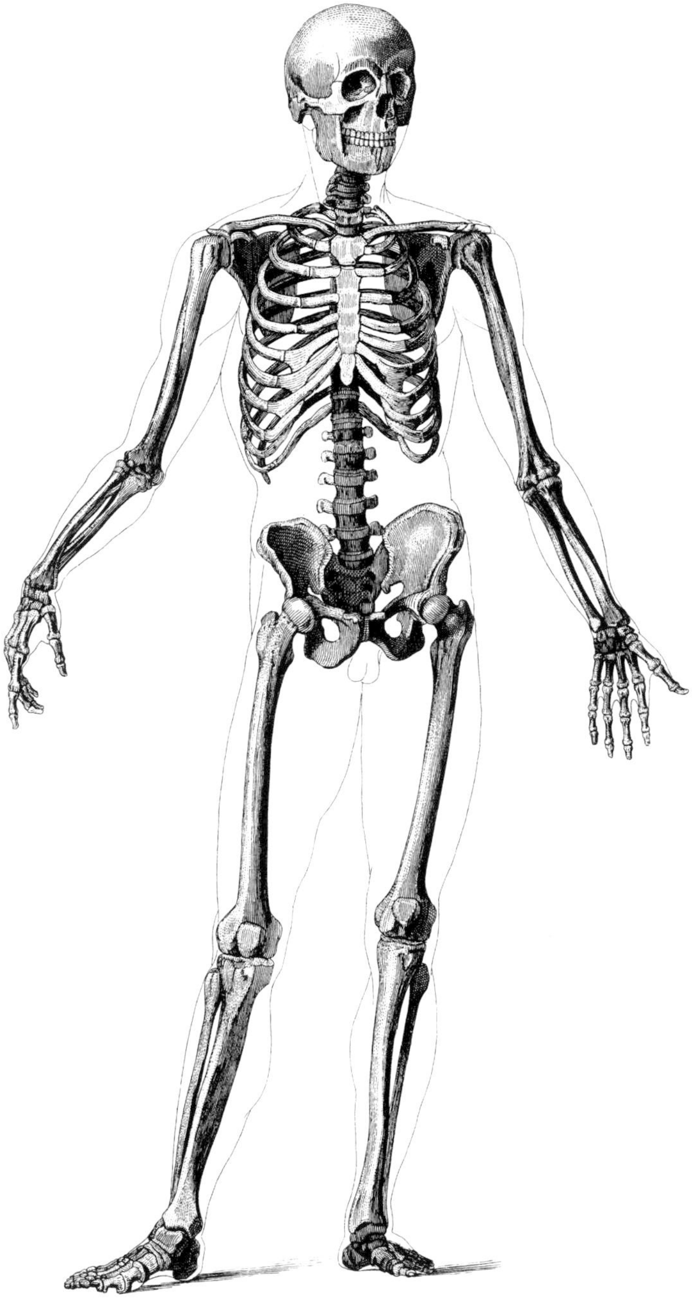

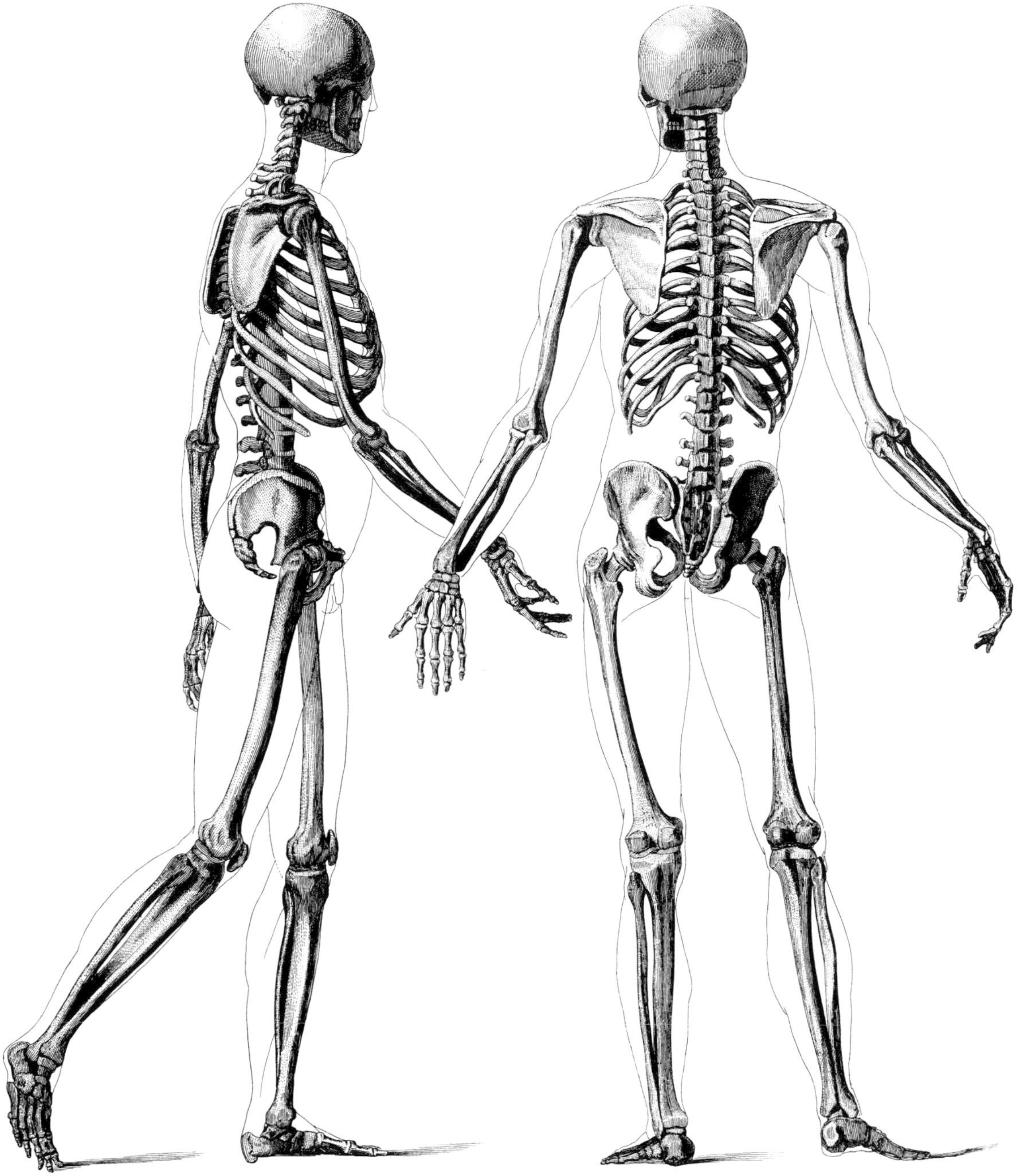

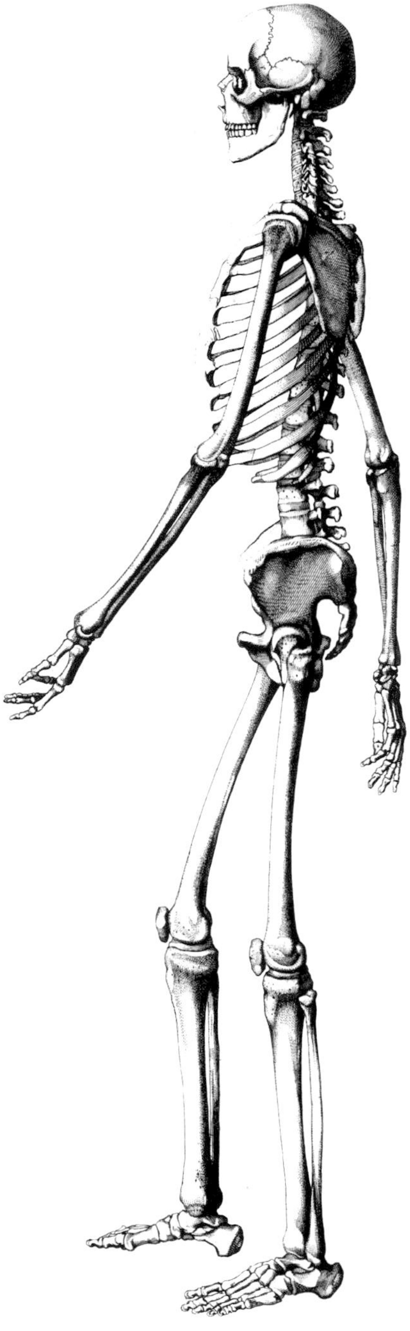

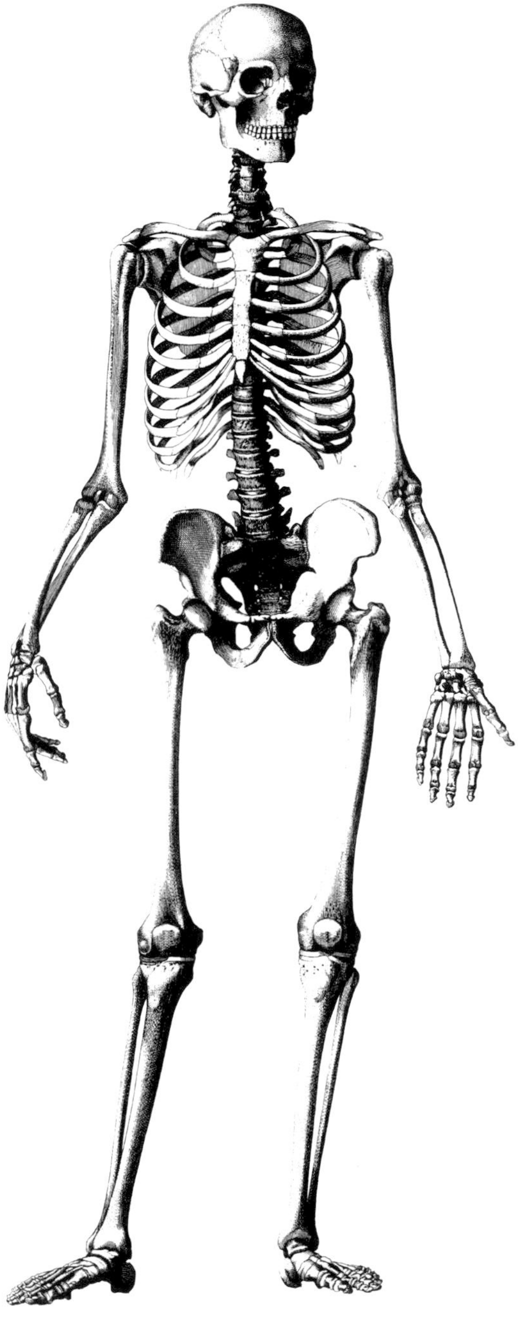

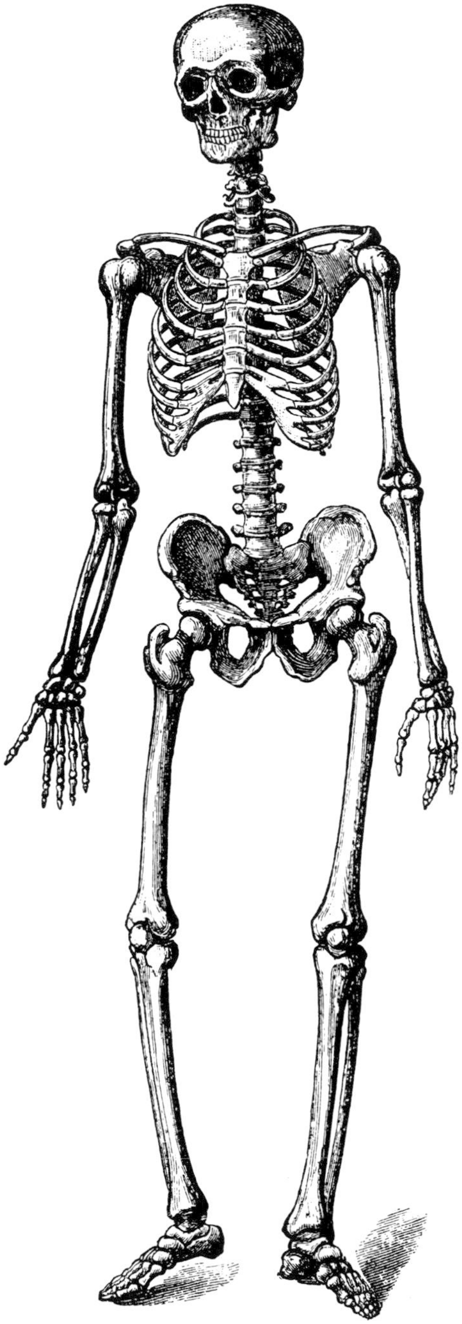
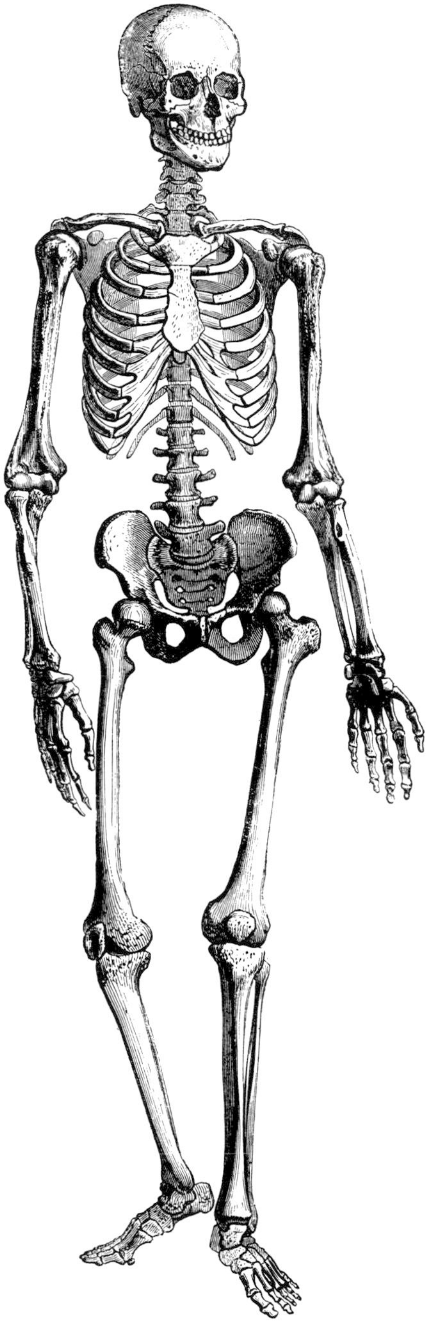

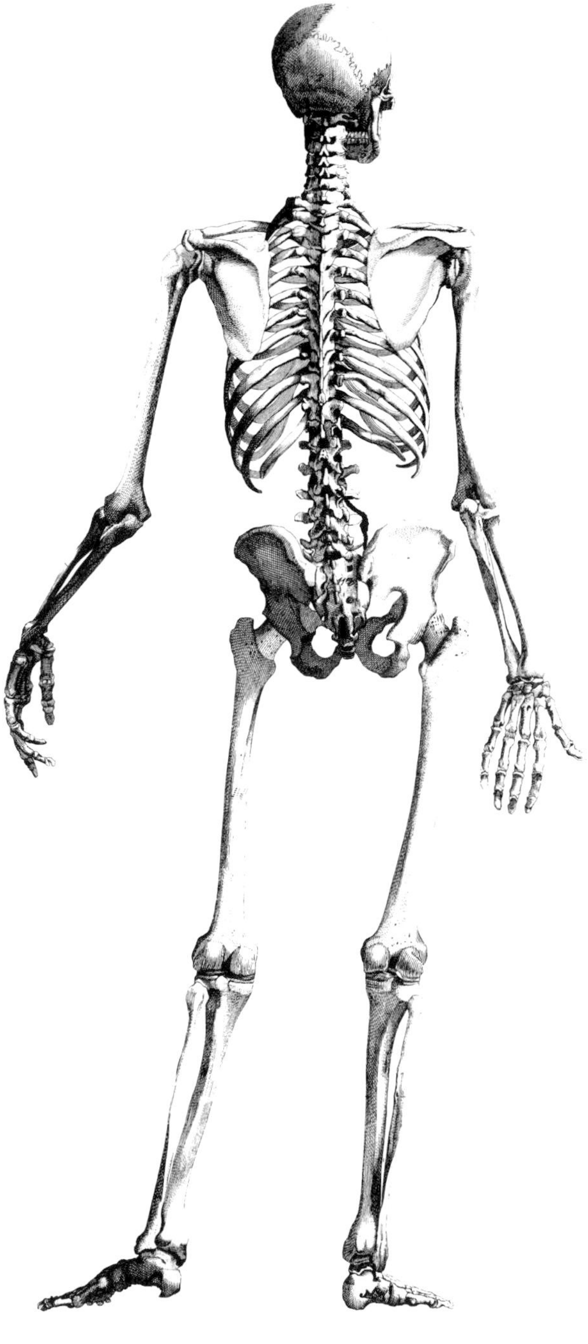

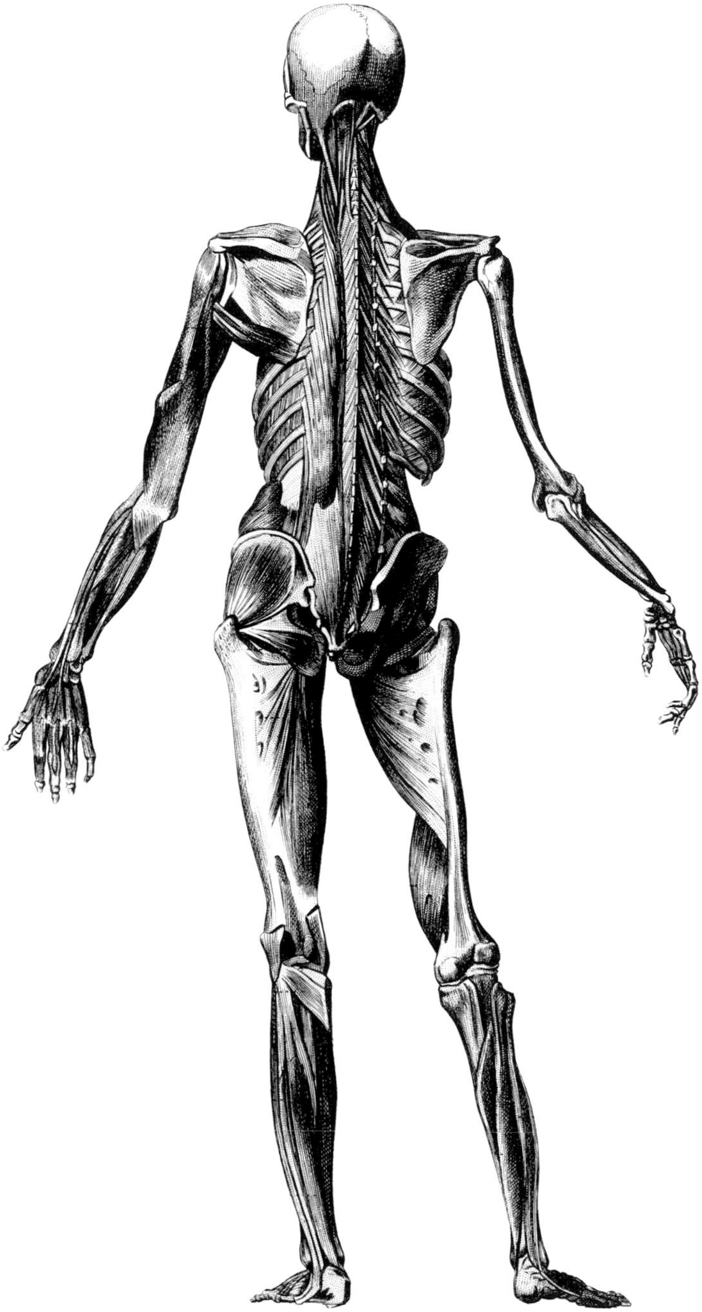

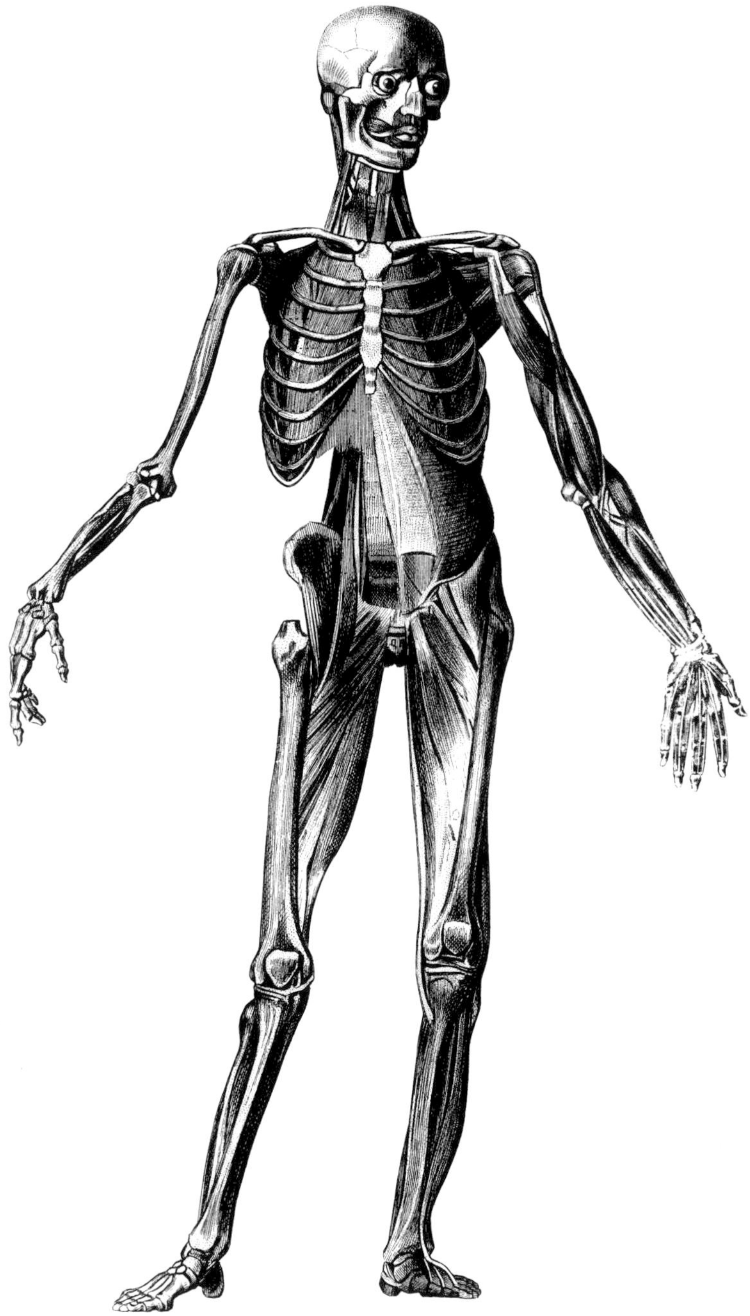

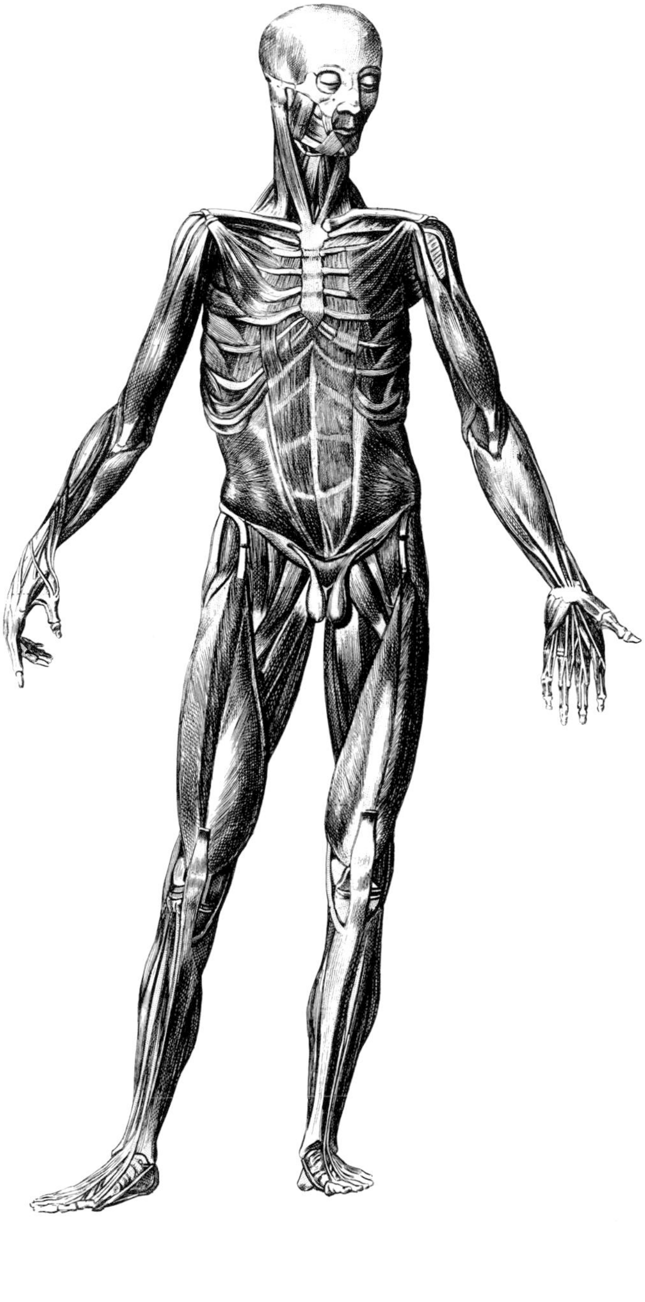

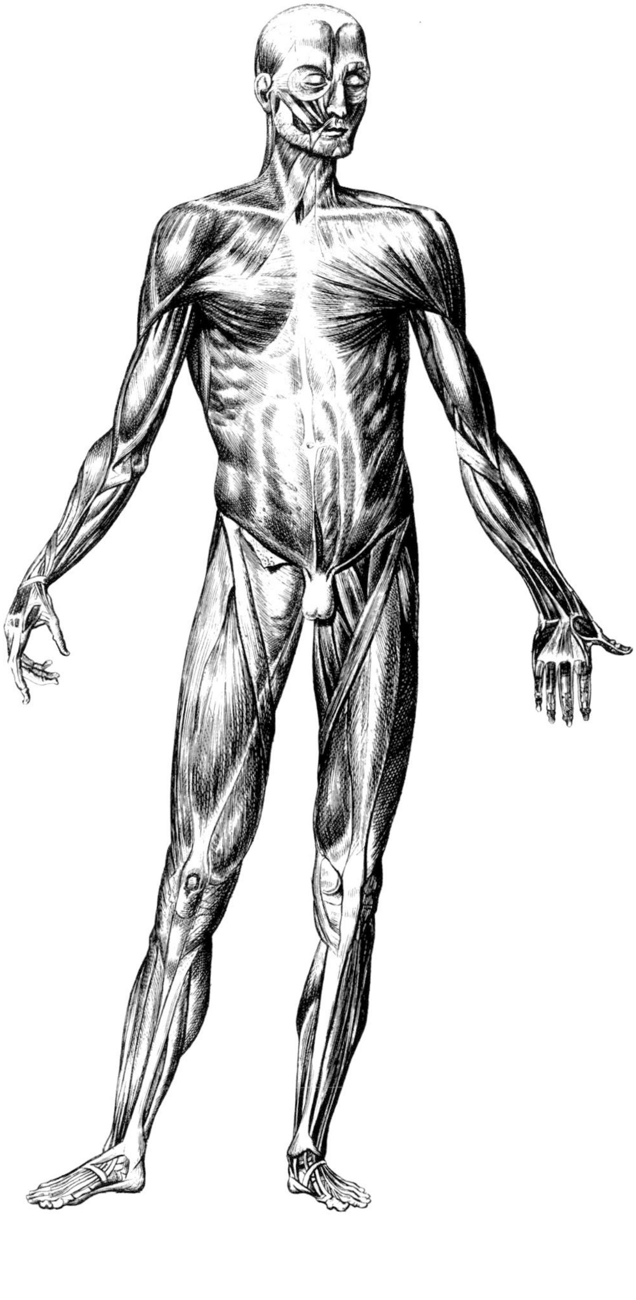

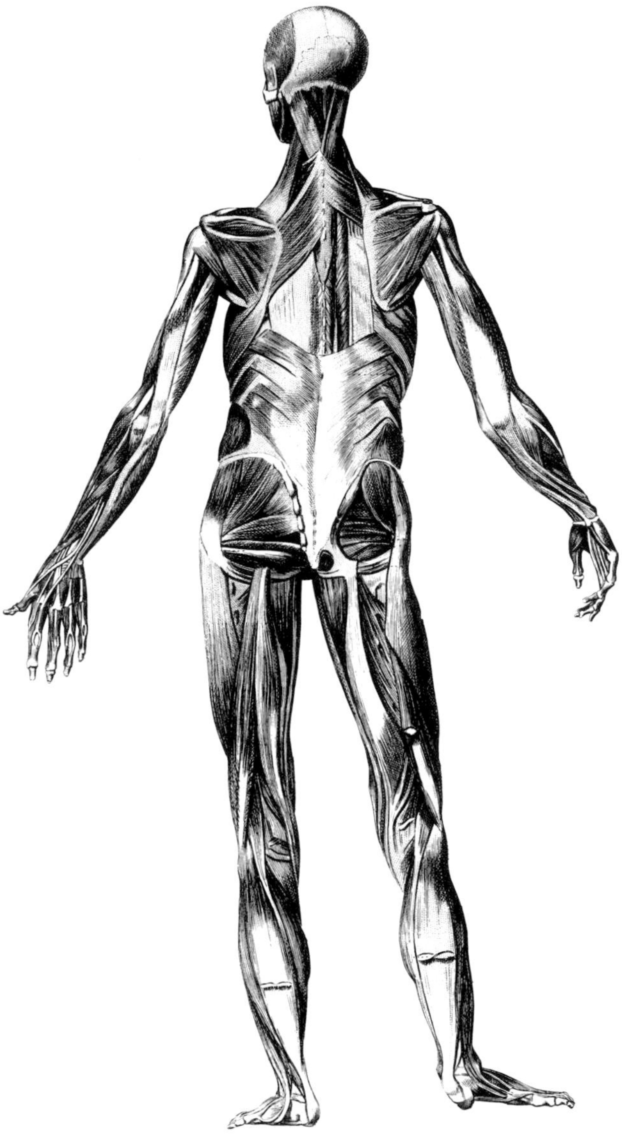

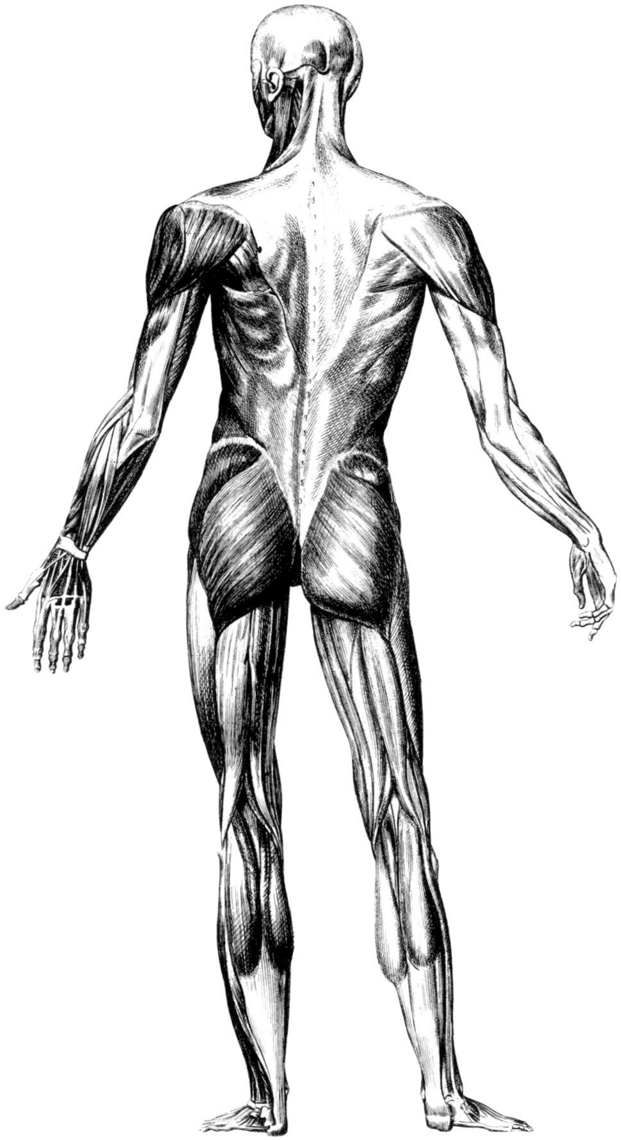

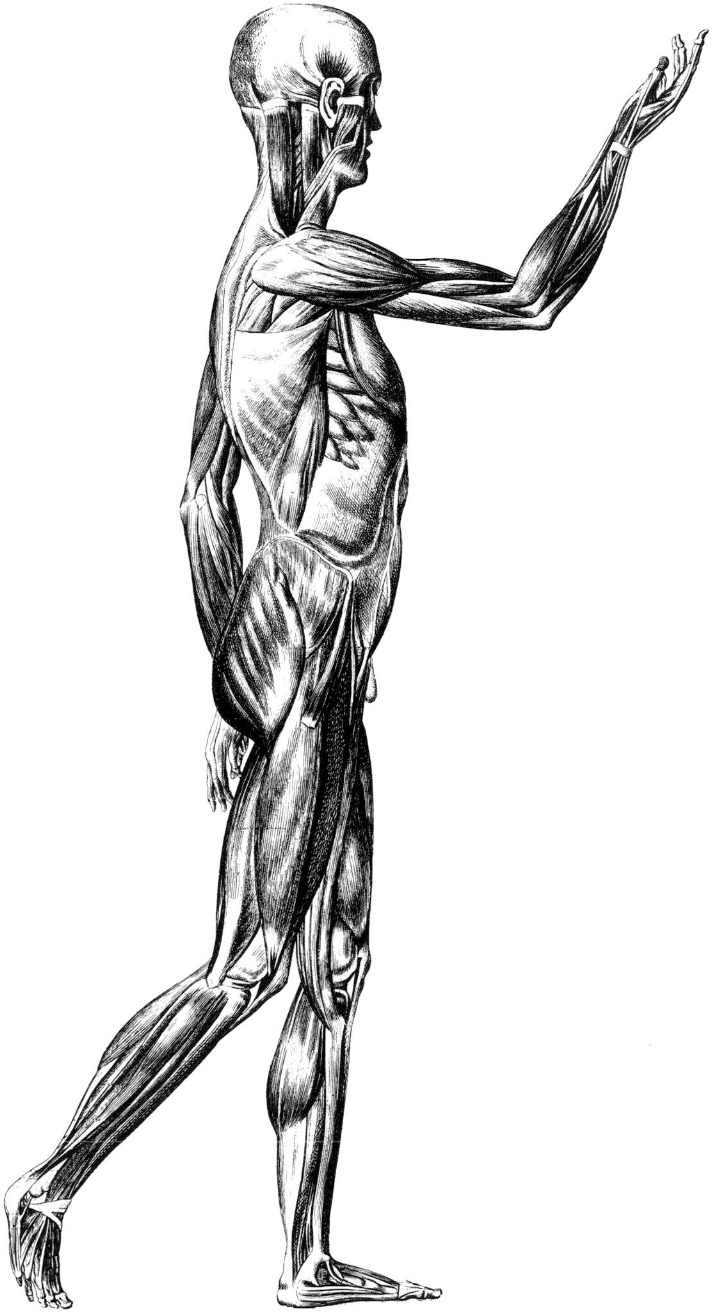

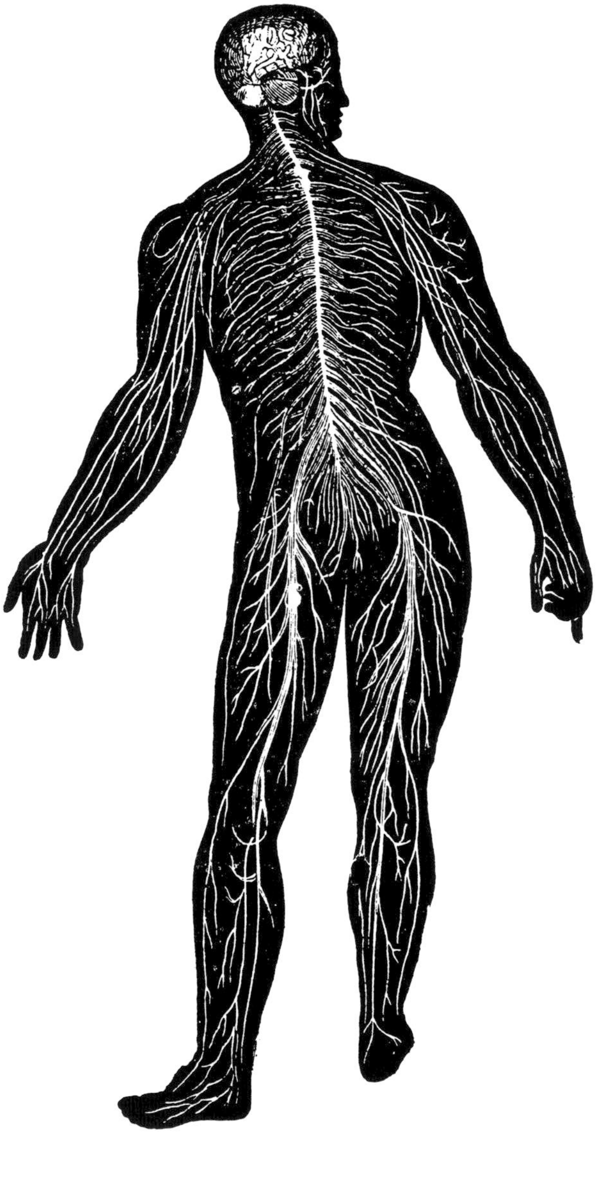

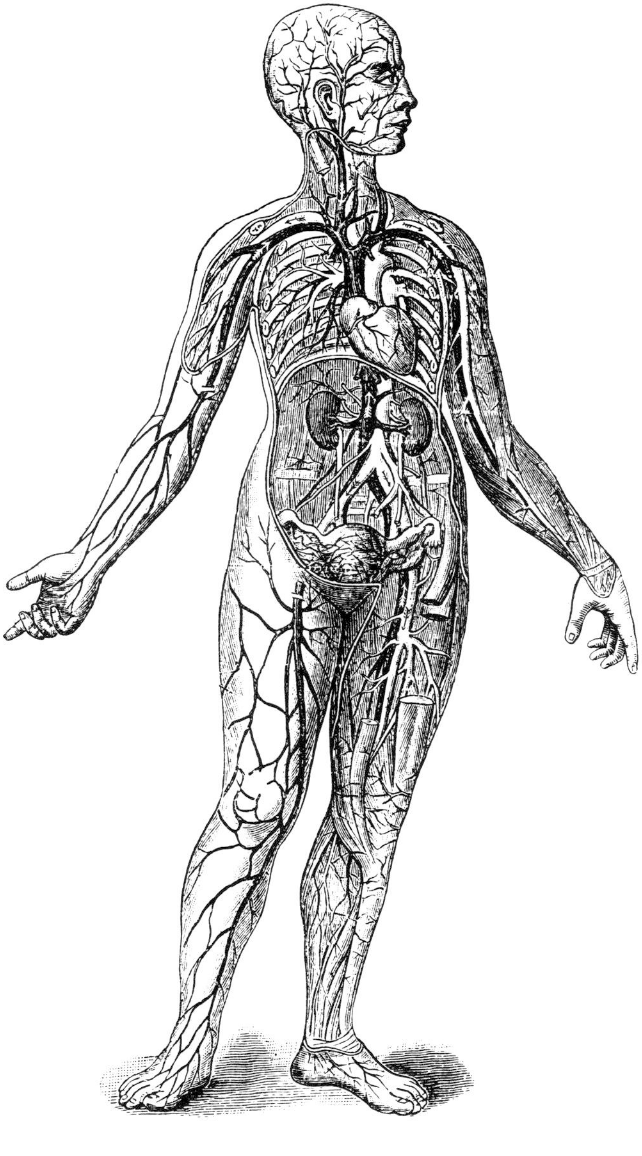

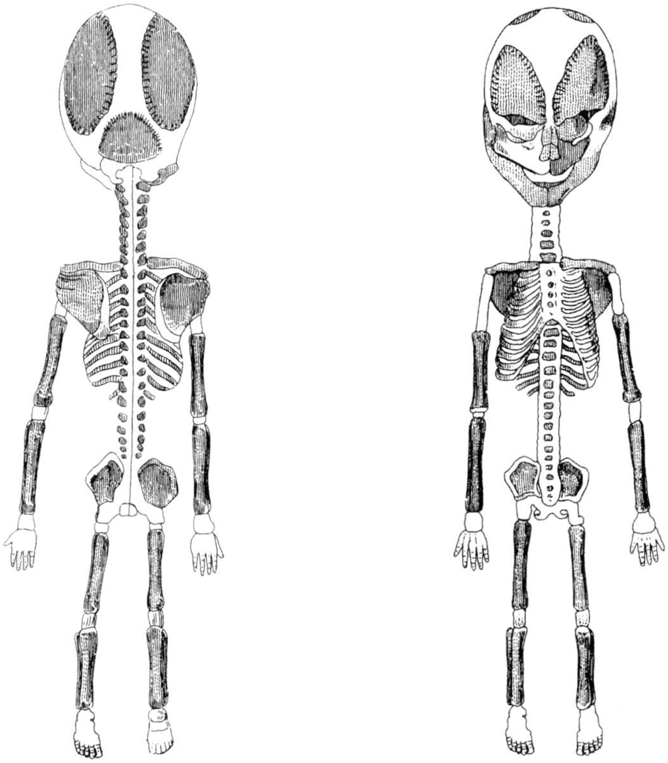

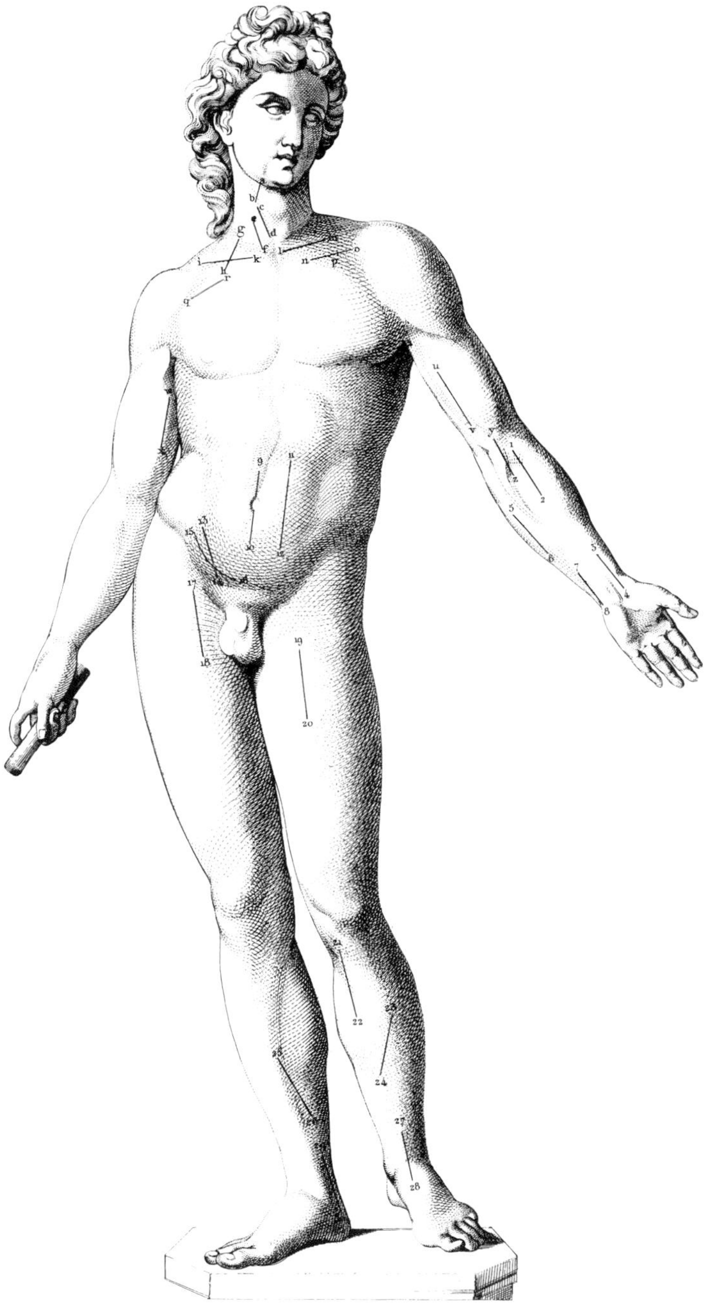

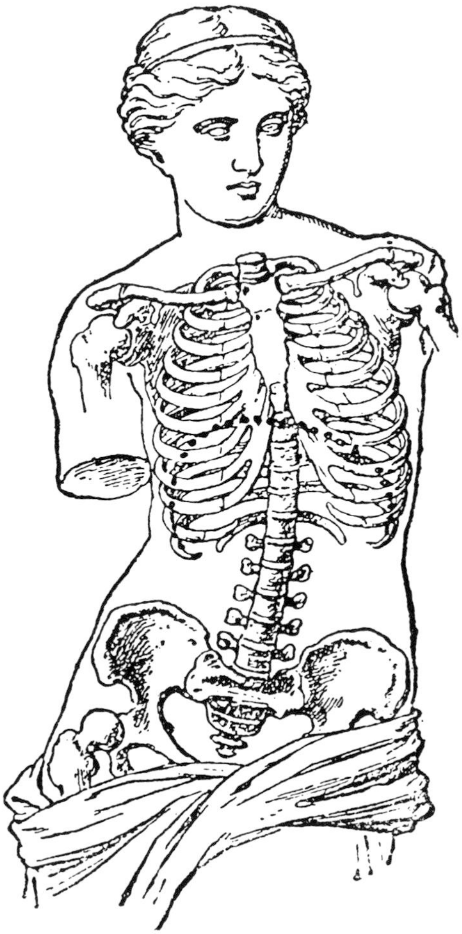

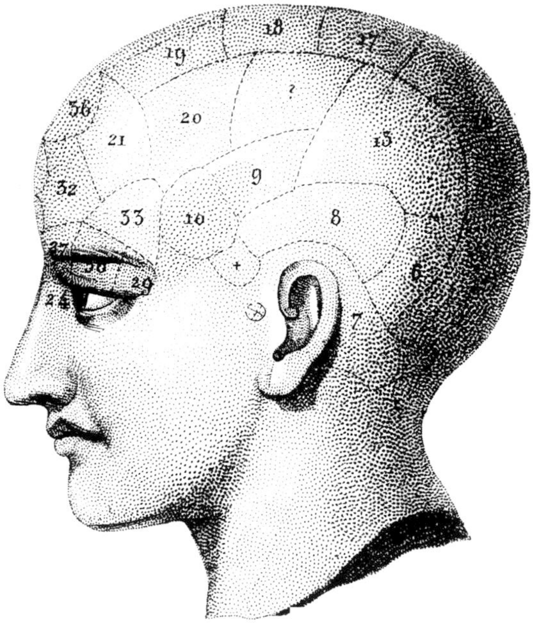
18
19
20
21
9
15
32
33
10
8

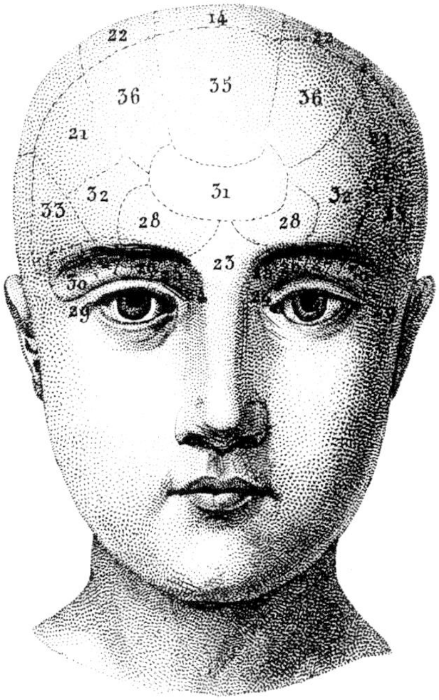
14
22
36
35
36
21
31
32
33
28
28
23

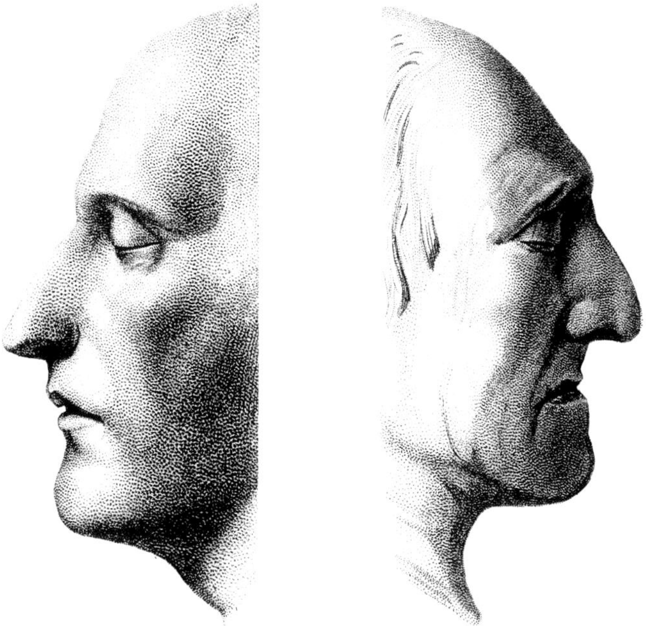

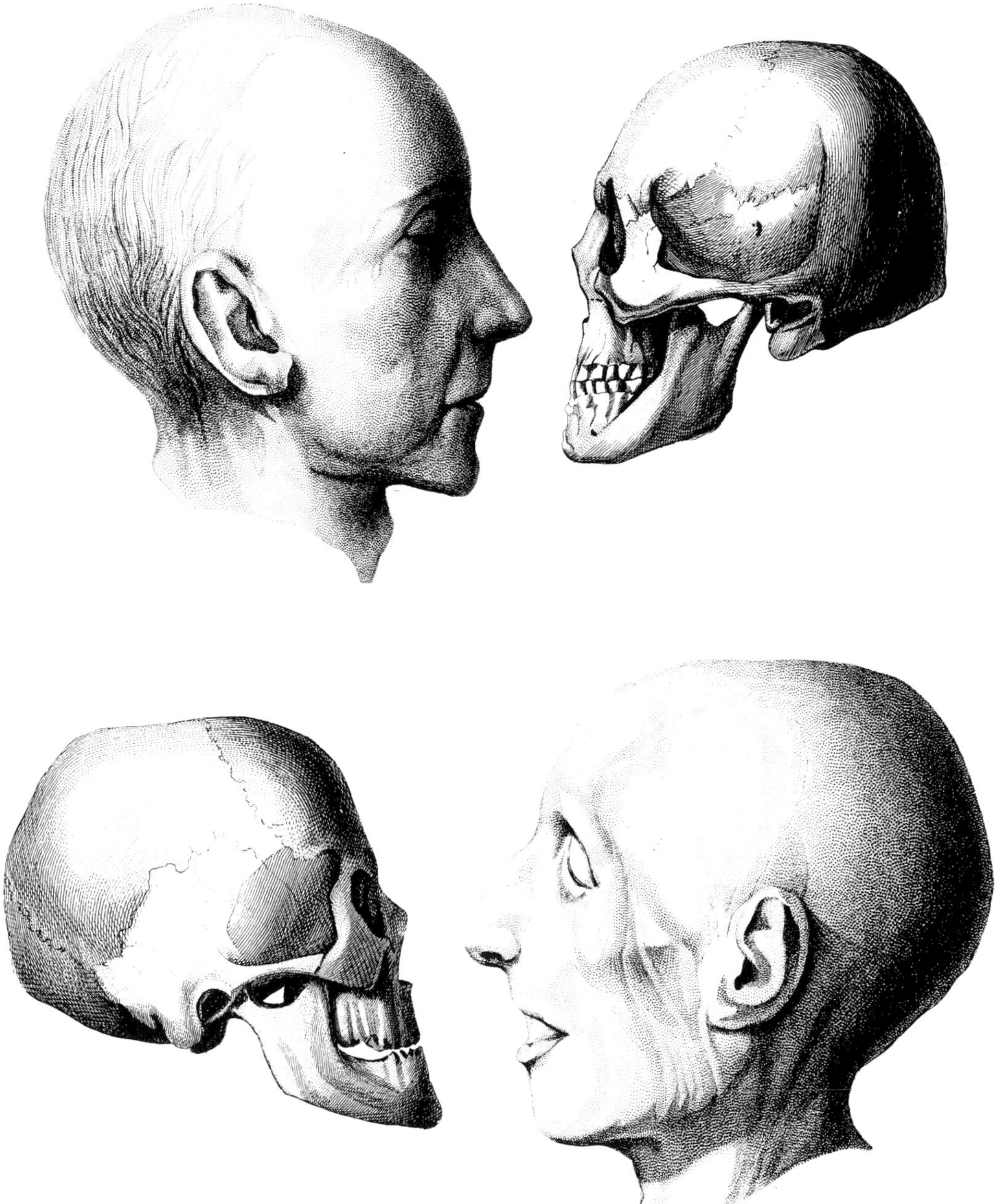

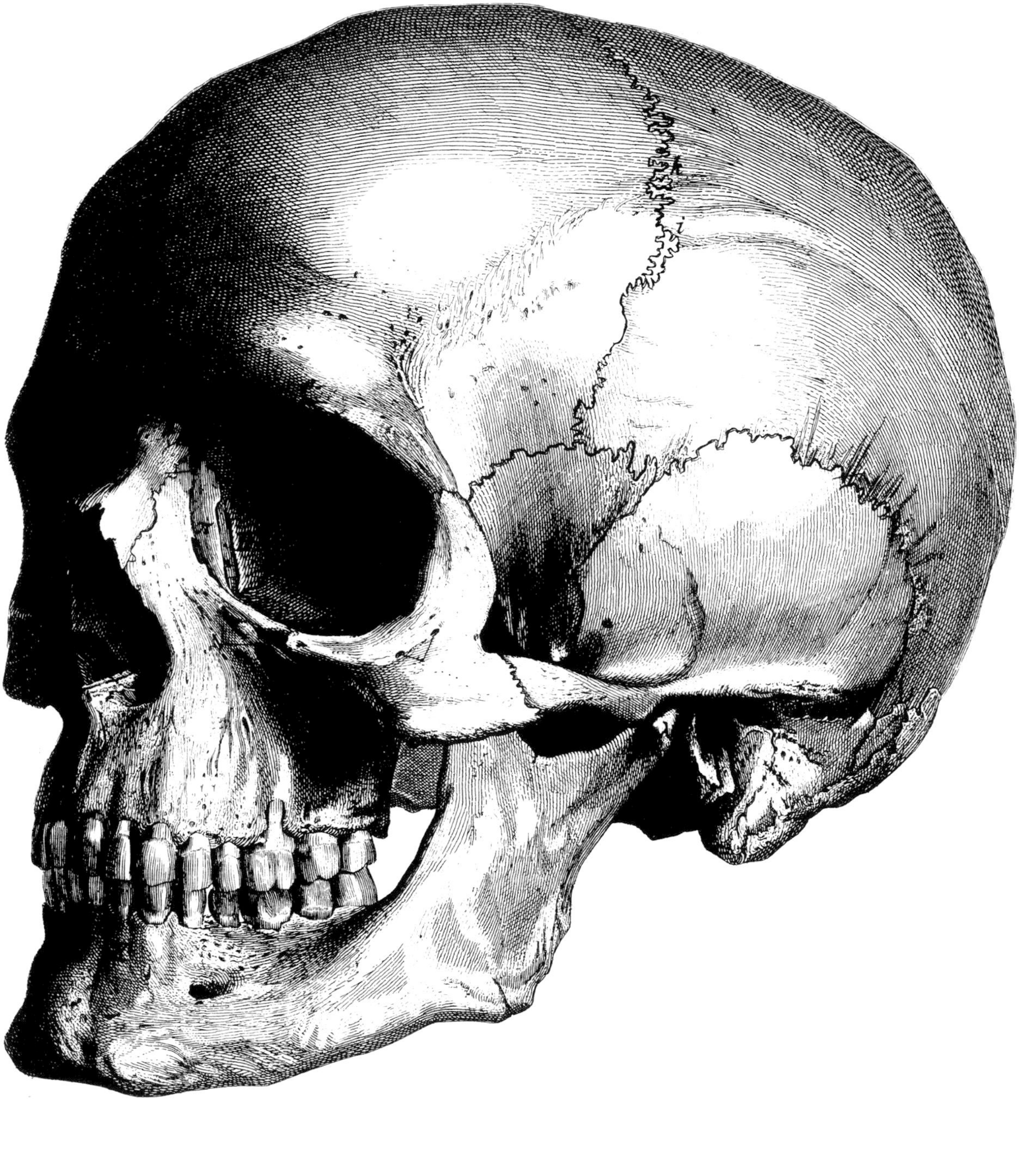

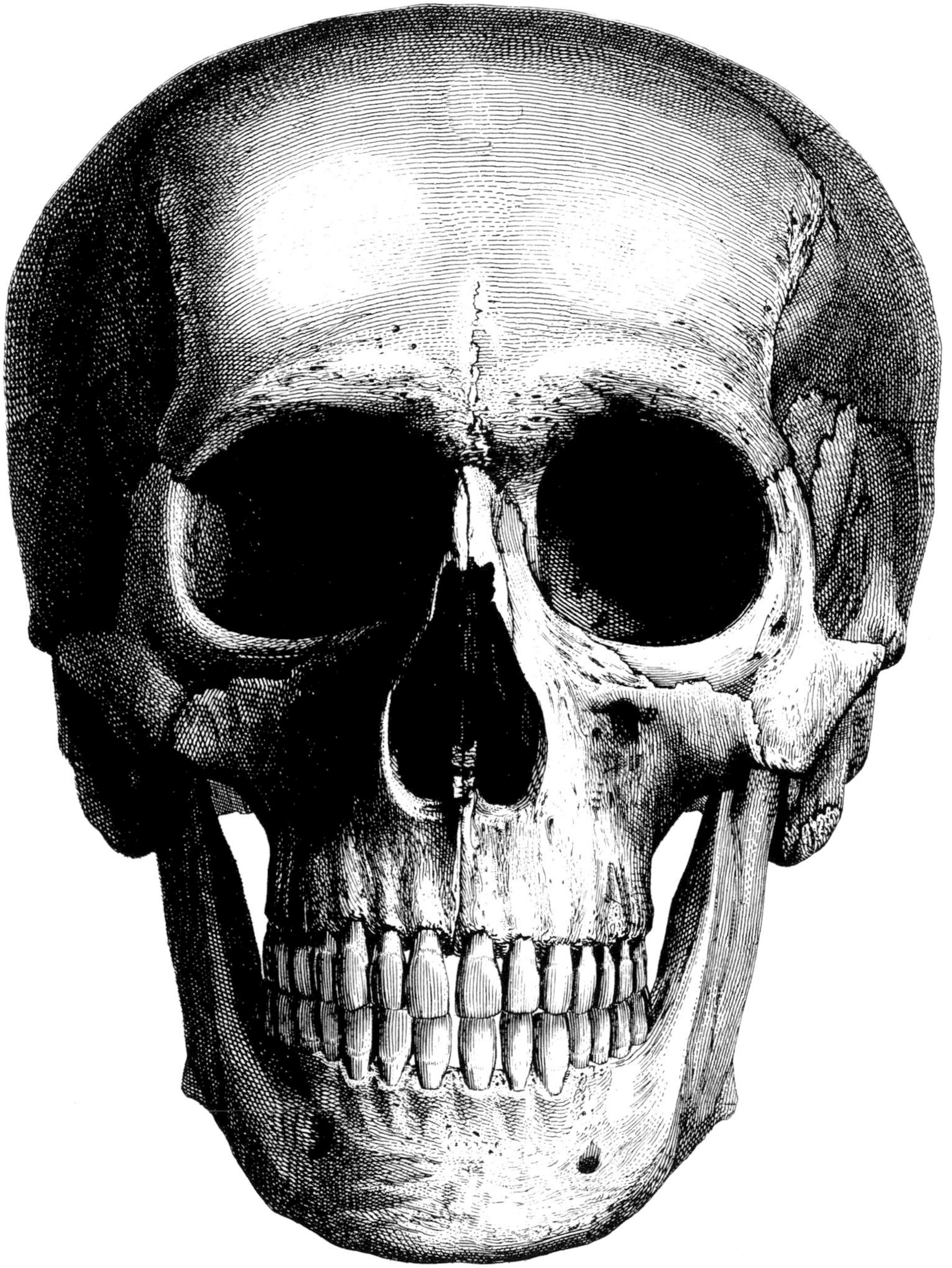

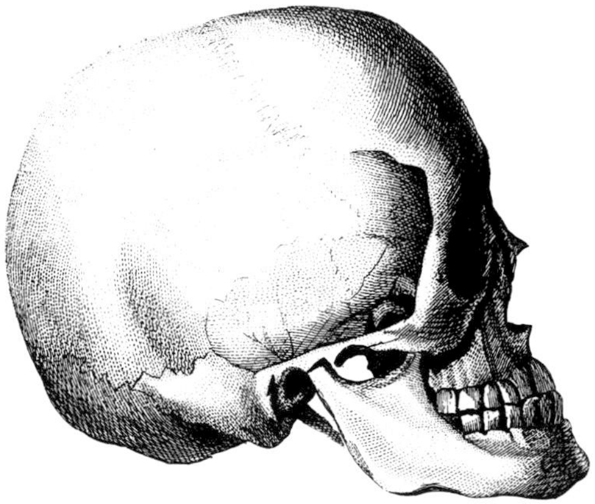

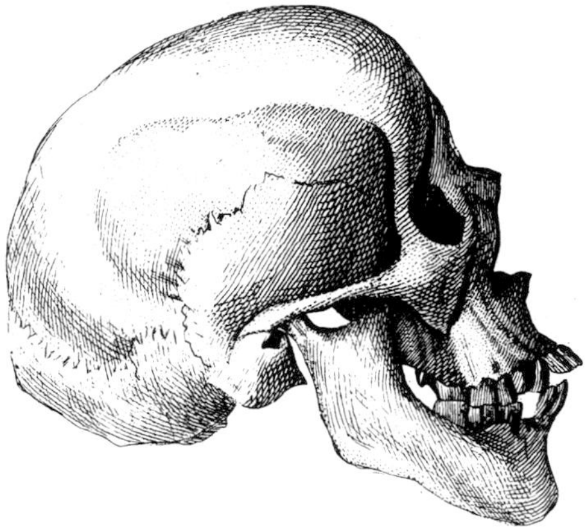

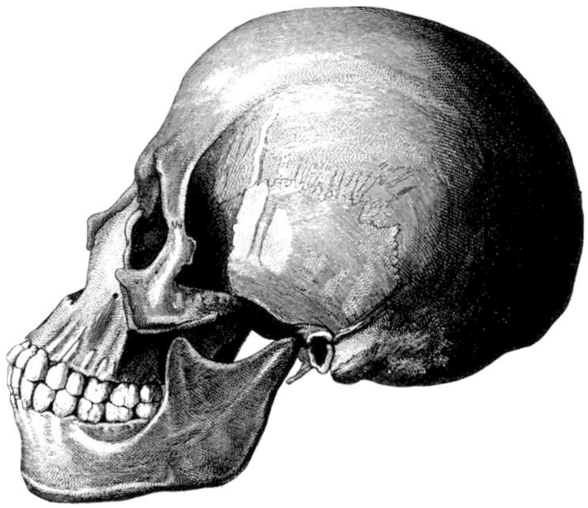

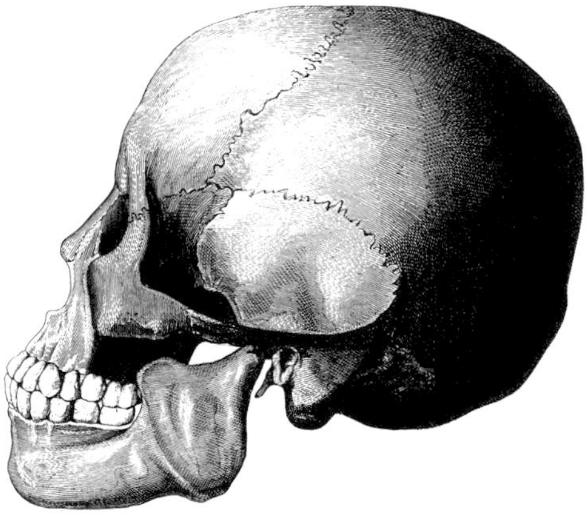

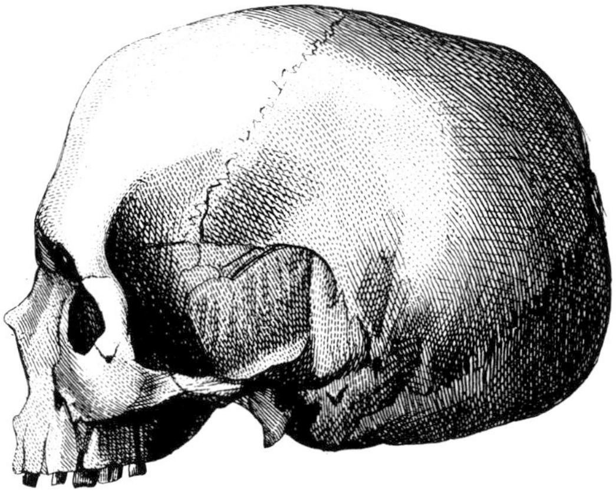

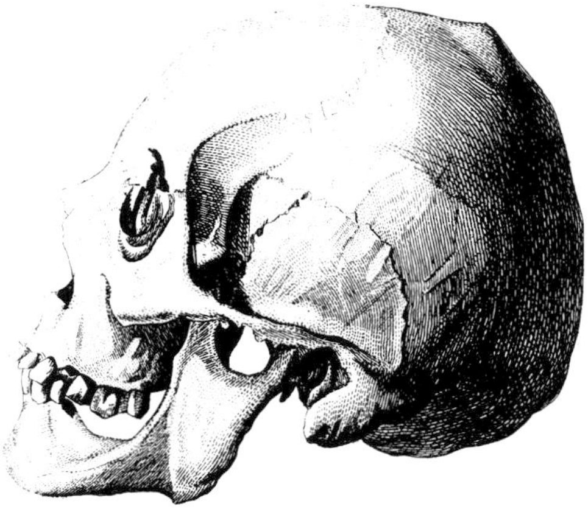

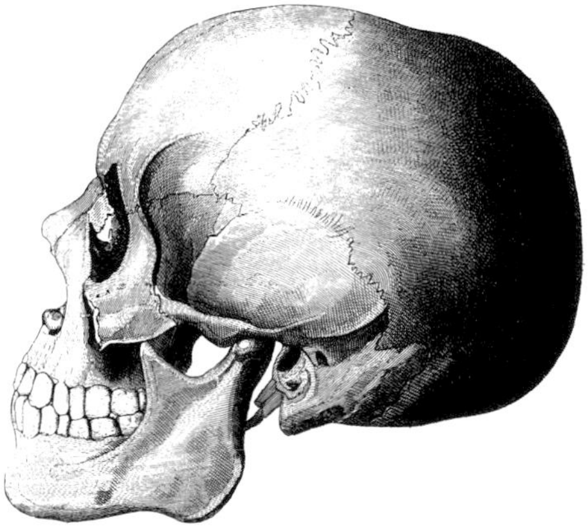

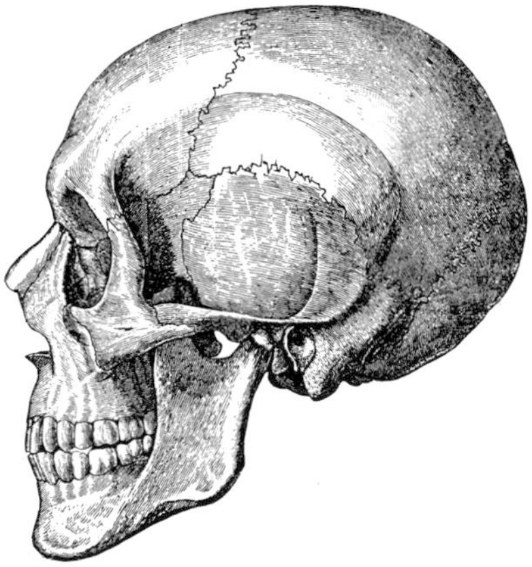

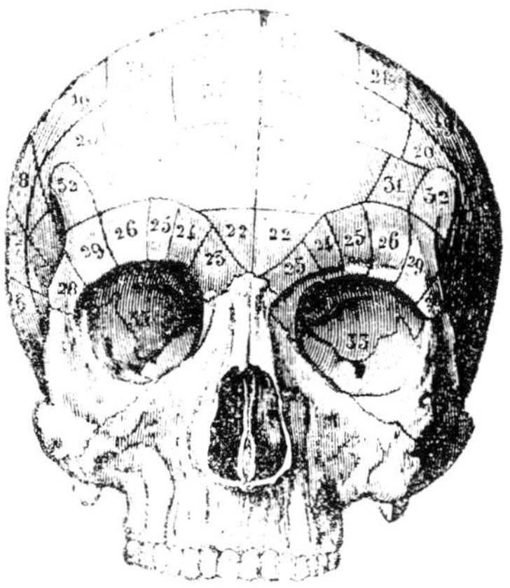

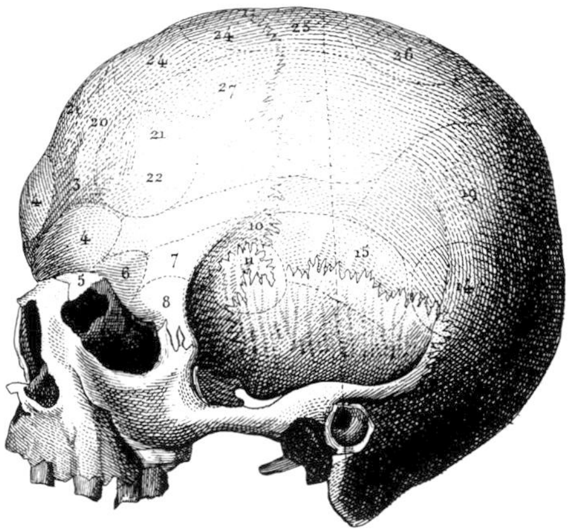

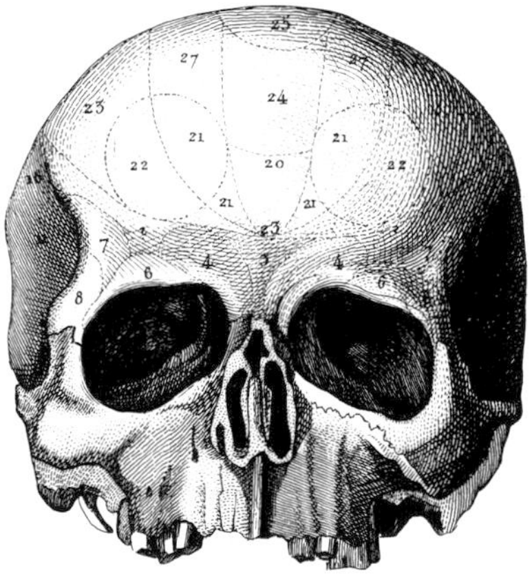

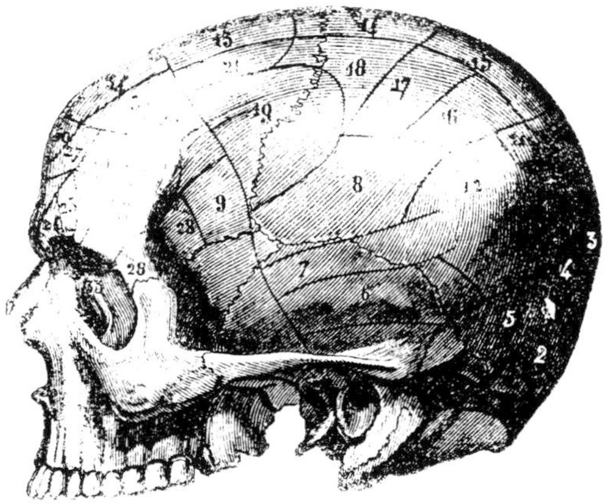

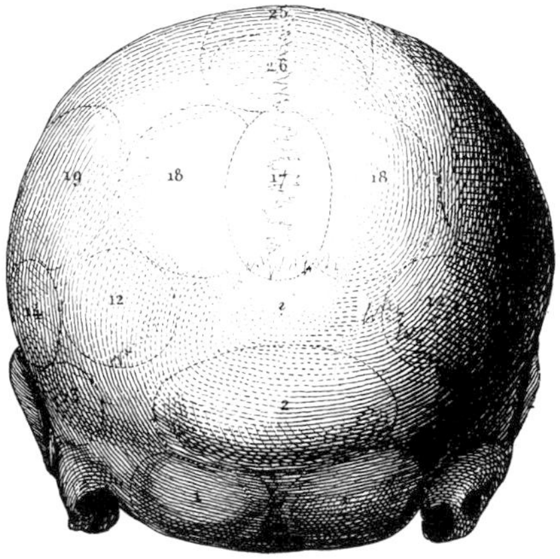

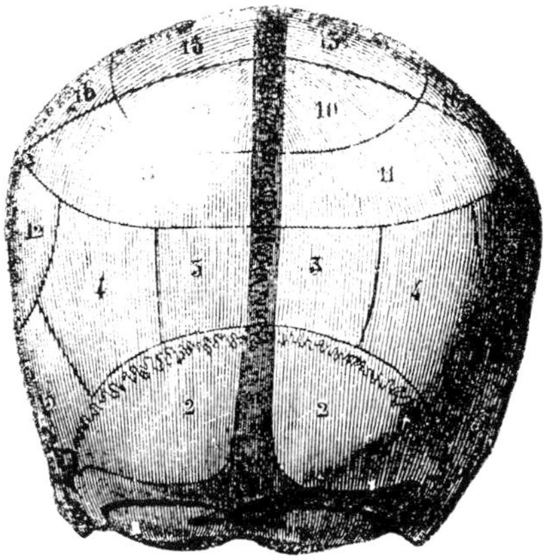

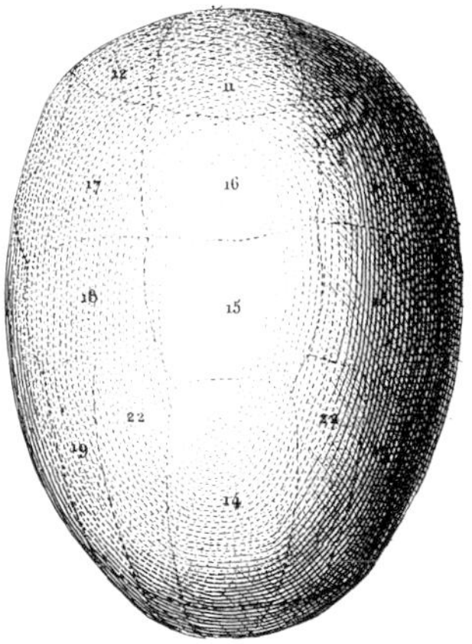

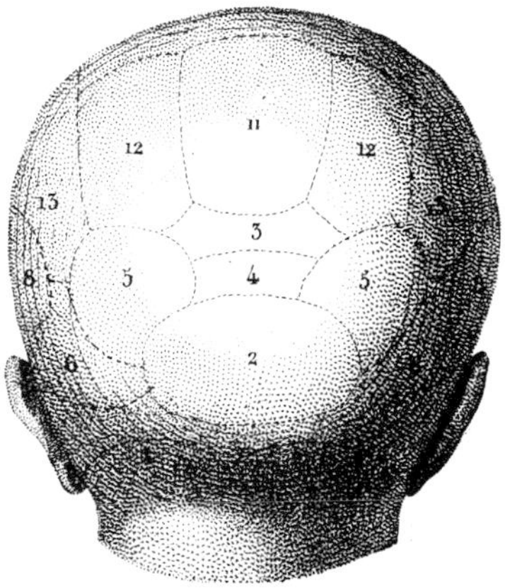

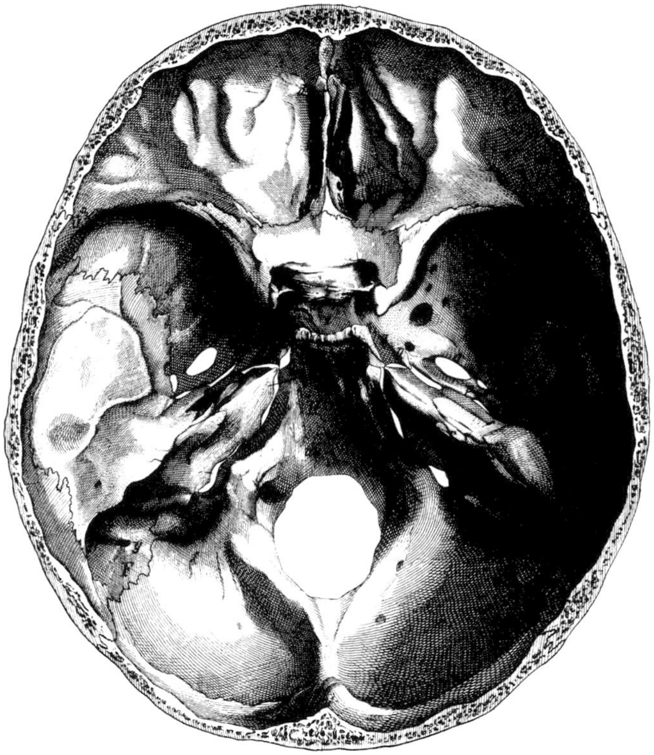

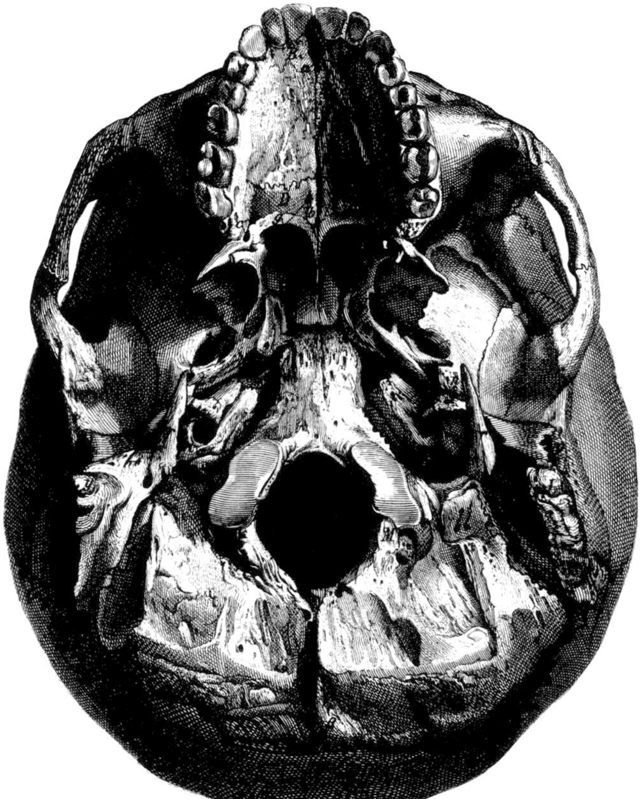

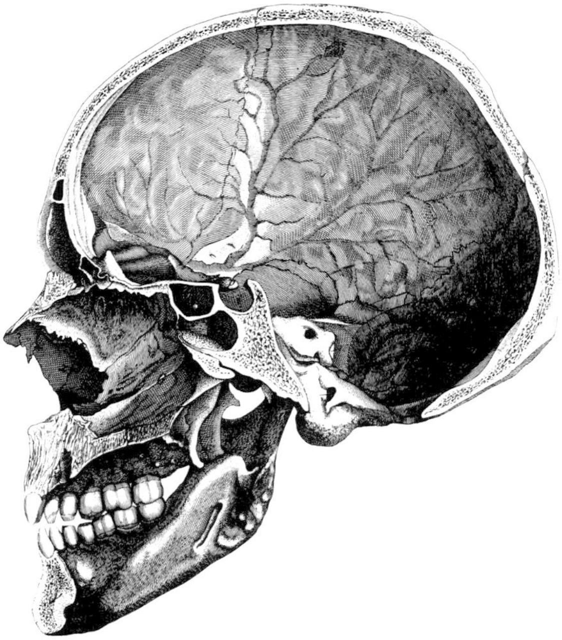
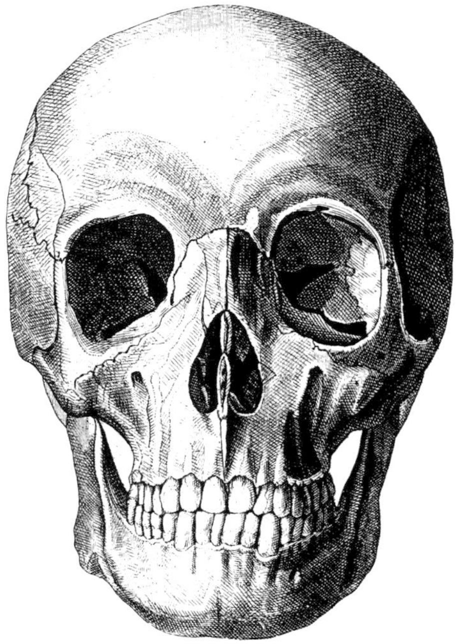
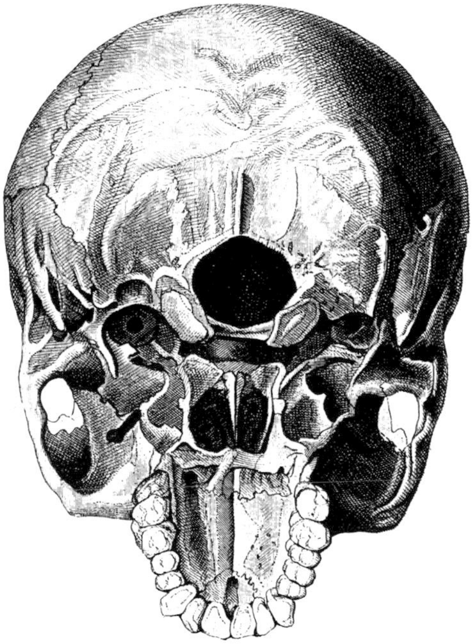
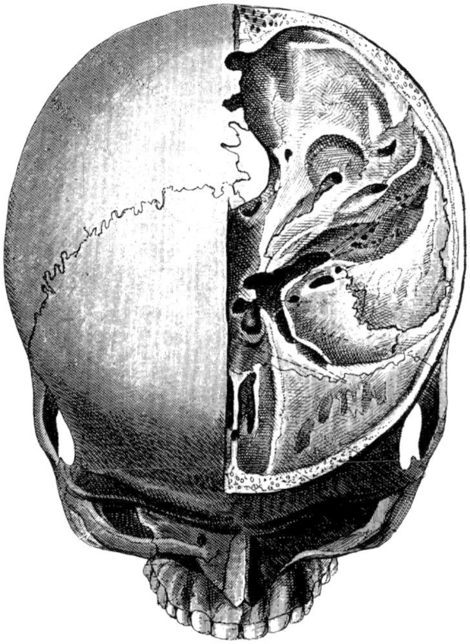

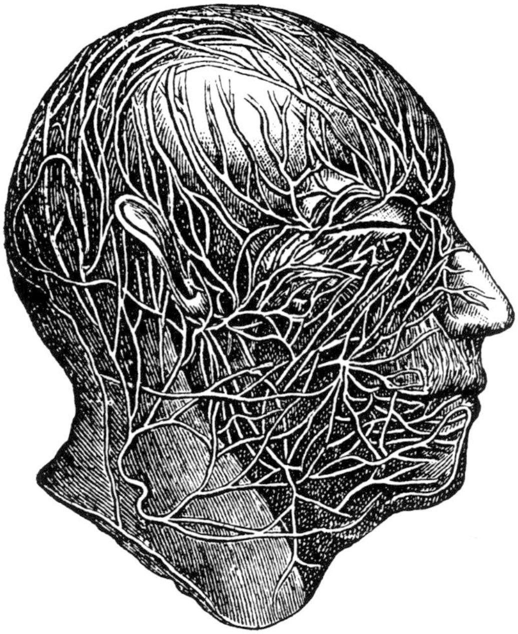

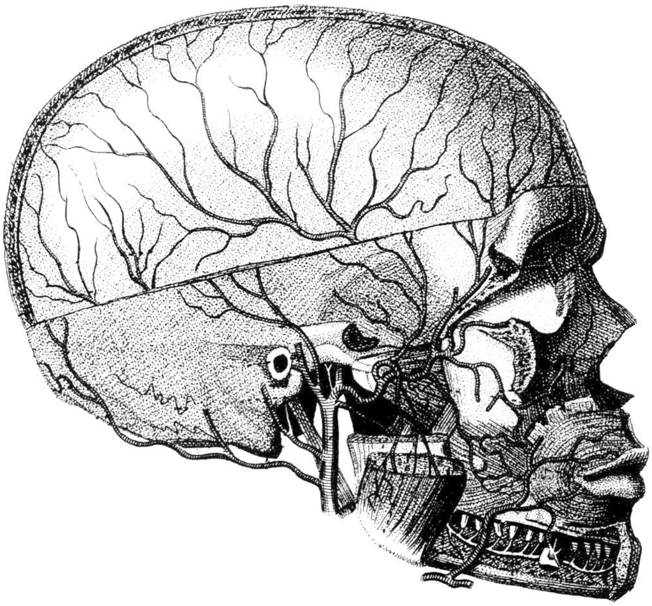

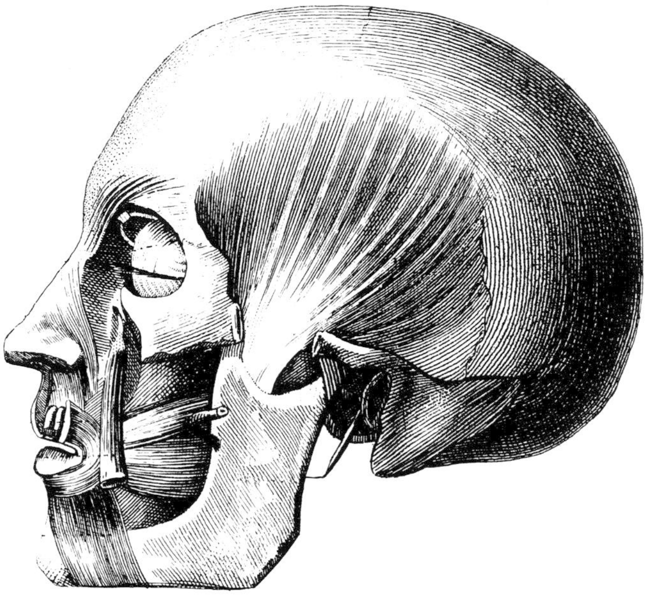

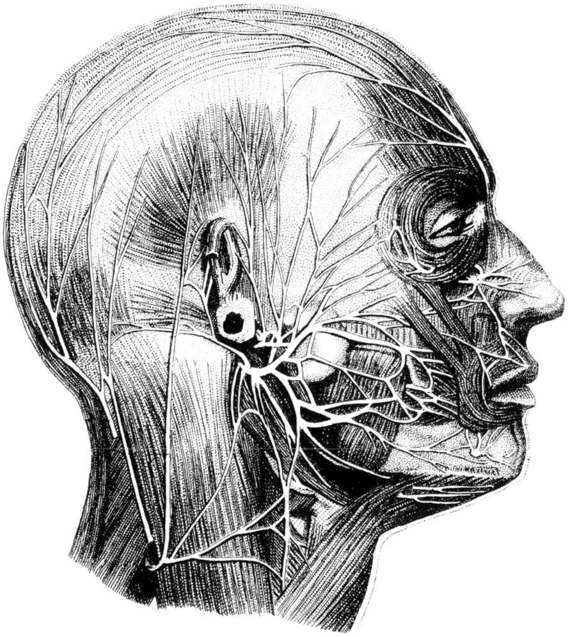

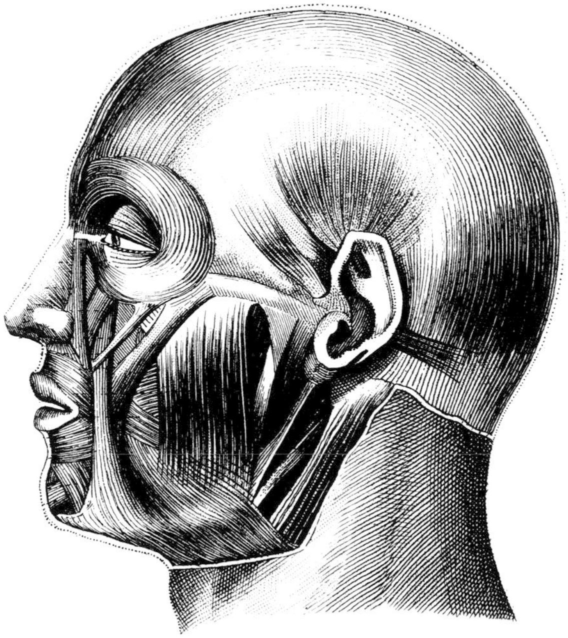

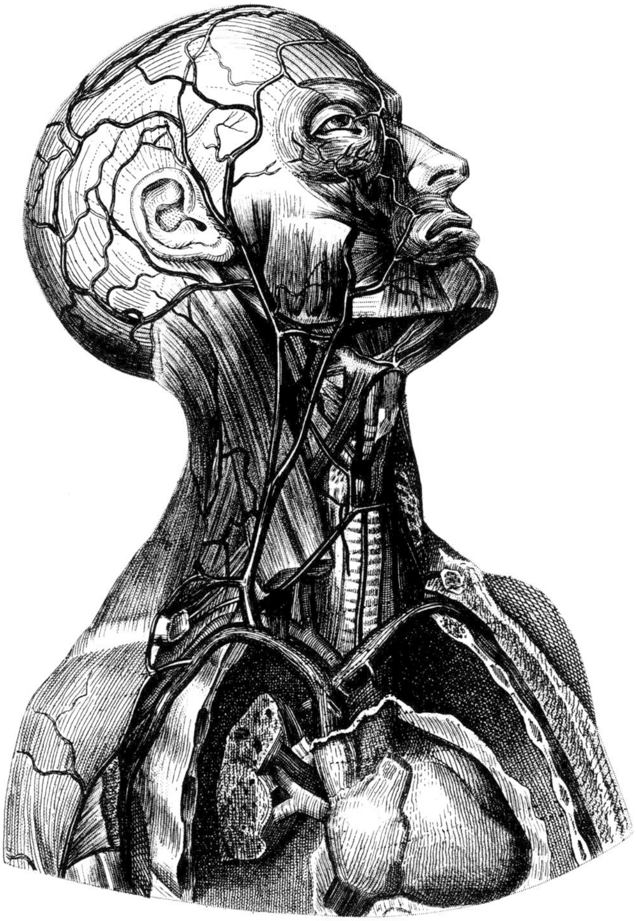

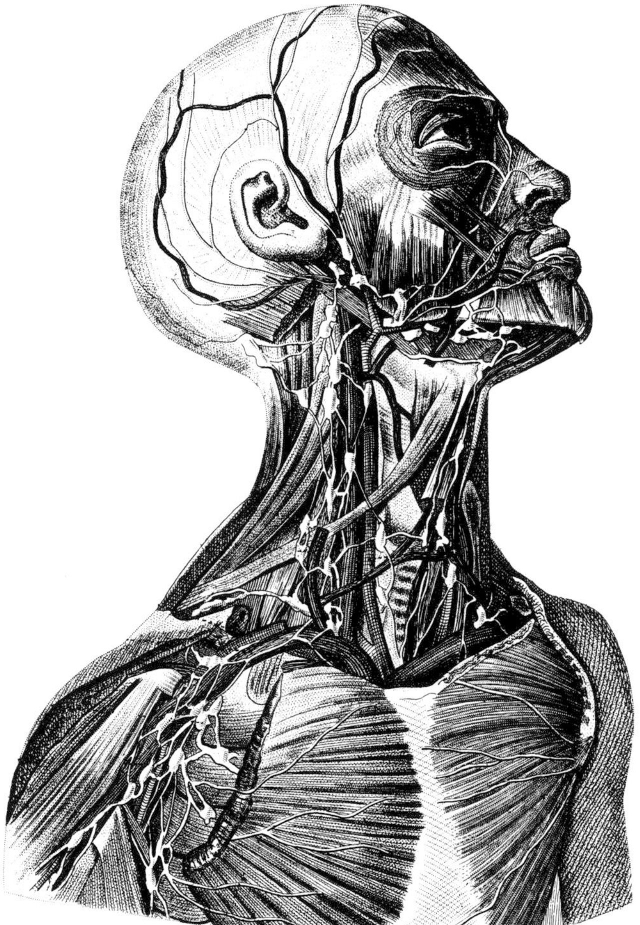

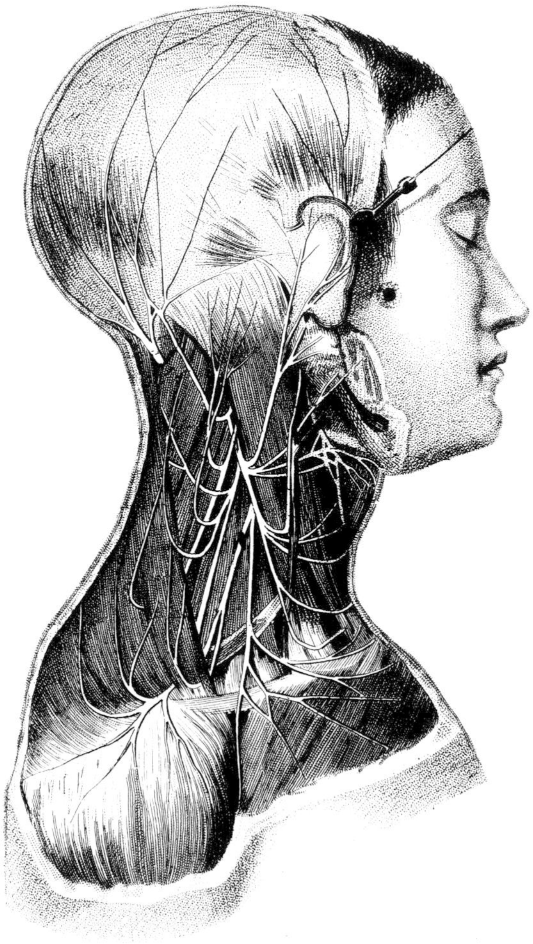

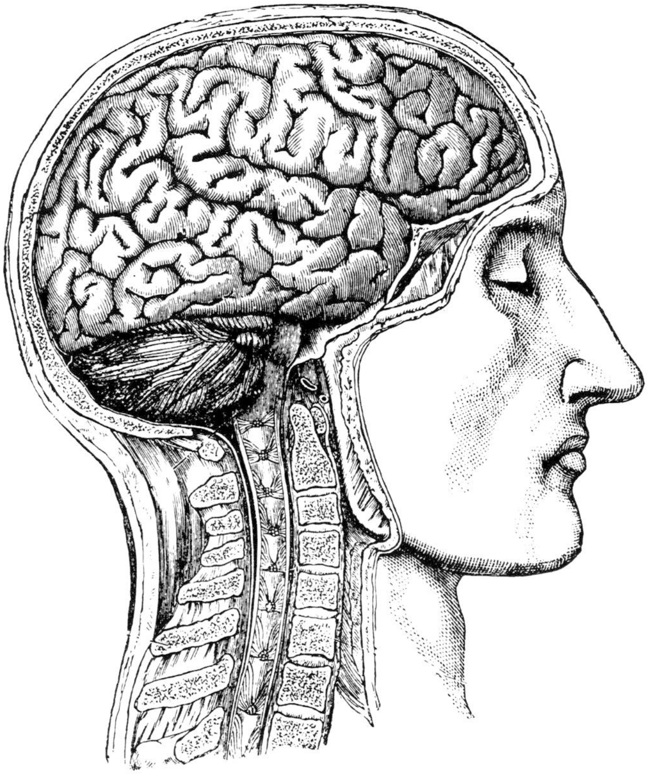

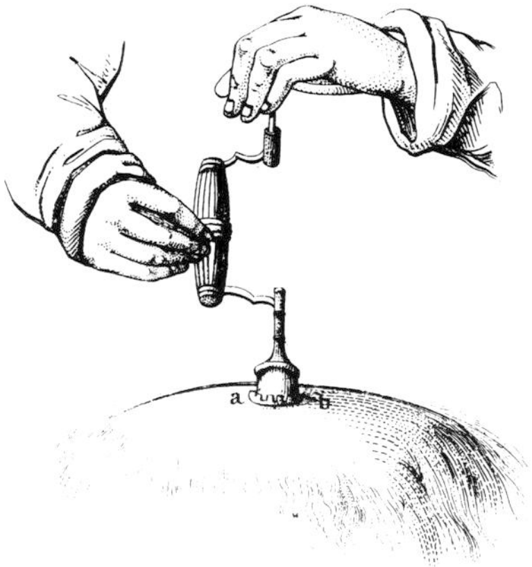
a
b

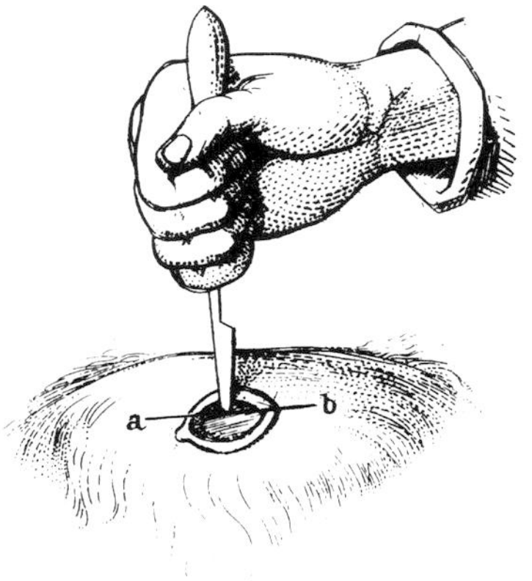
a
b

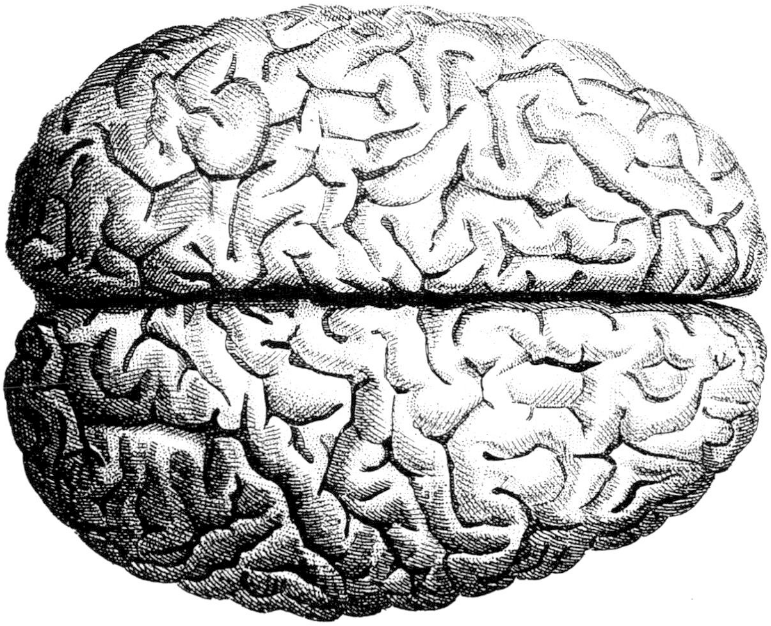

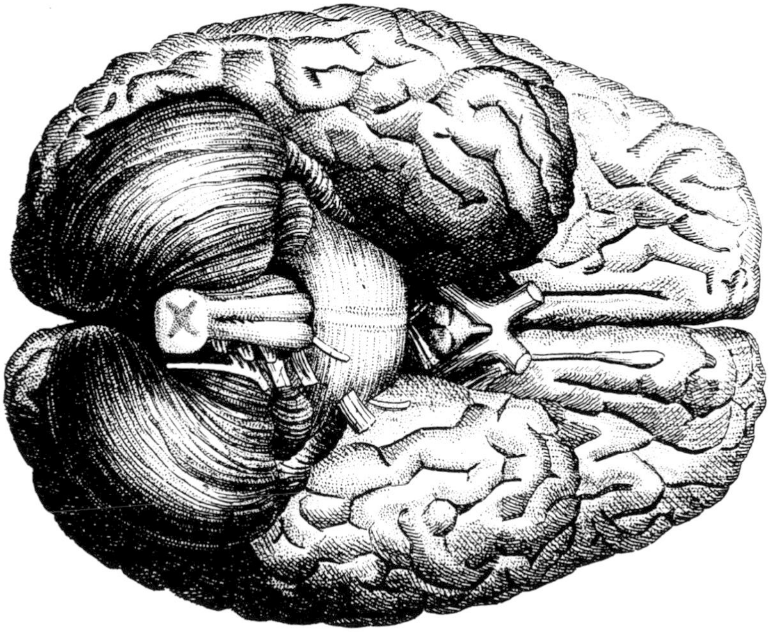

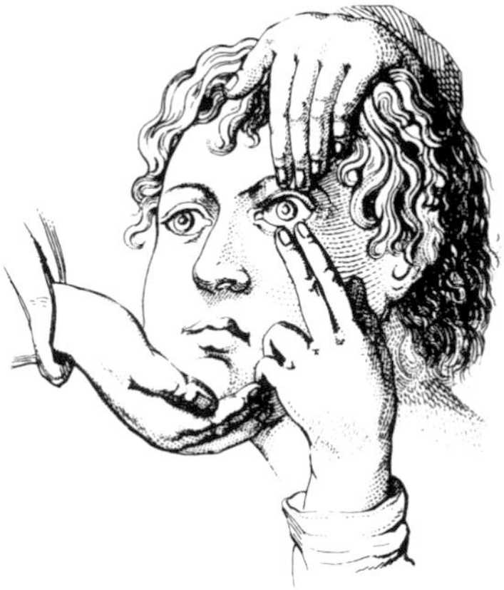

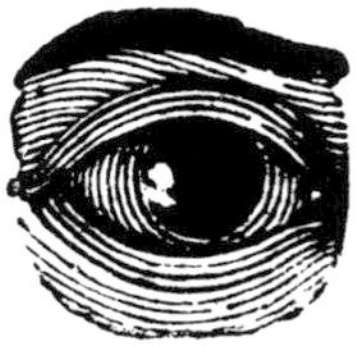
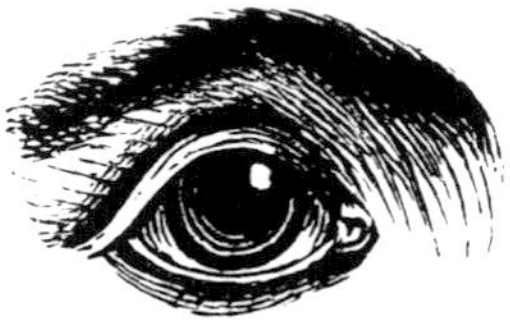
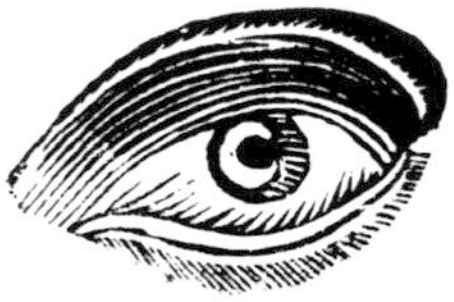
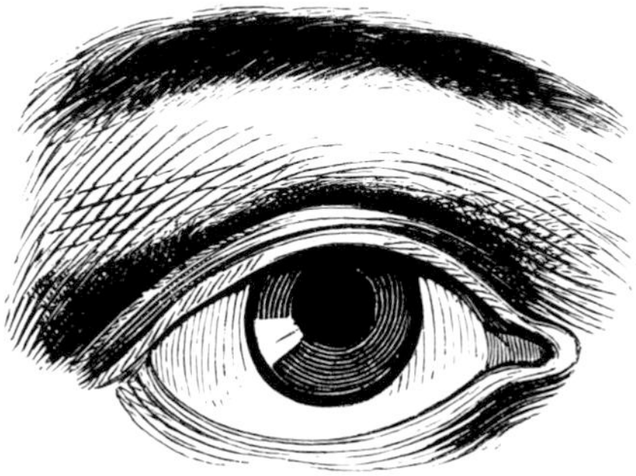
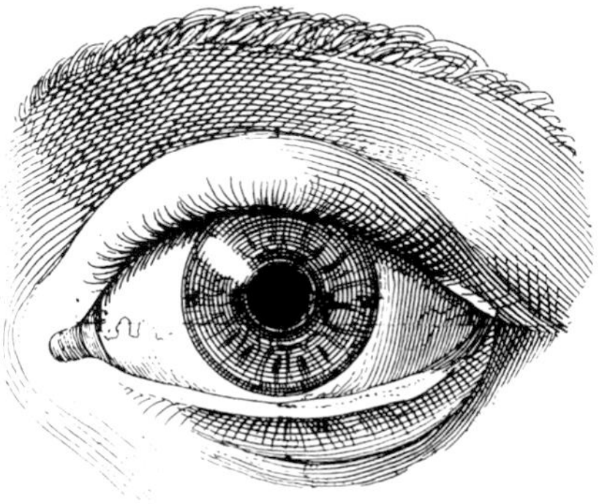
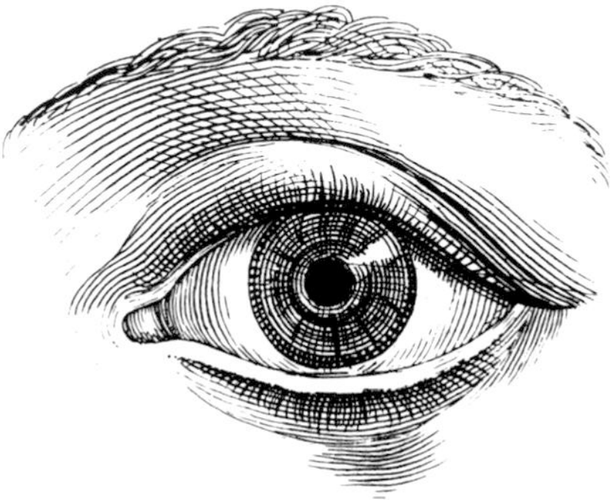
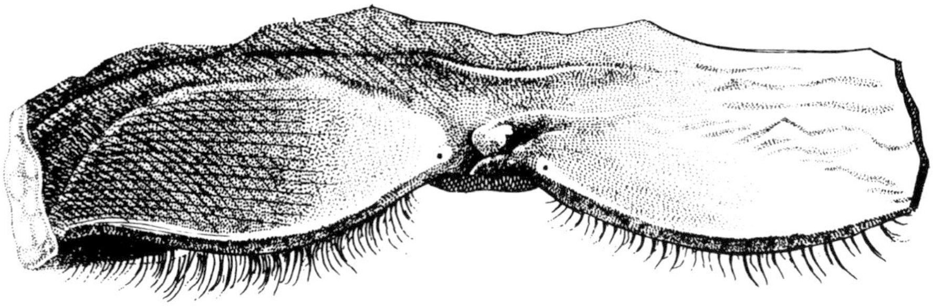
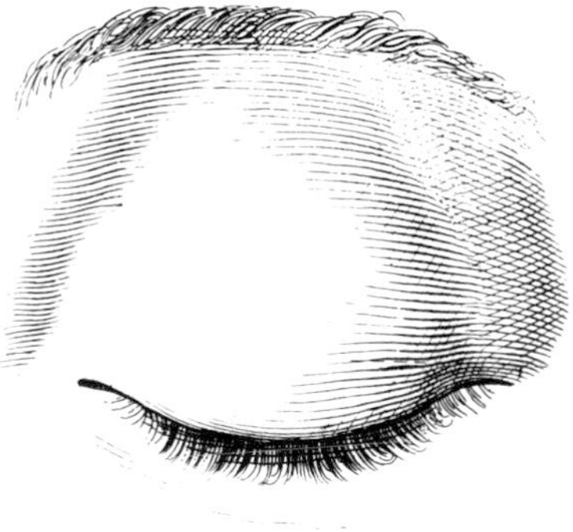

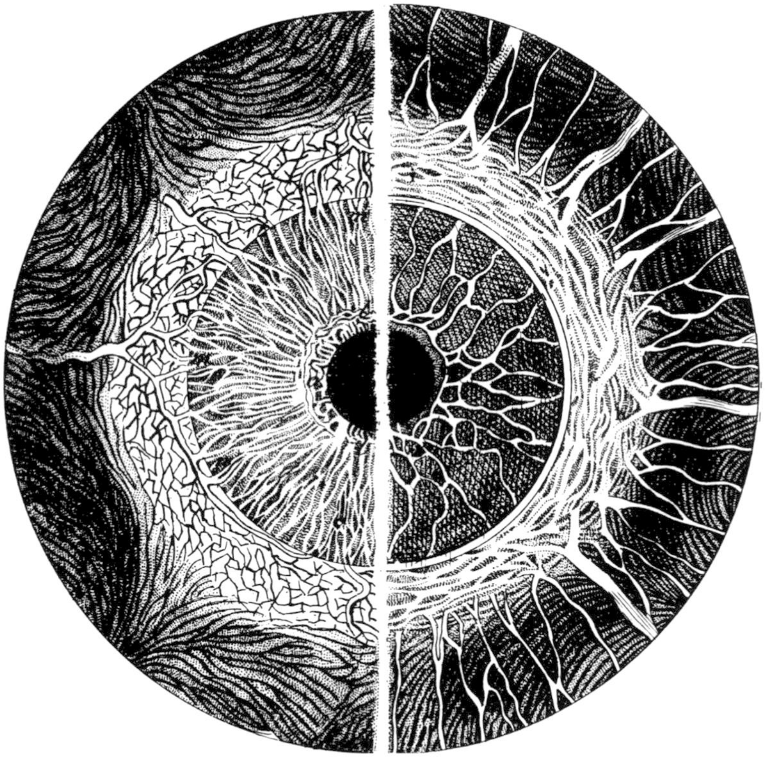

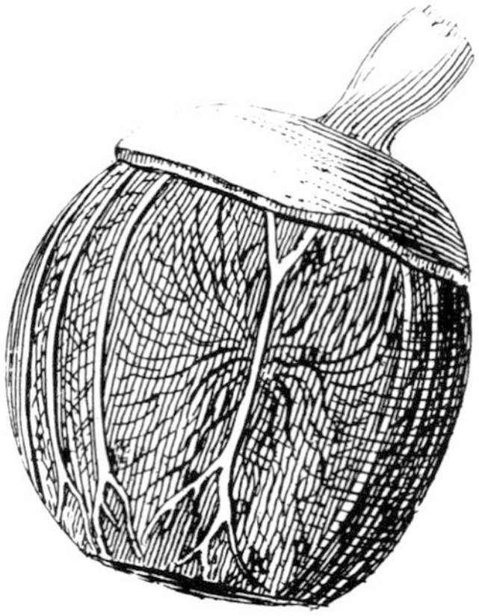
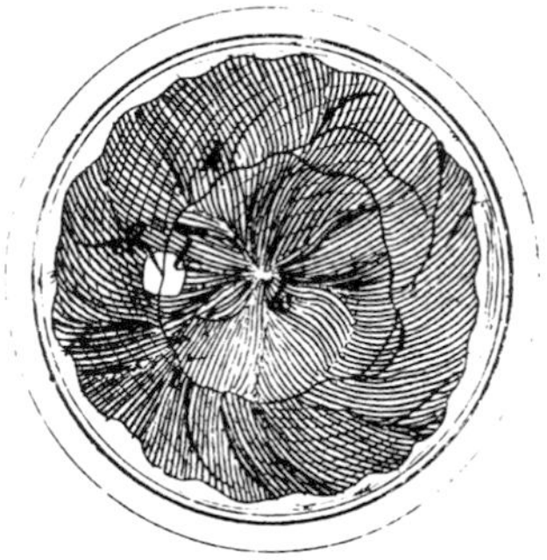
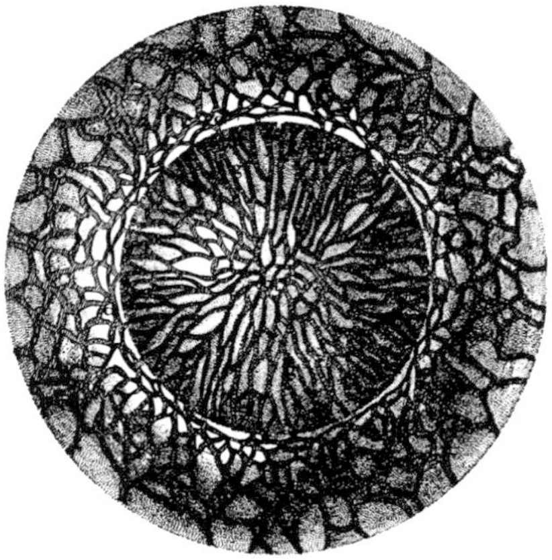
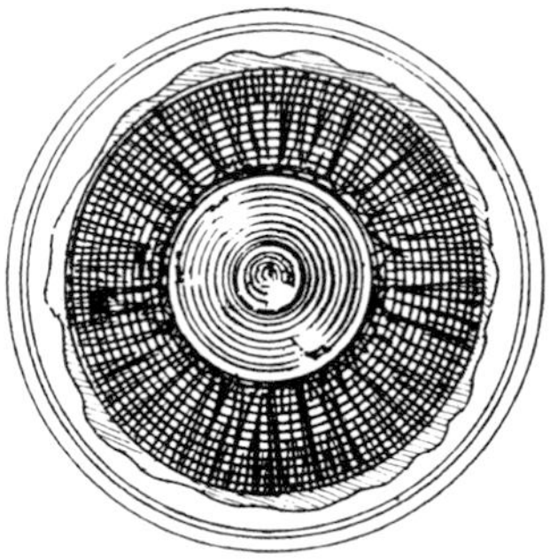
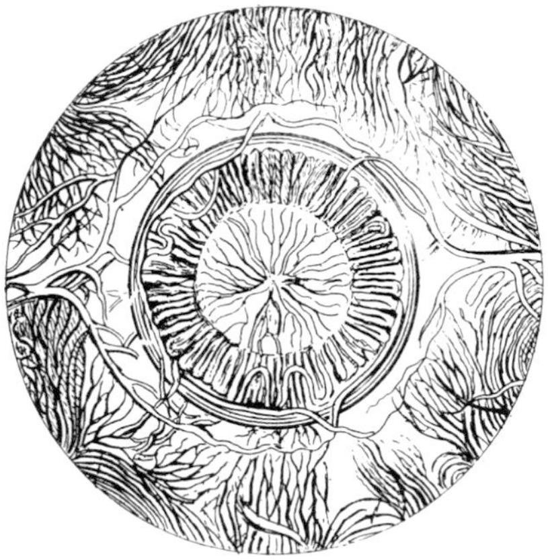
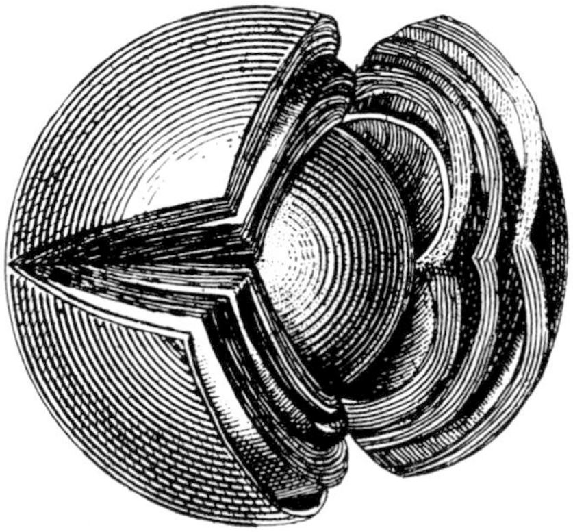
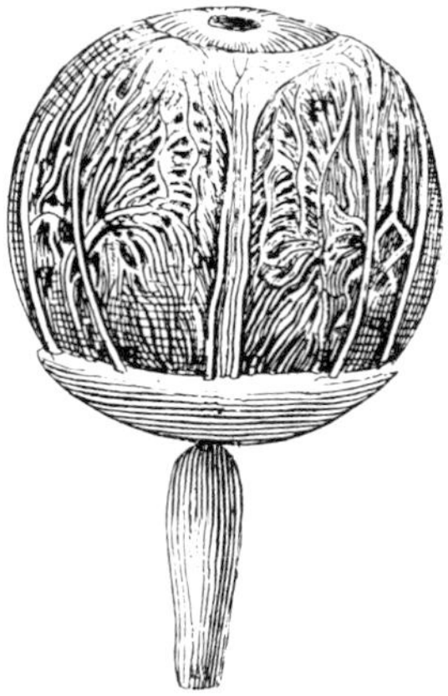
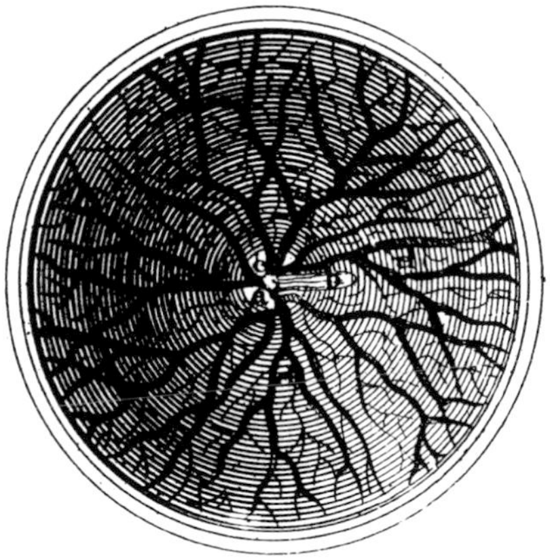
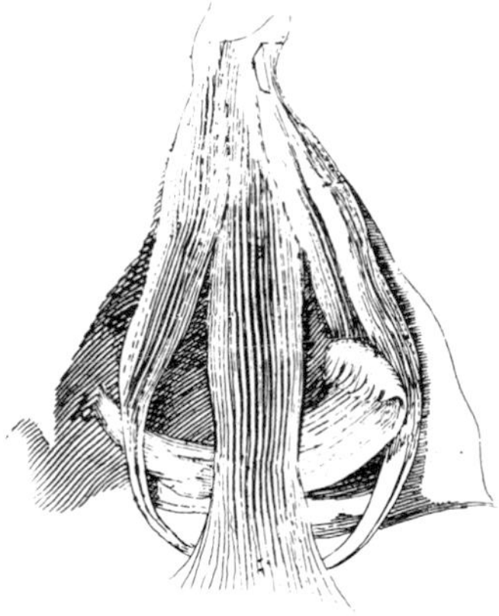

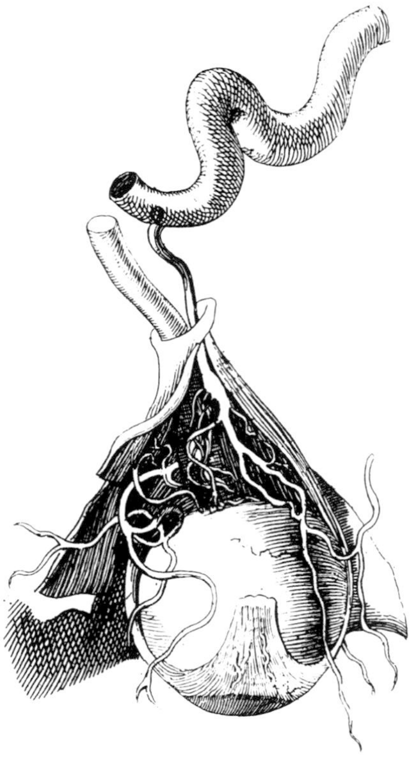

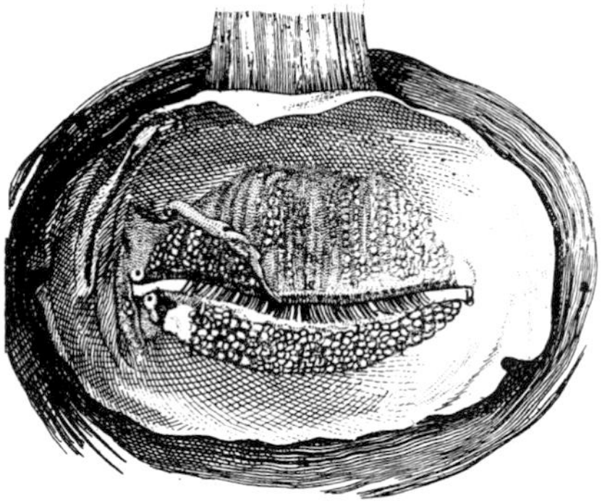

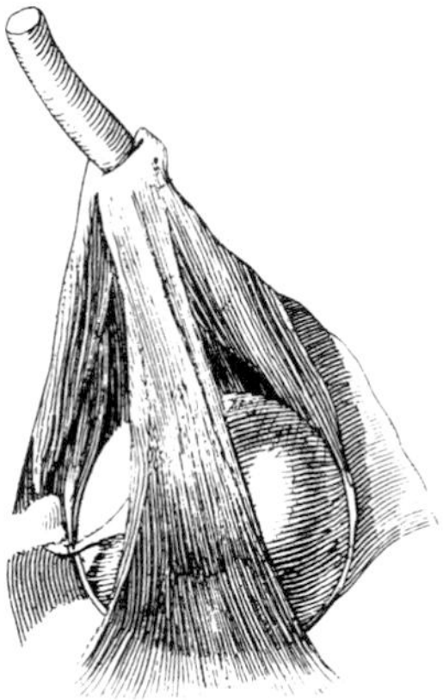

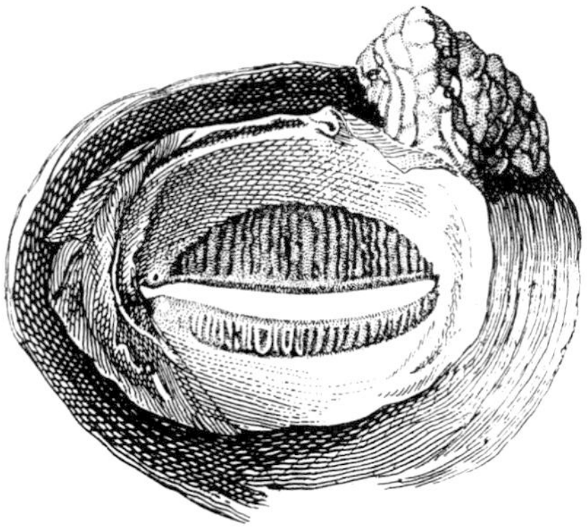

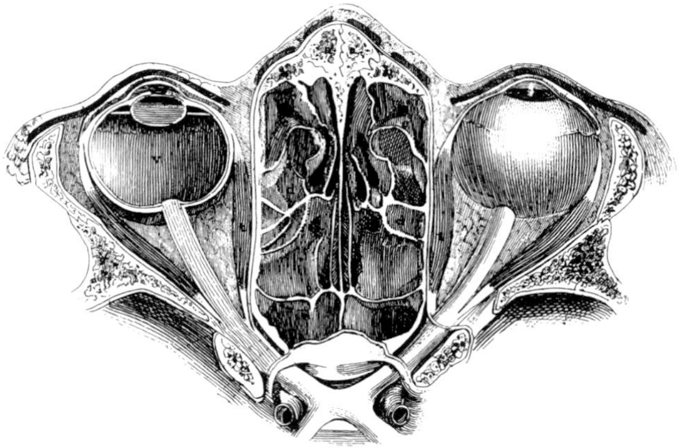

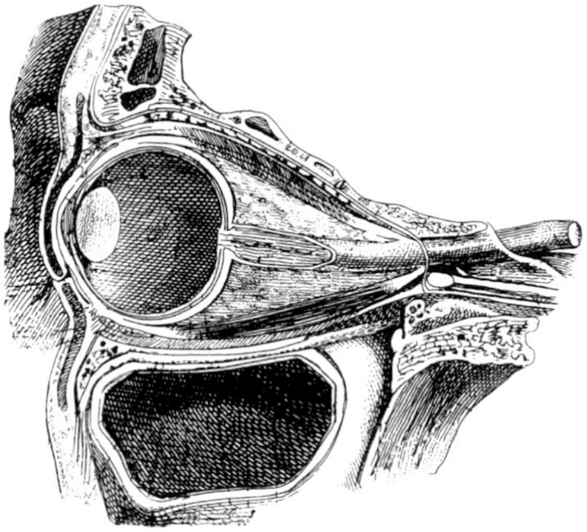

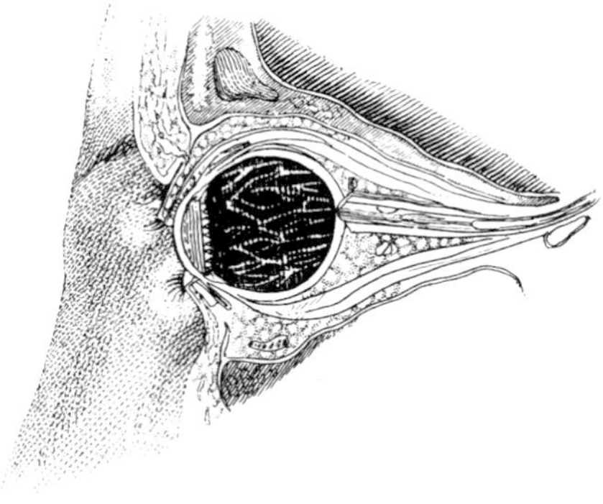

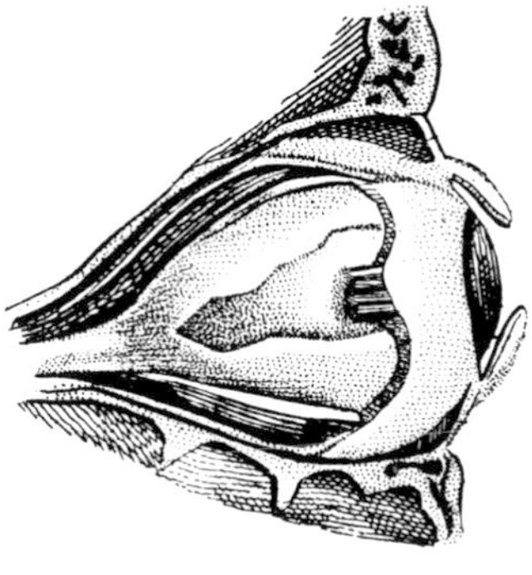

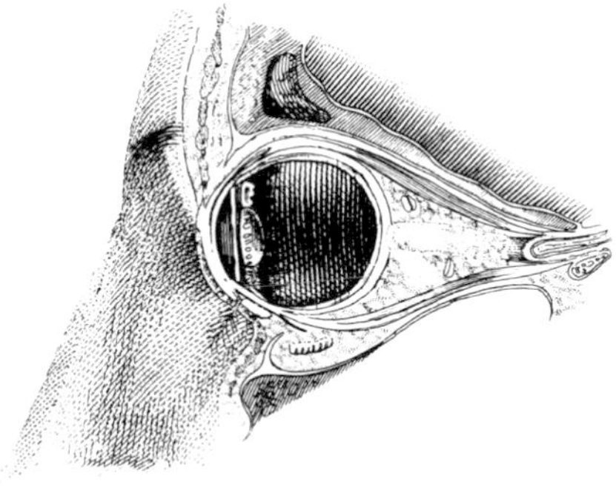

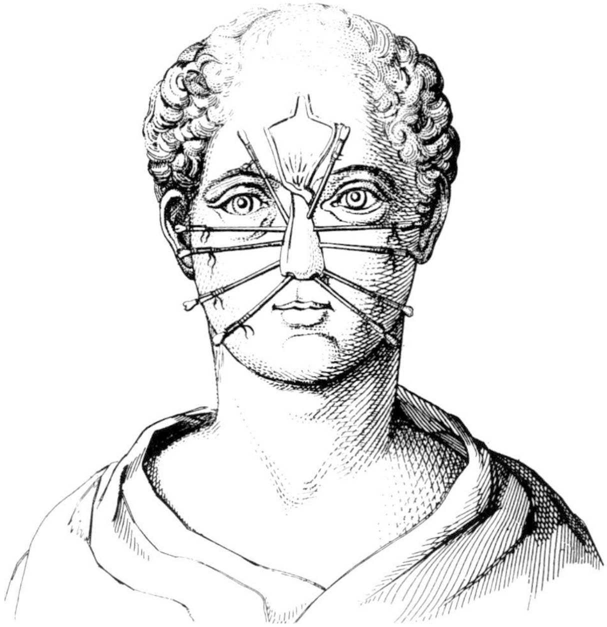
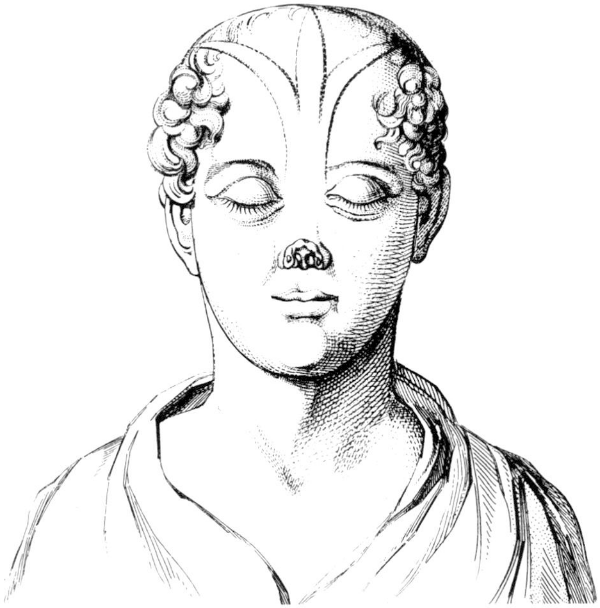
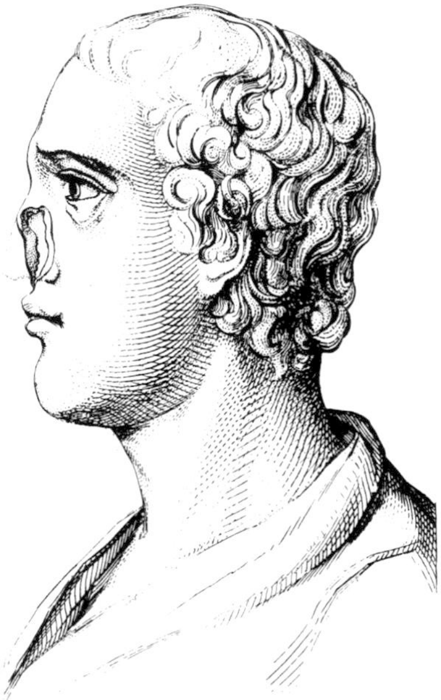
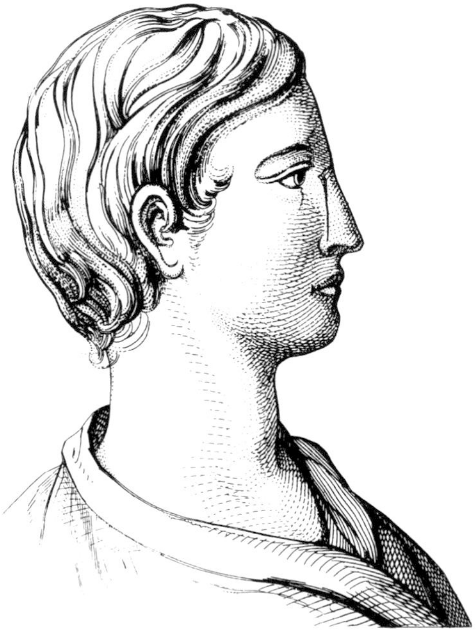

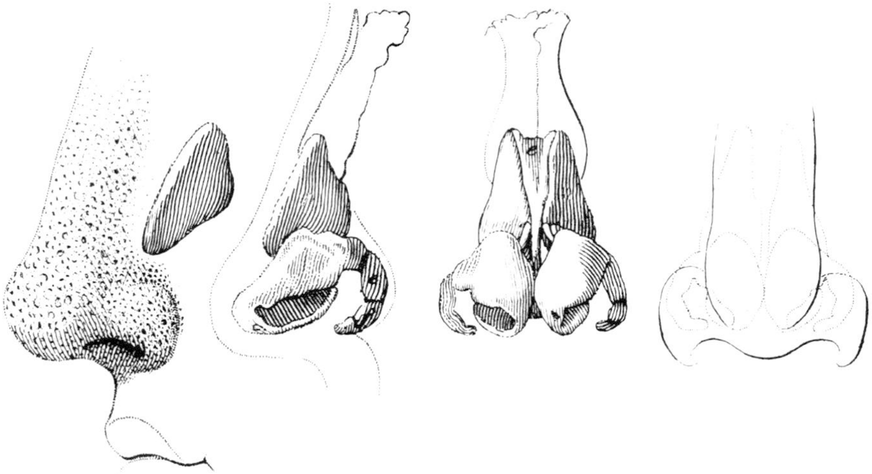

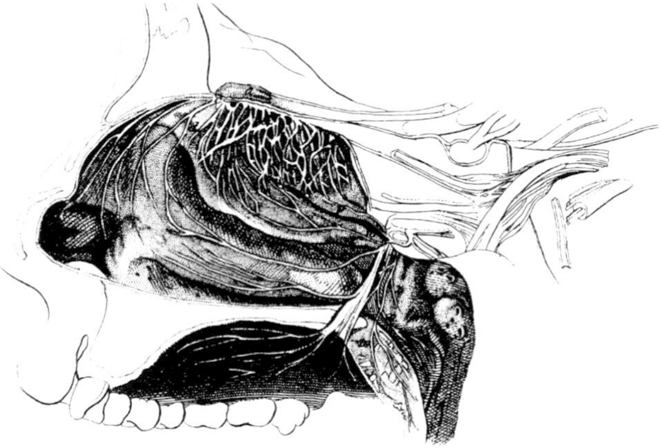

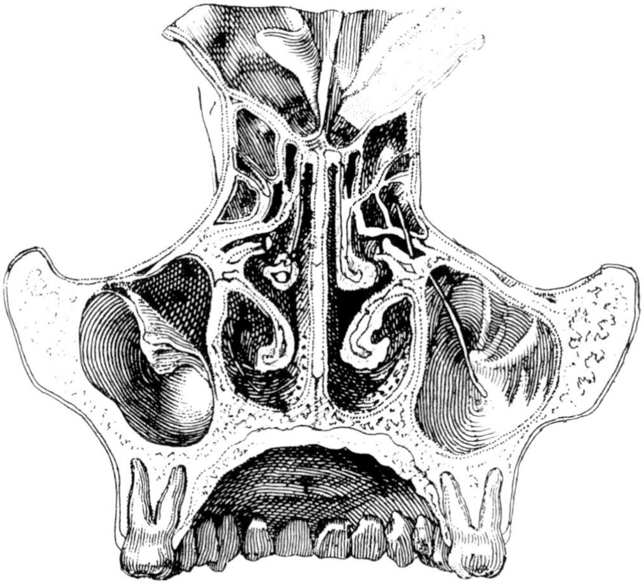

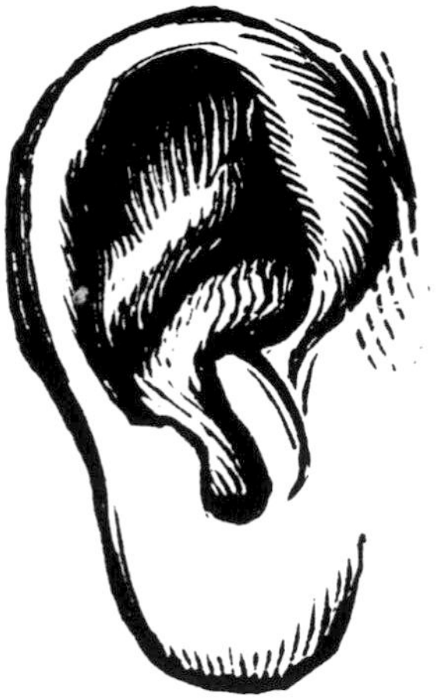

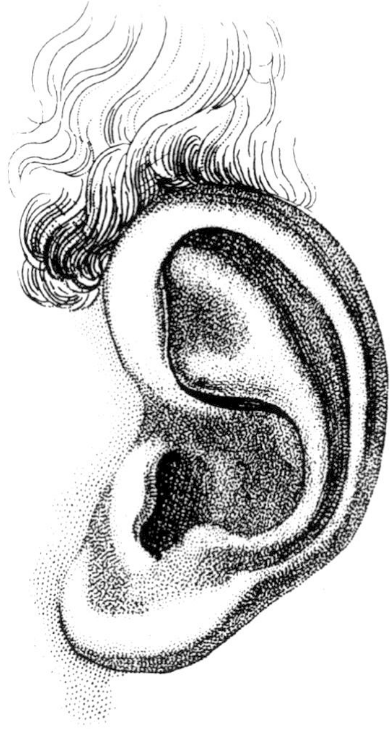

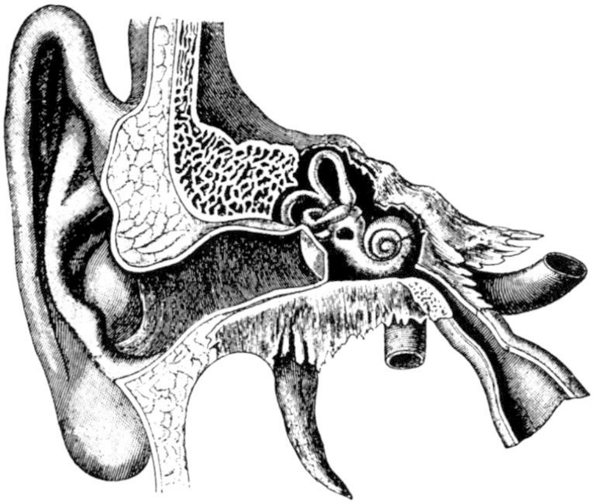
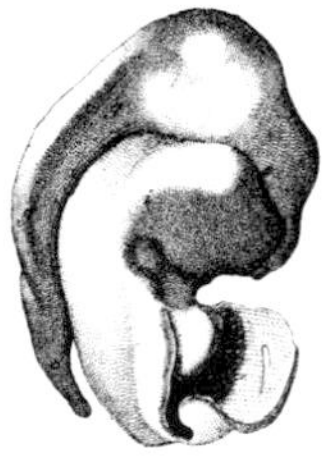
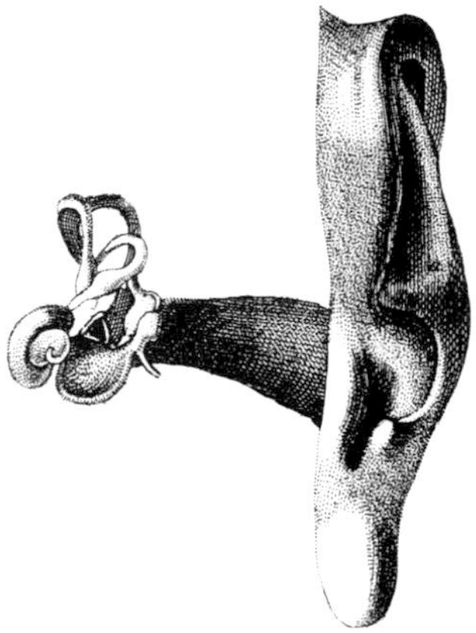
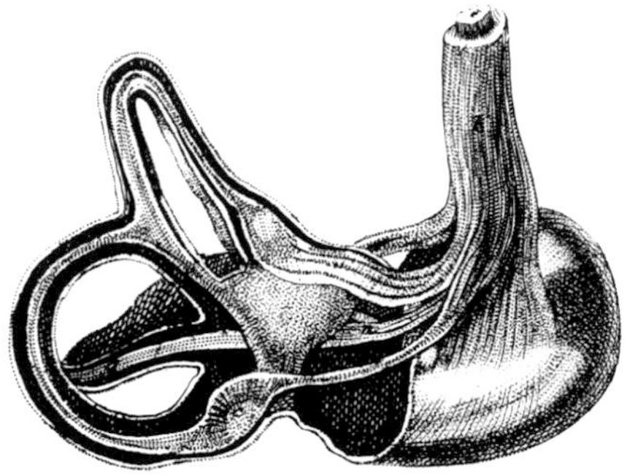
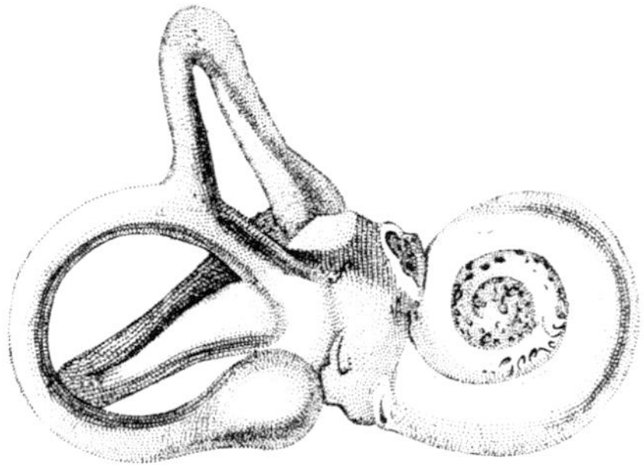
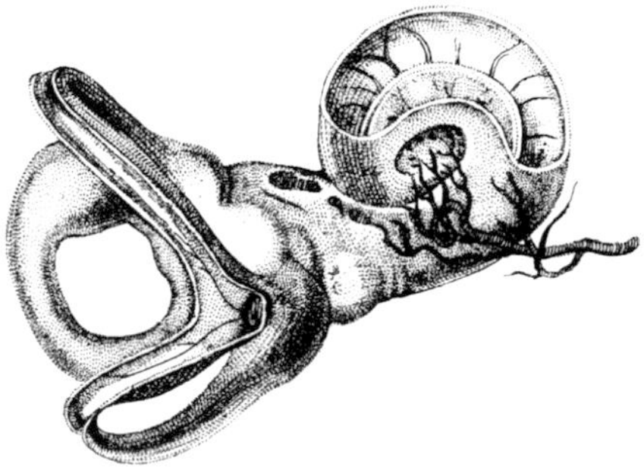
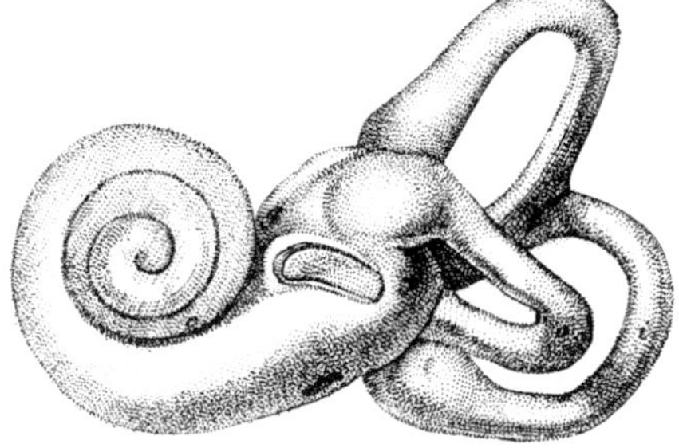
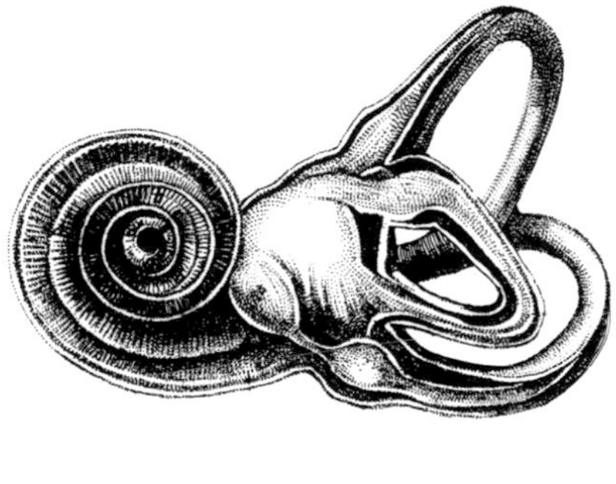
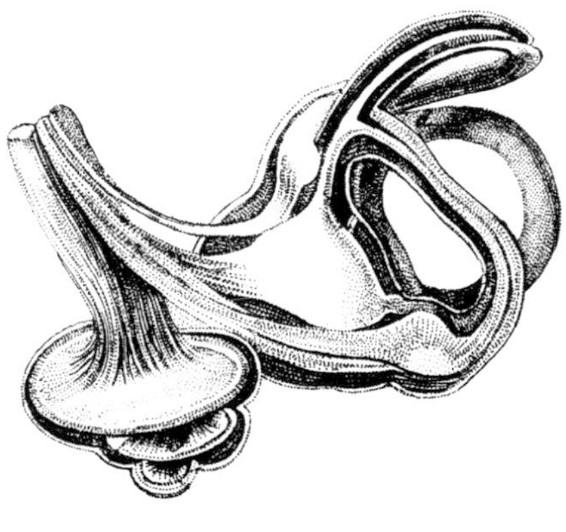

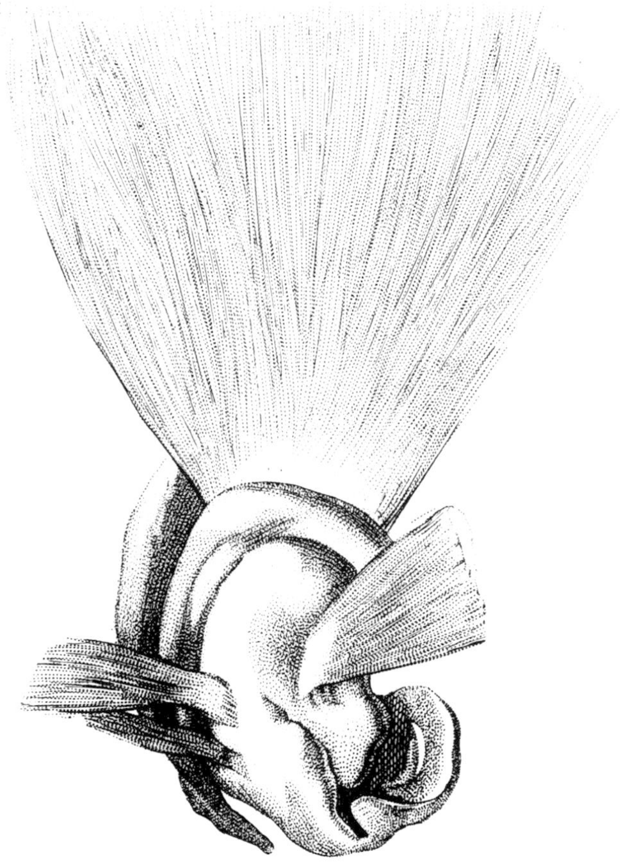

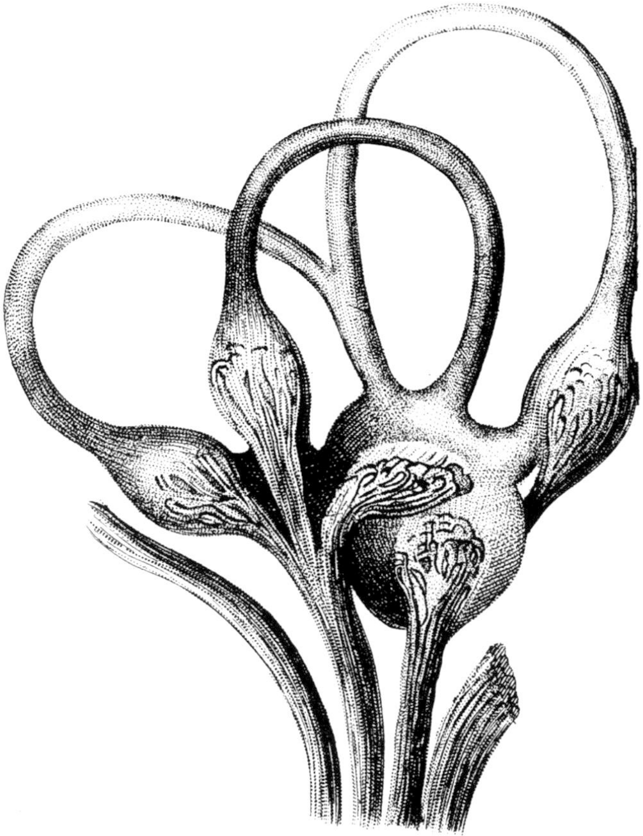

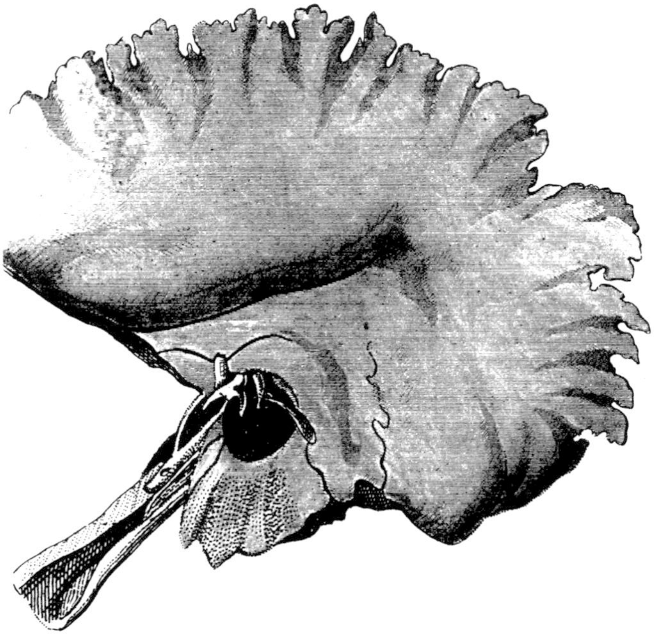
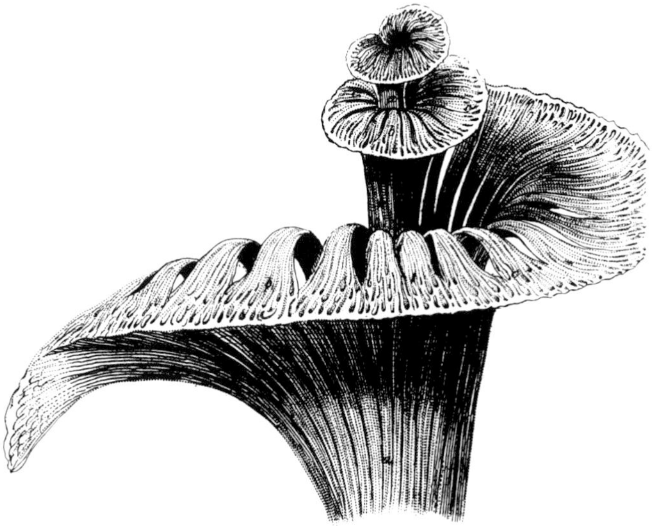
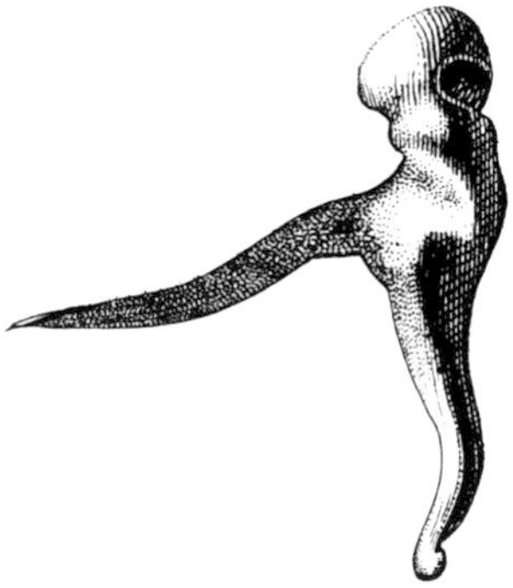
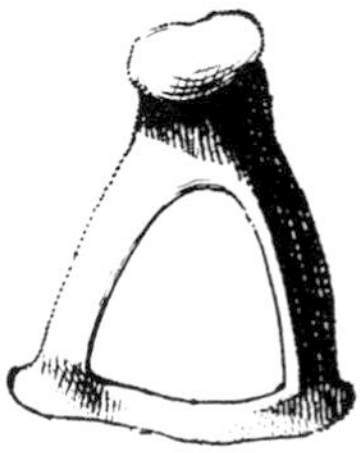
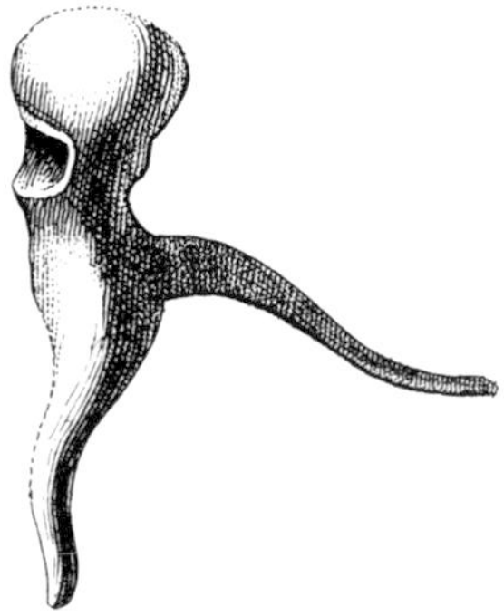

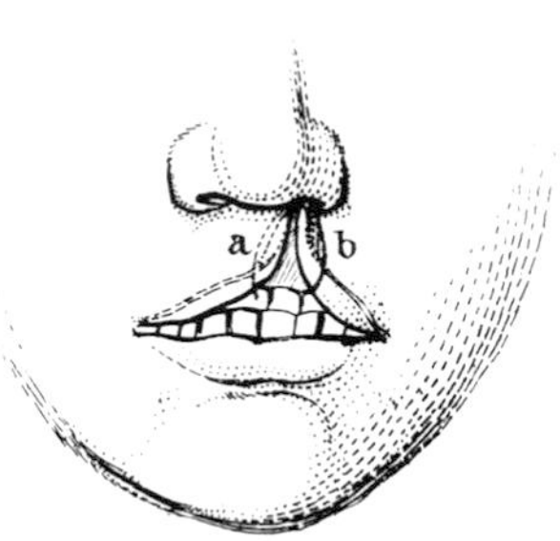
a
b

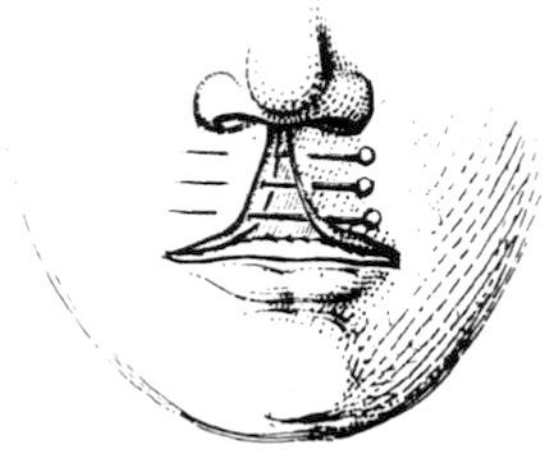

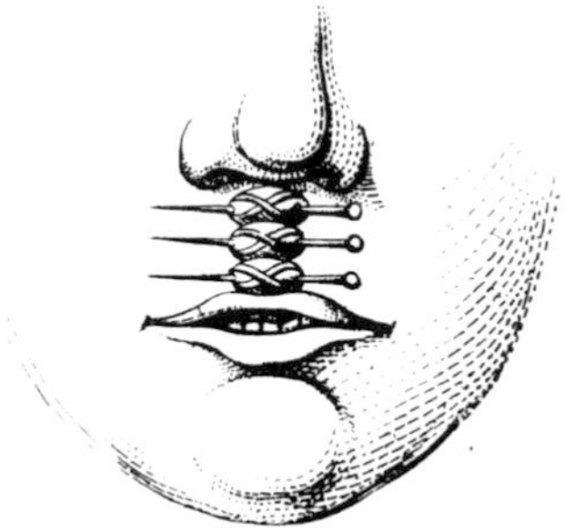

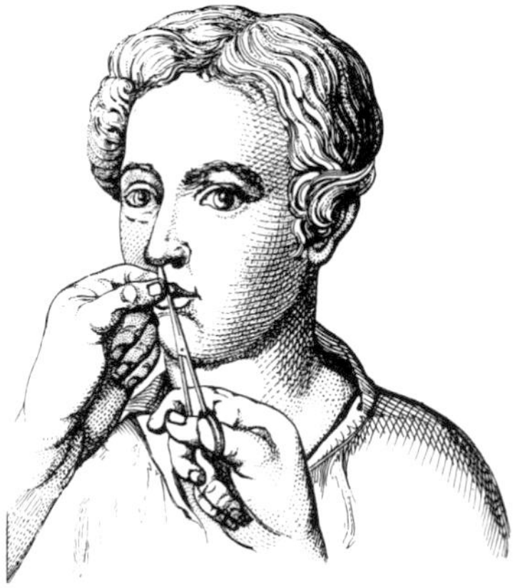

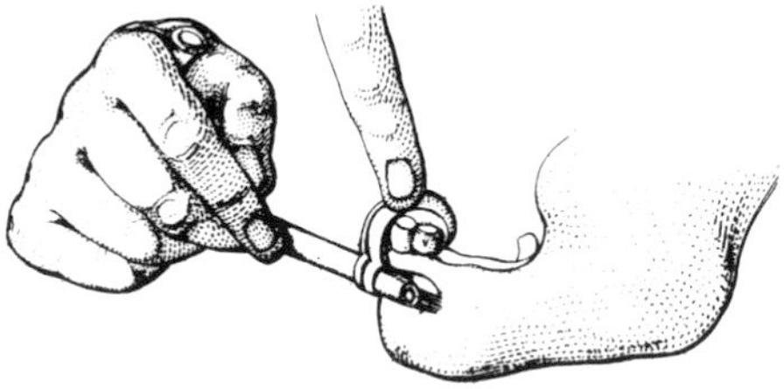

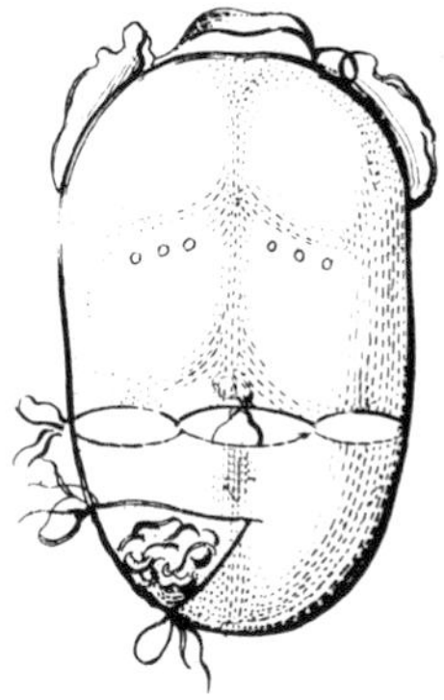

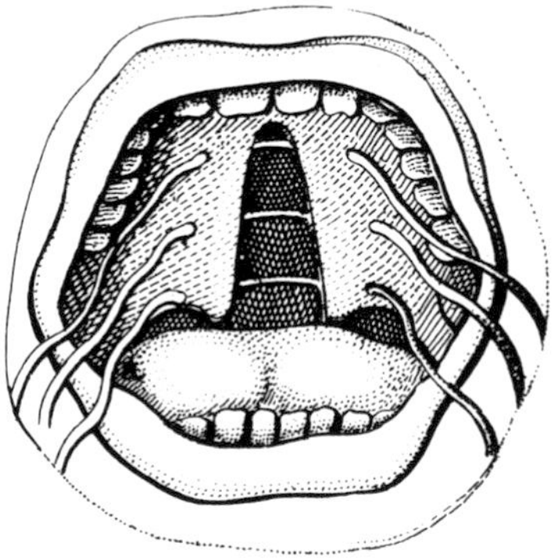

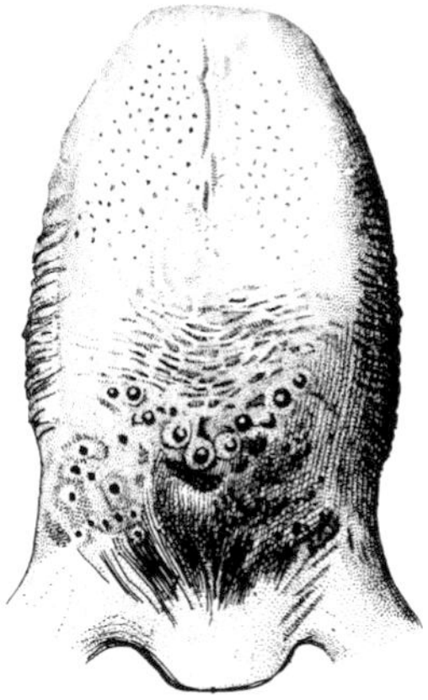

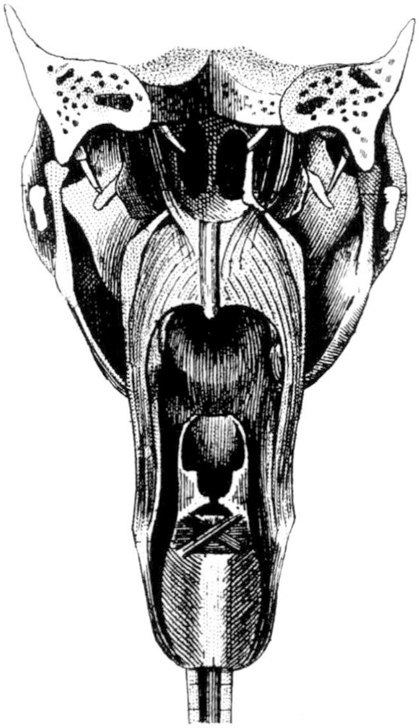
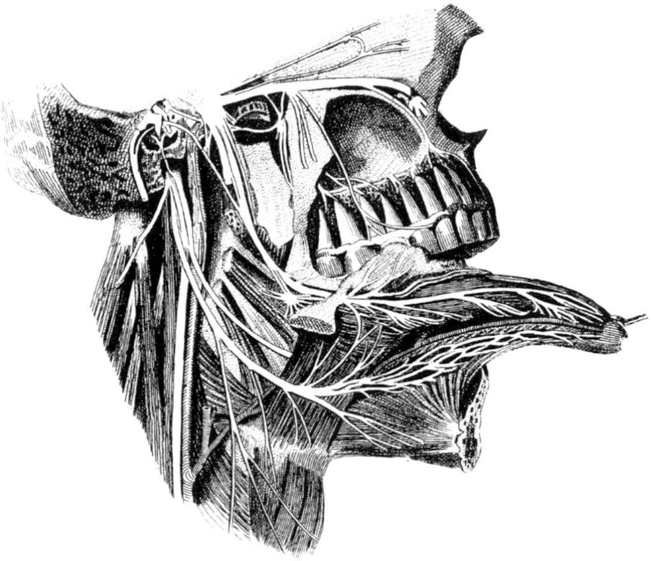
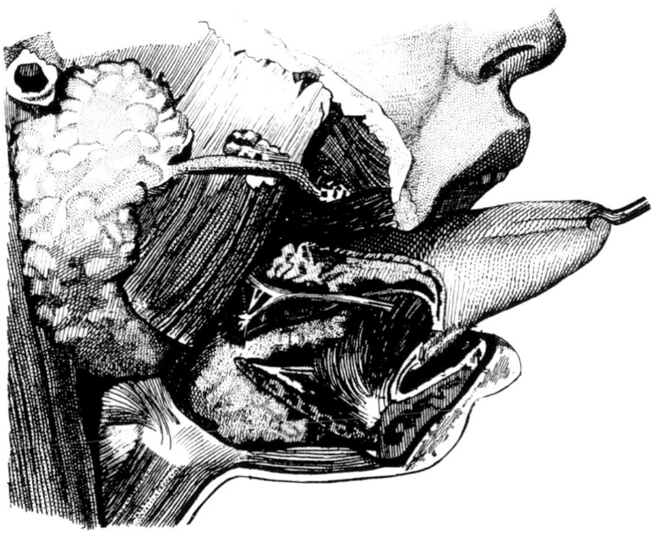
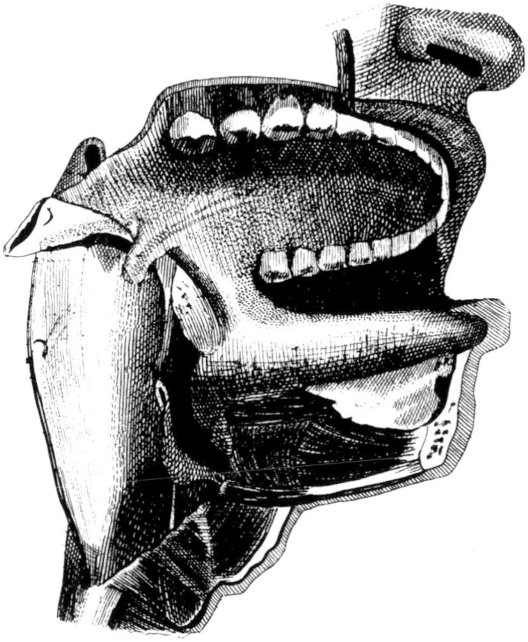

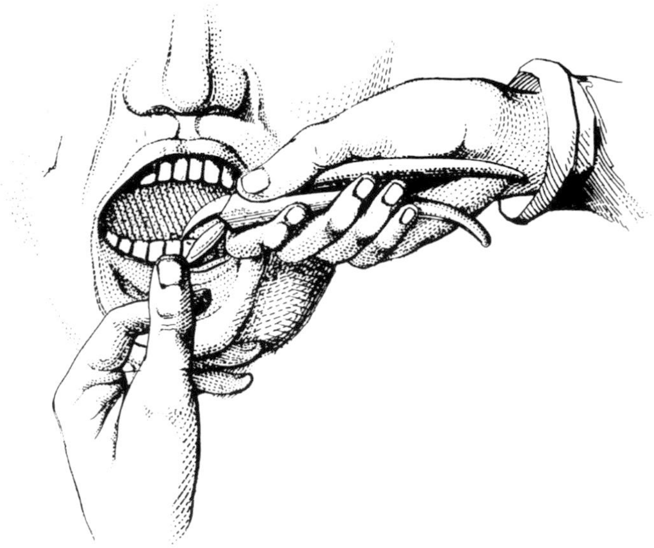

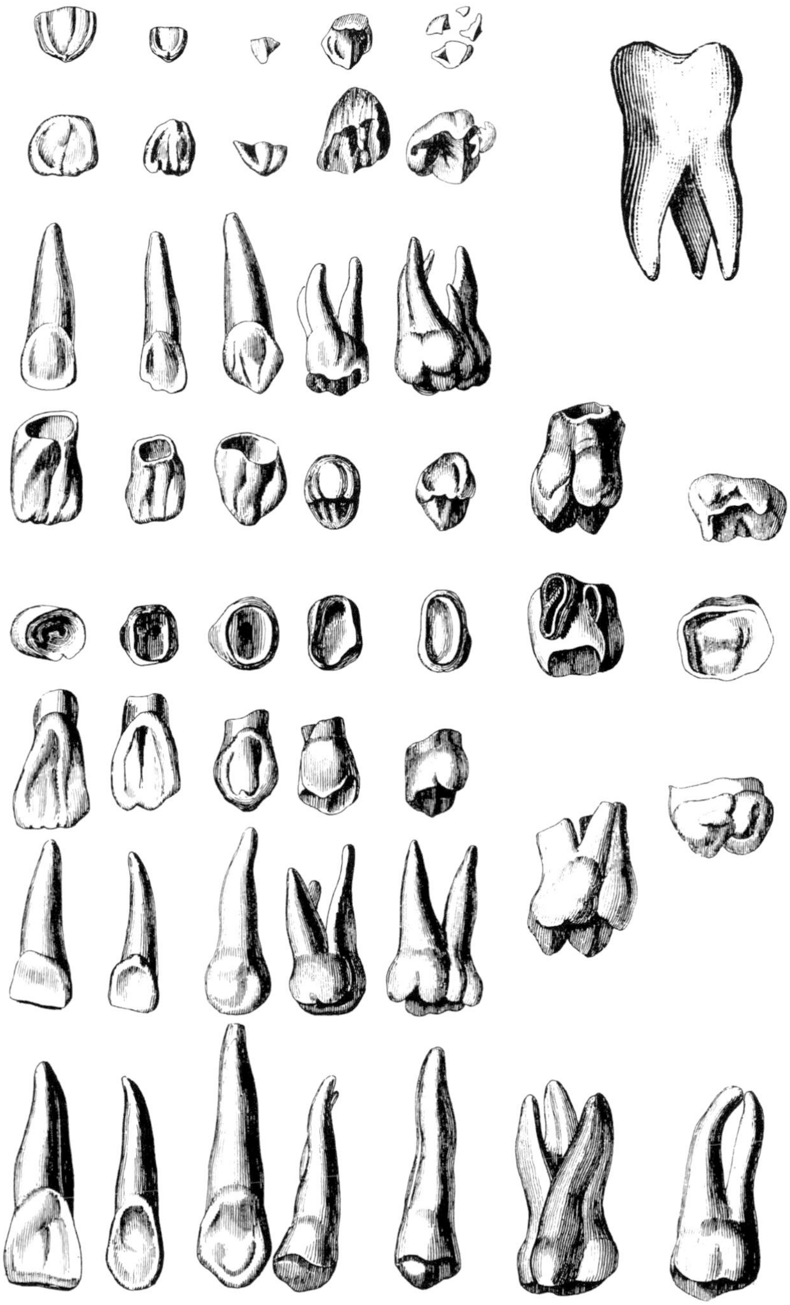

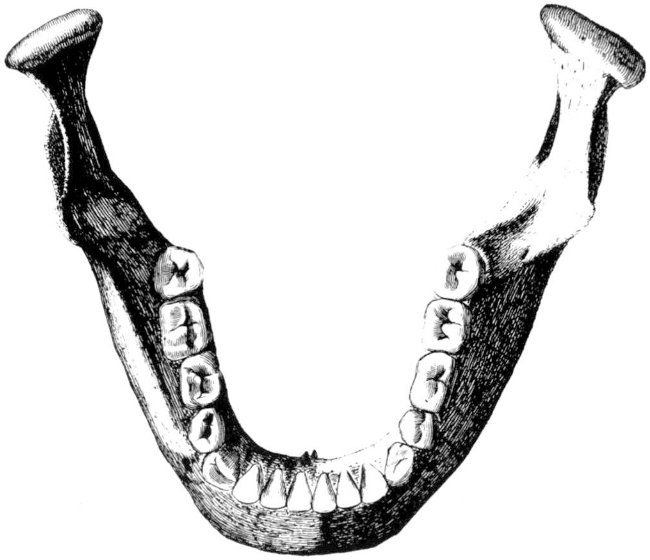

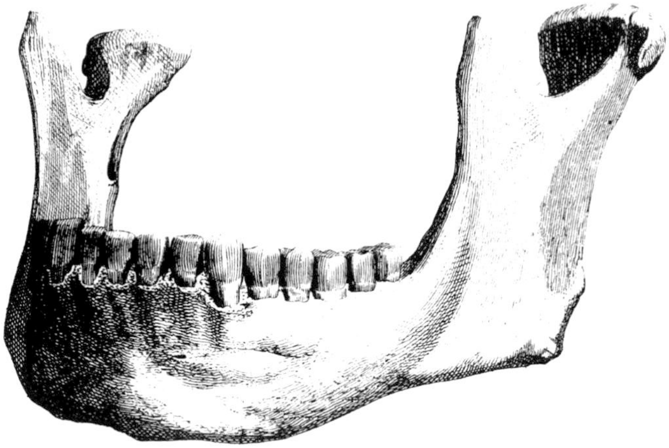

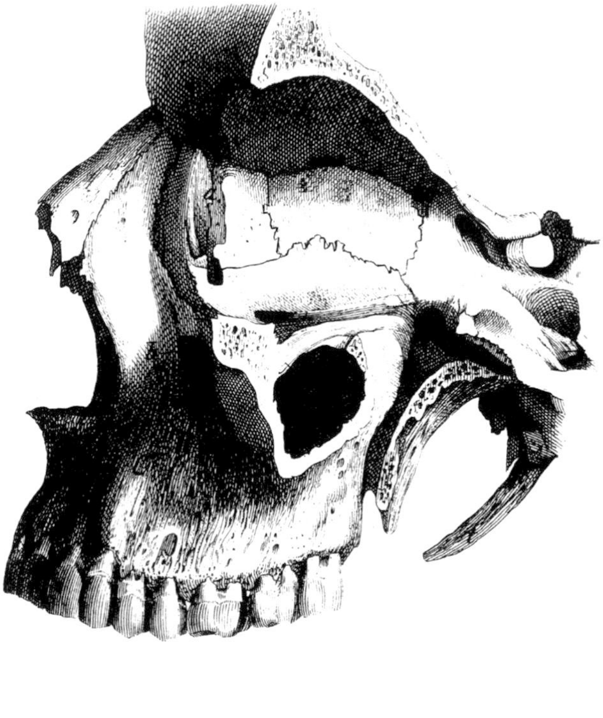

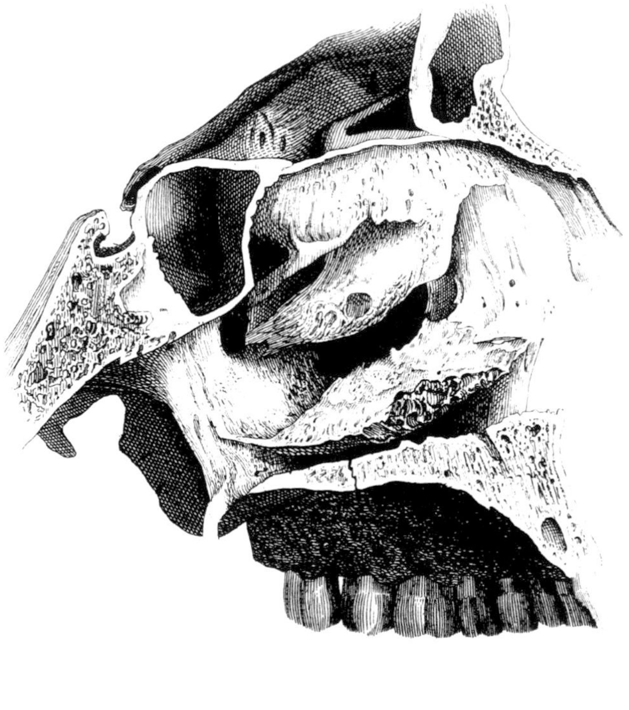

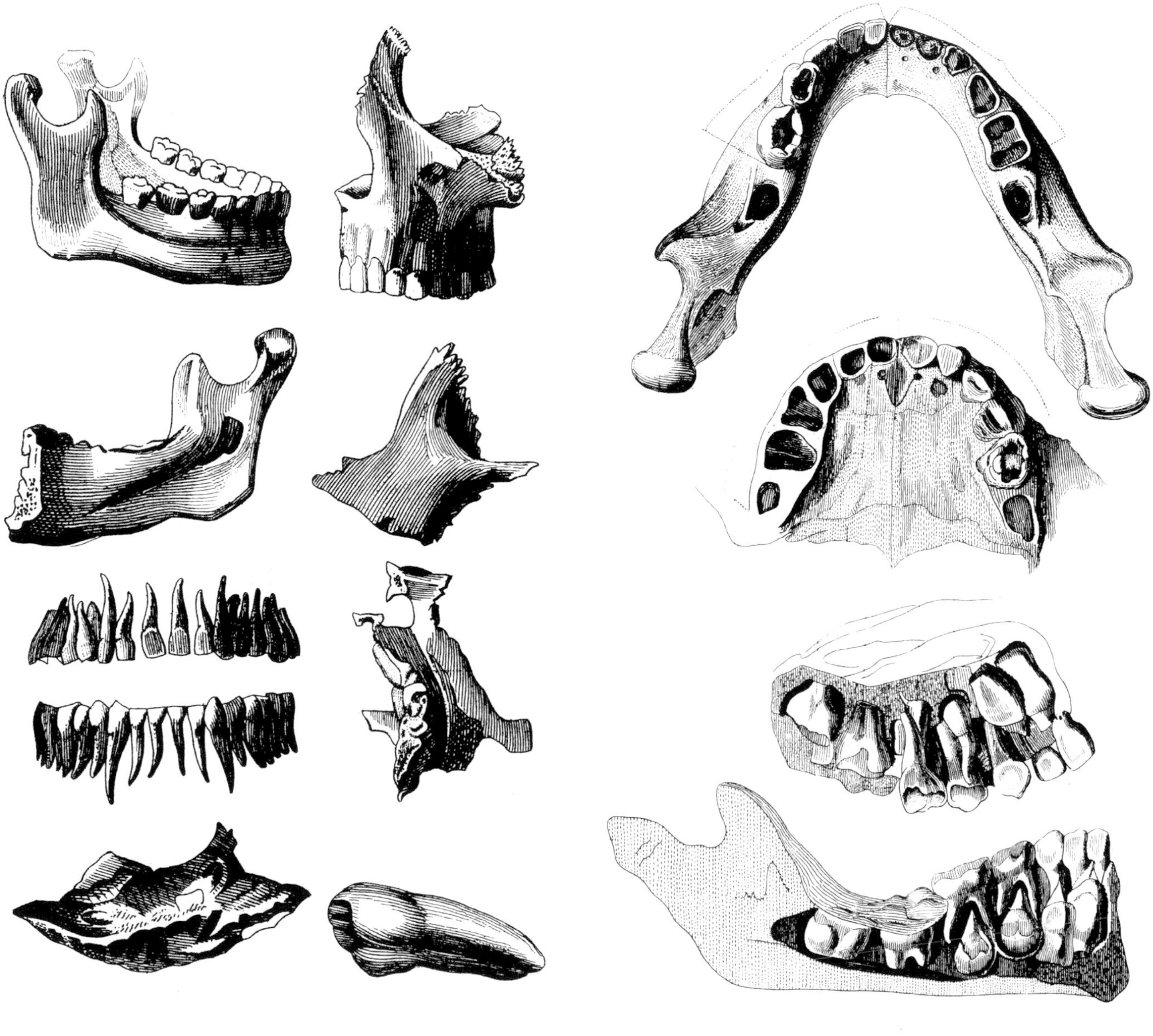

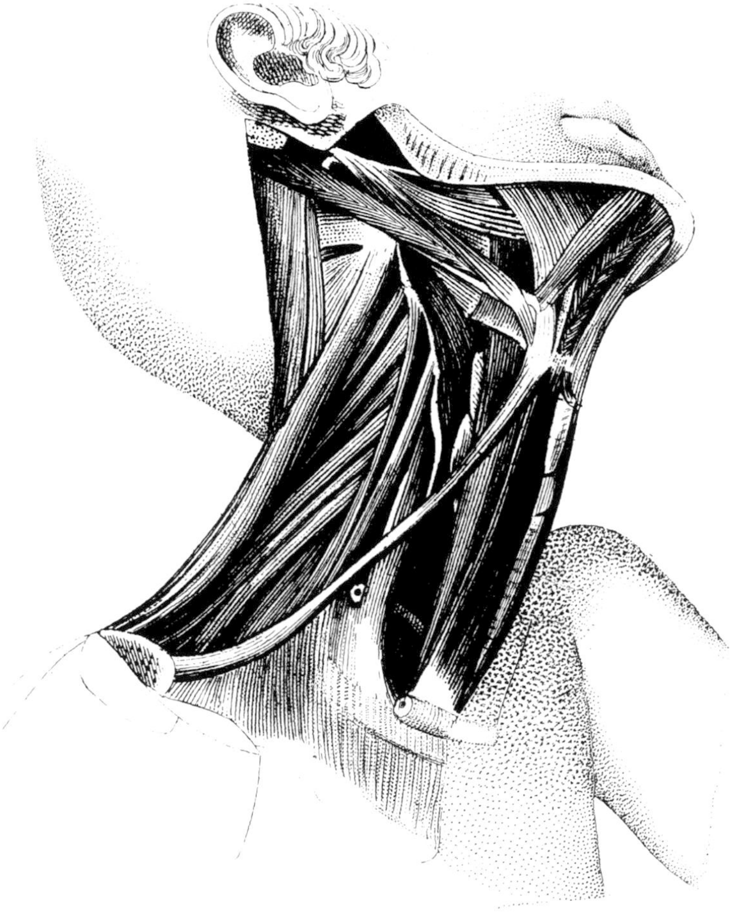

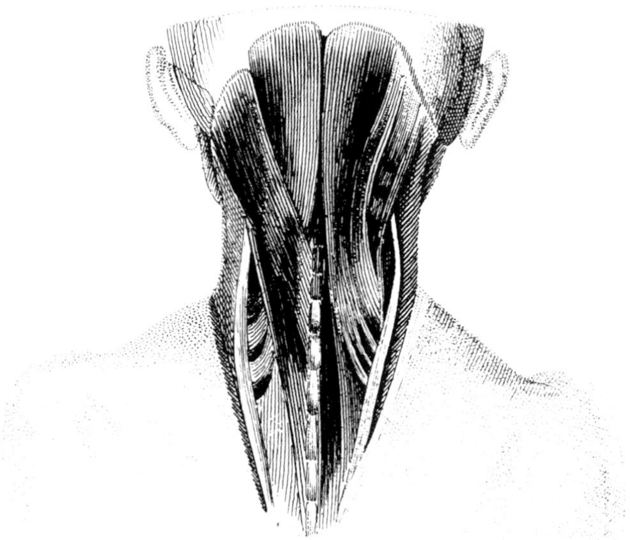
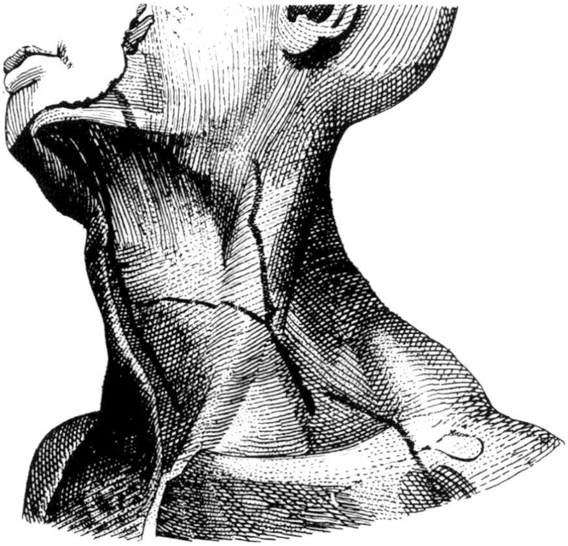
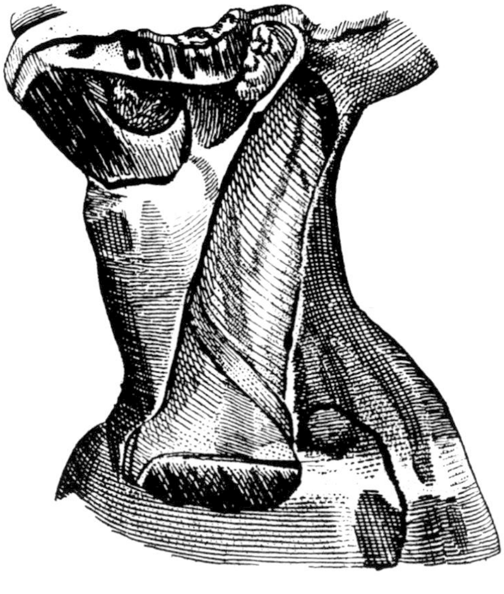
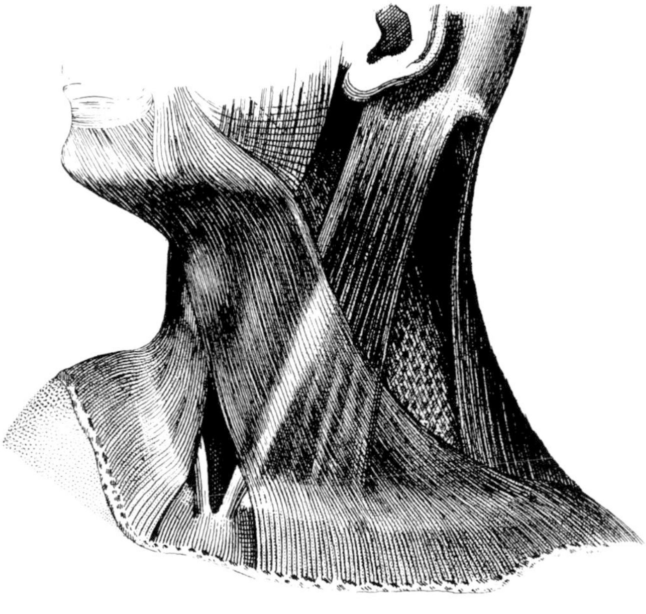

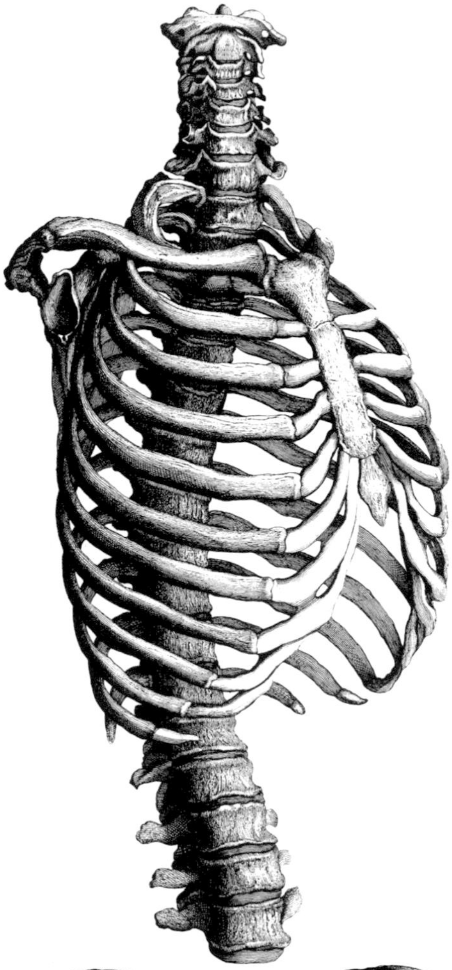

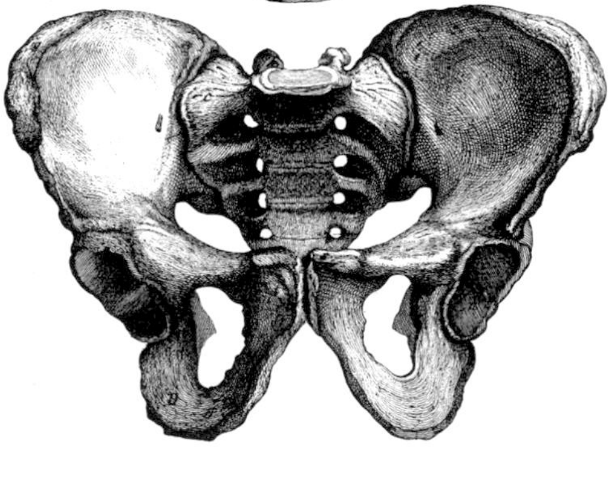

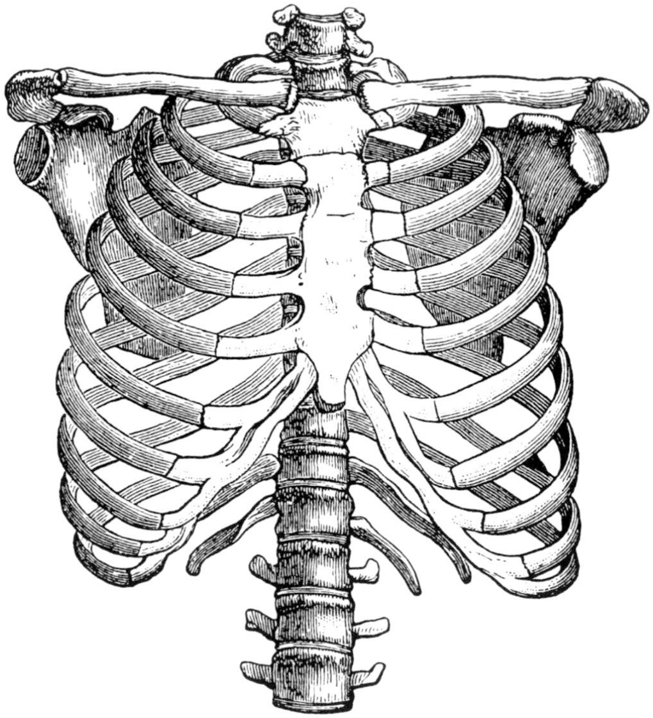

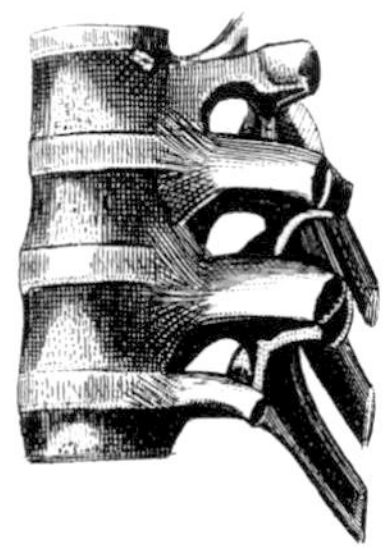

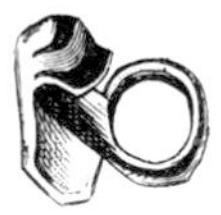

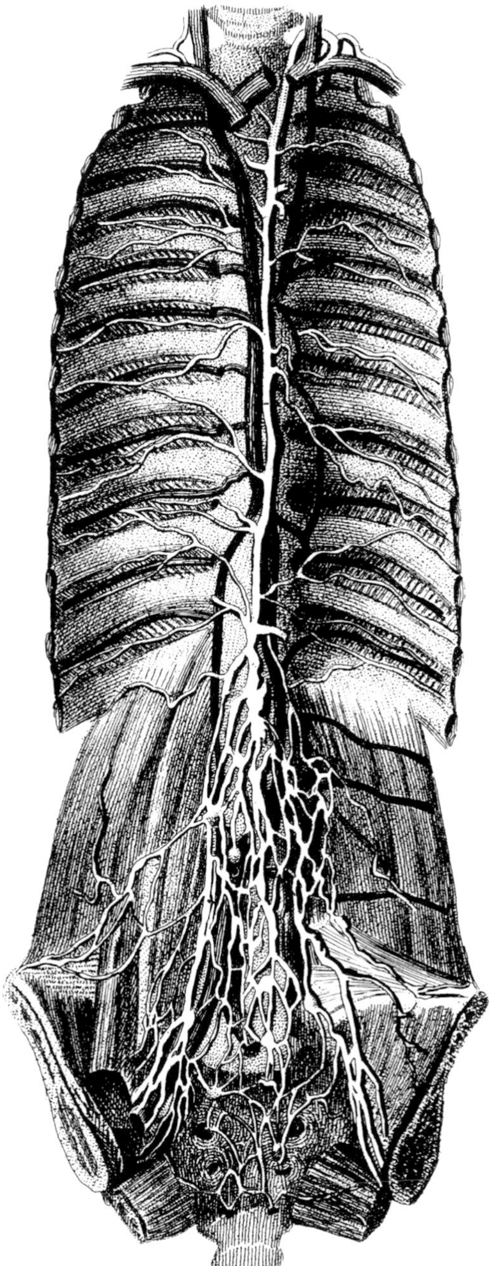 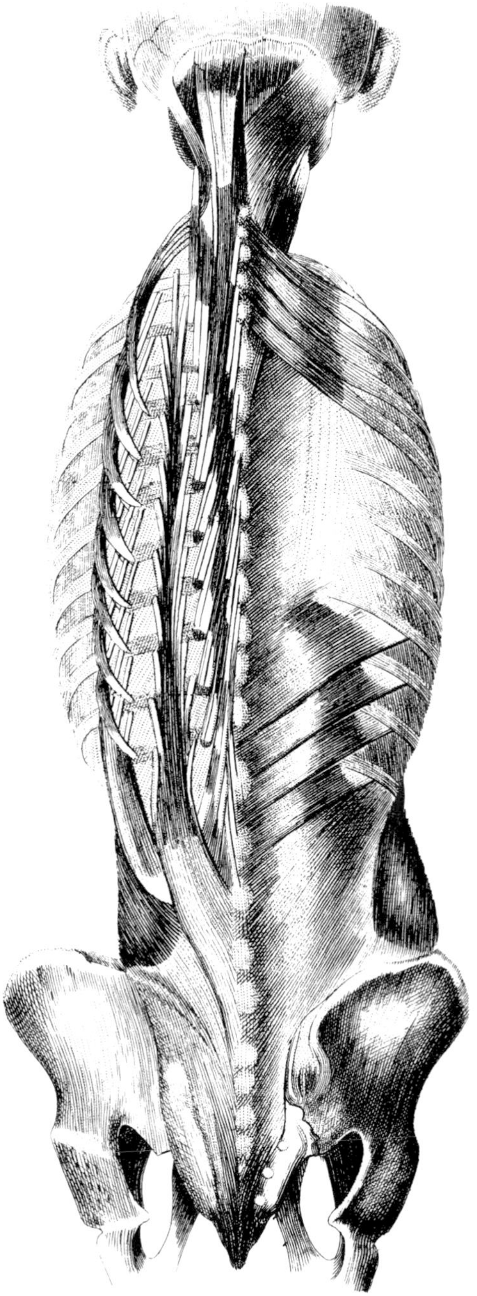 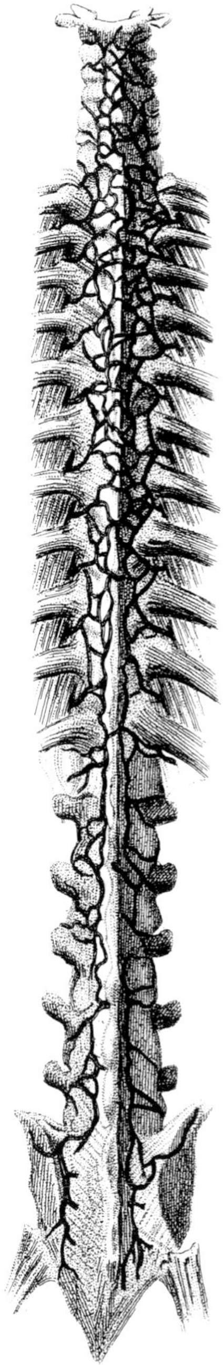

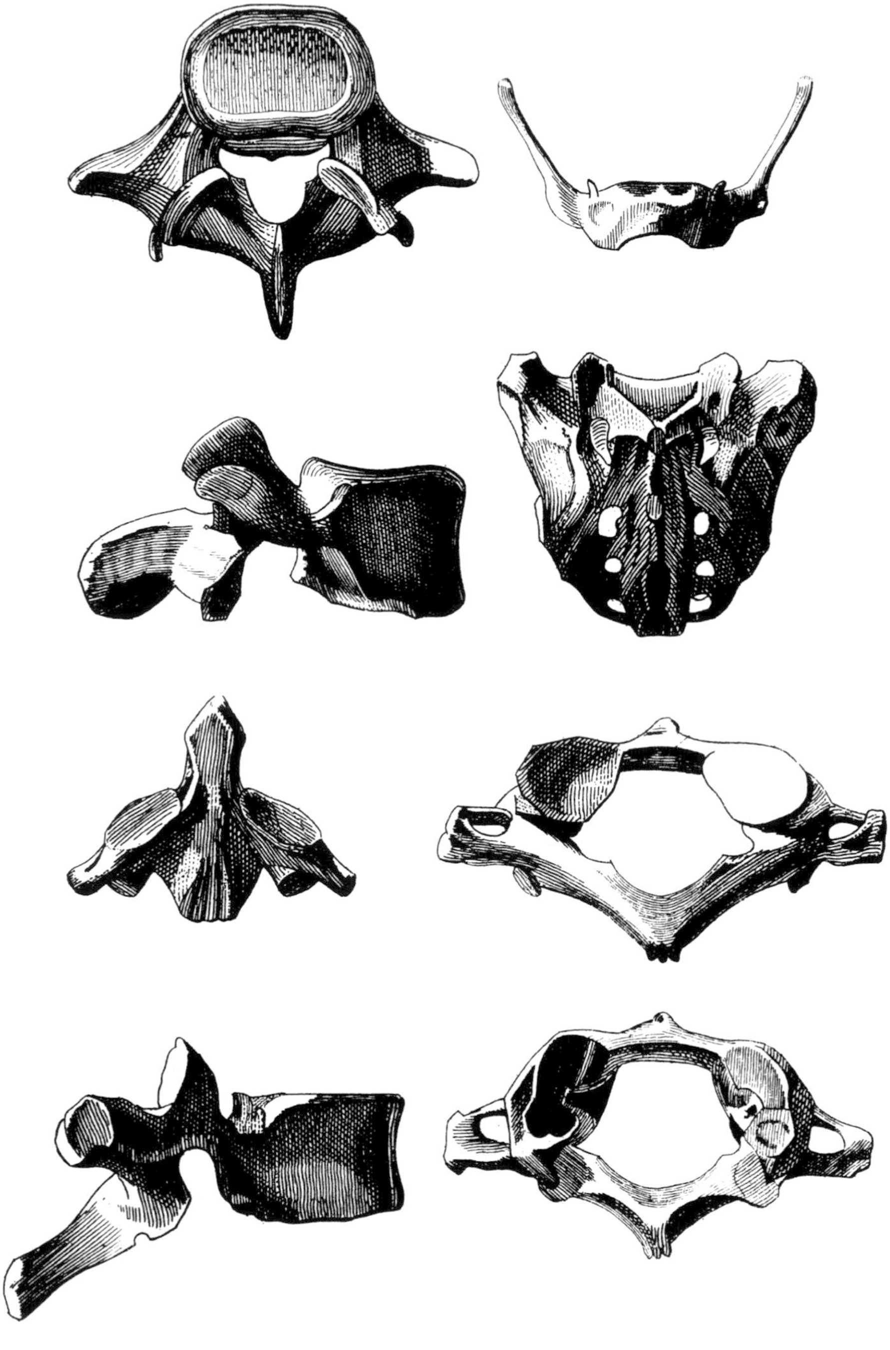

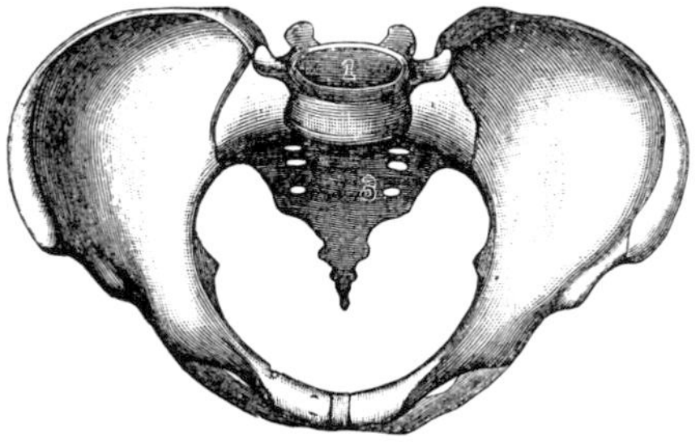
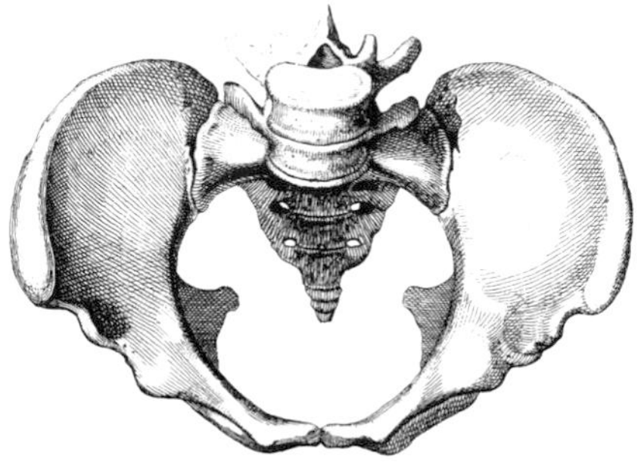
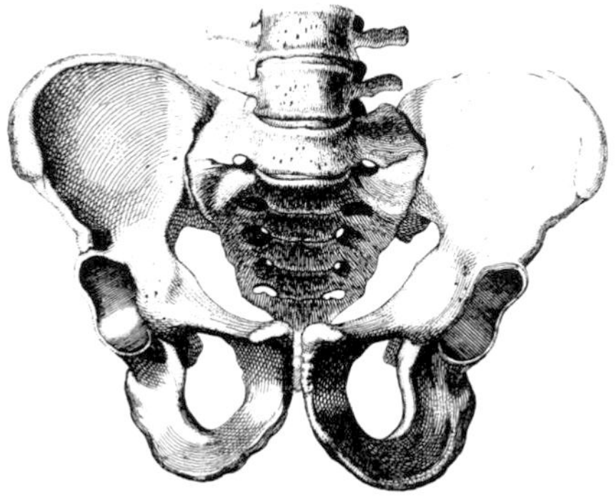
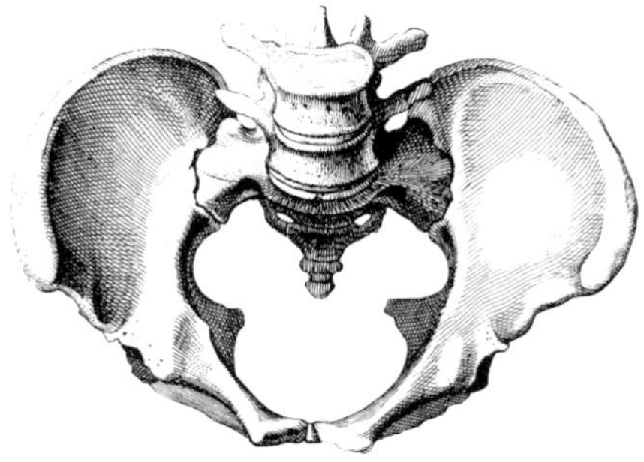
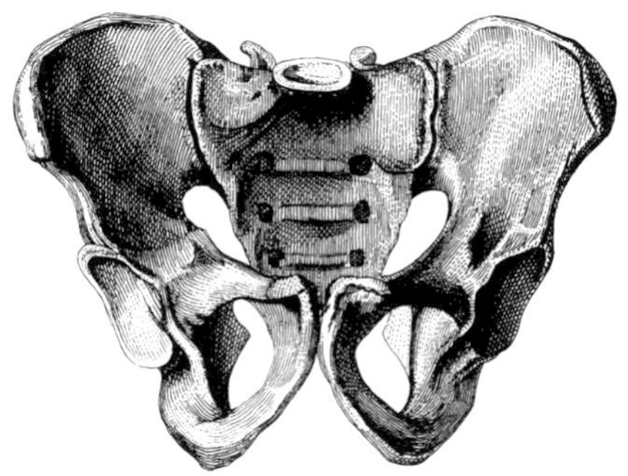
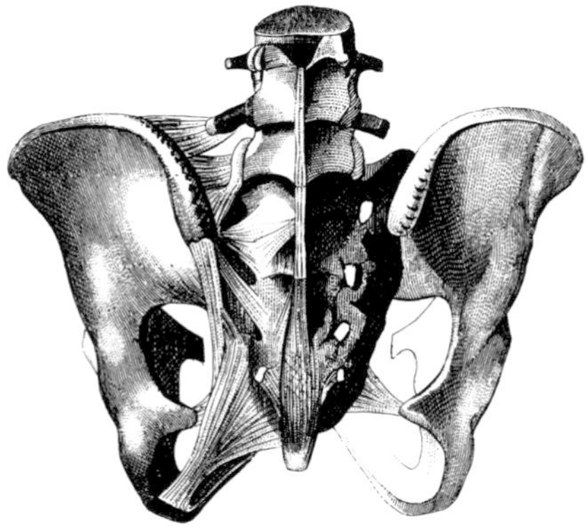
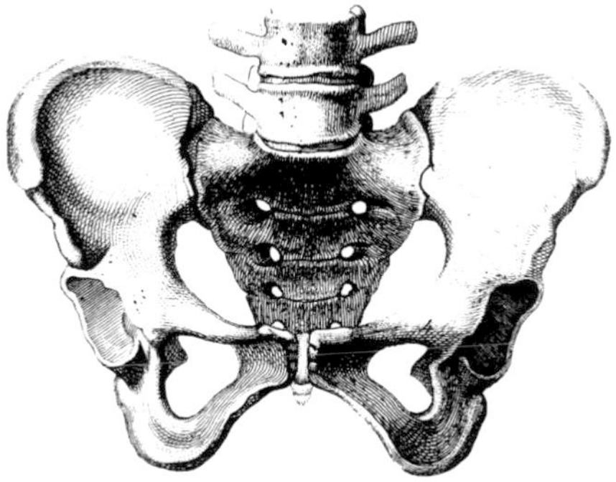
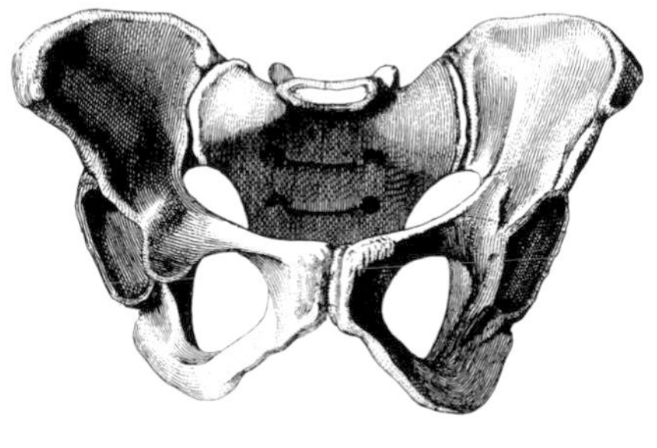
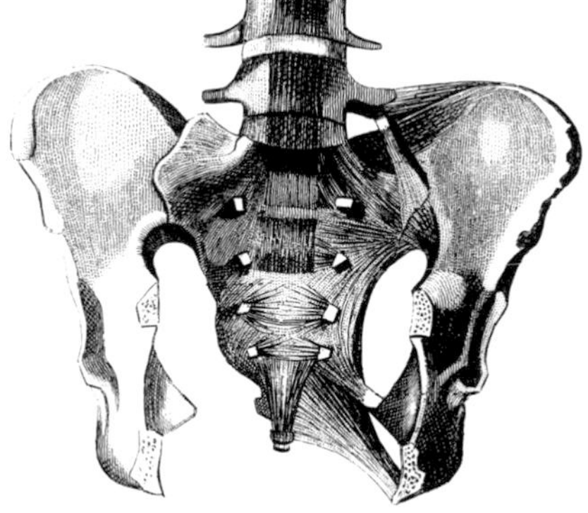

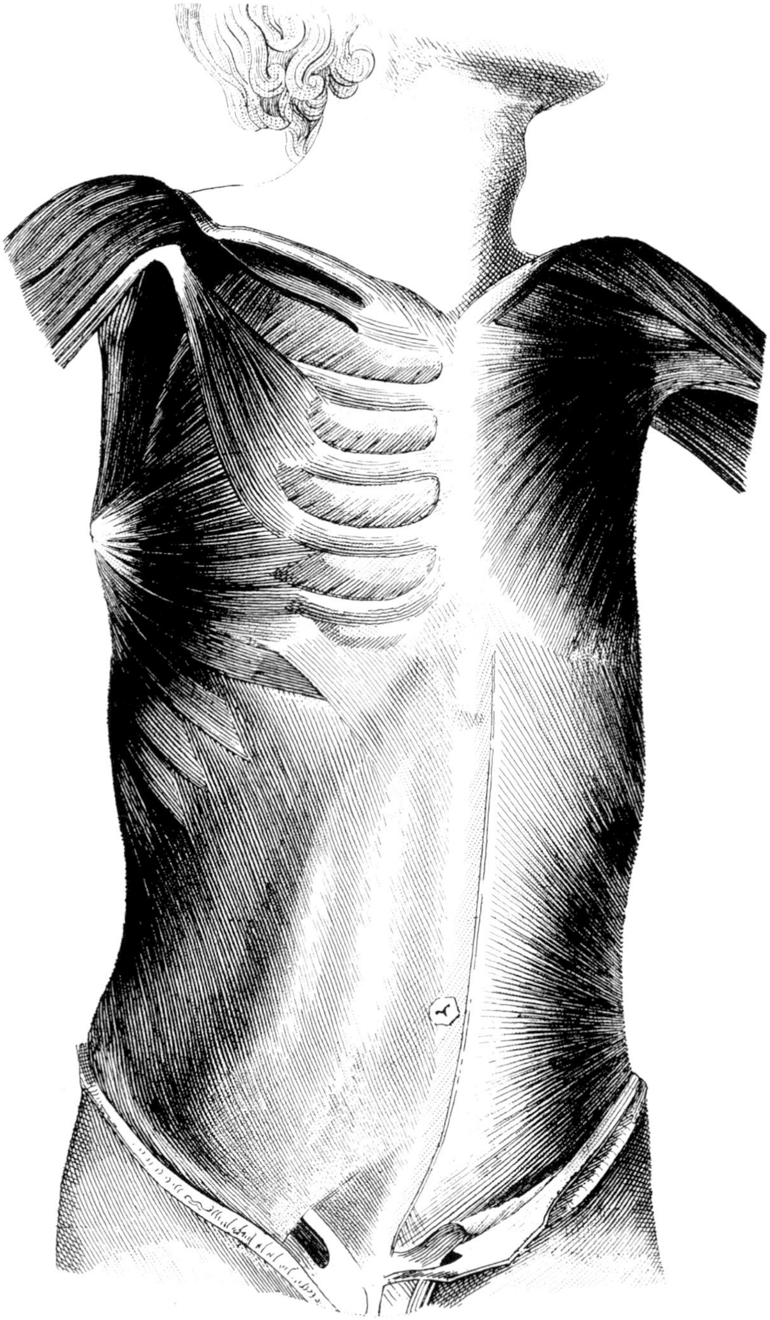

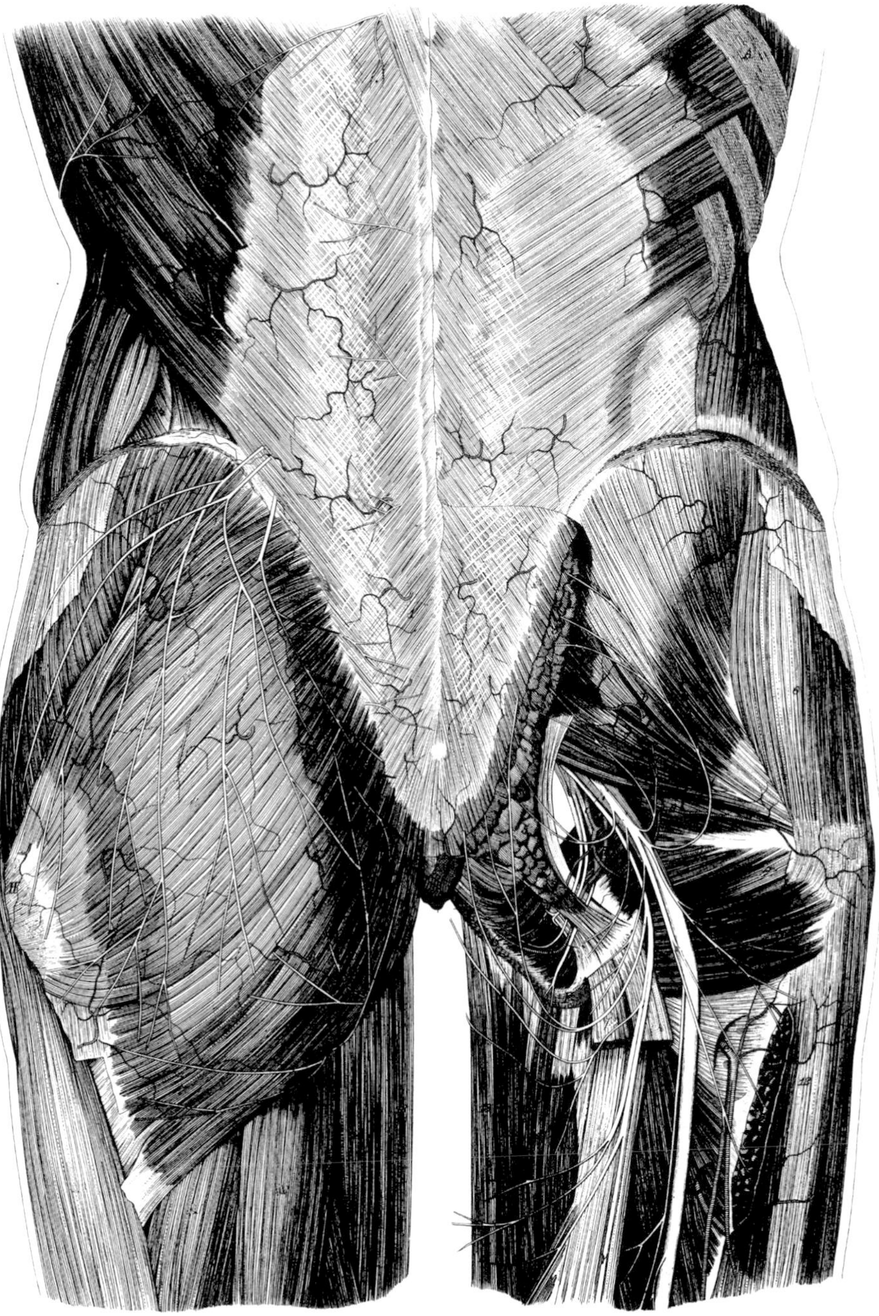

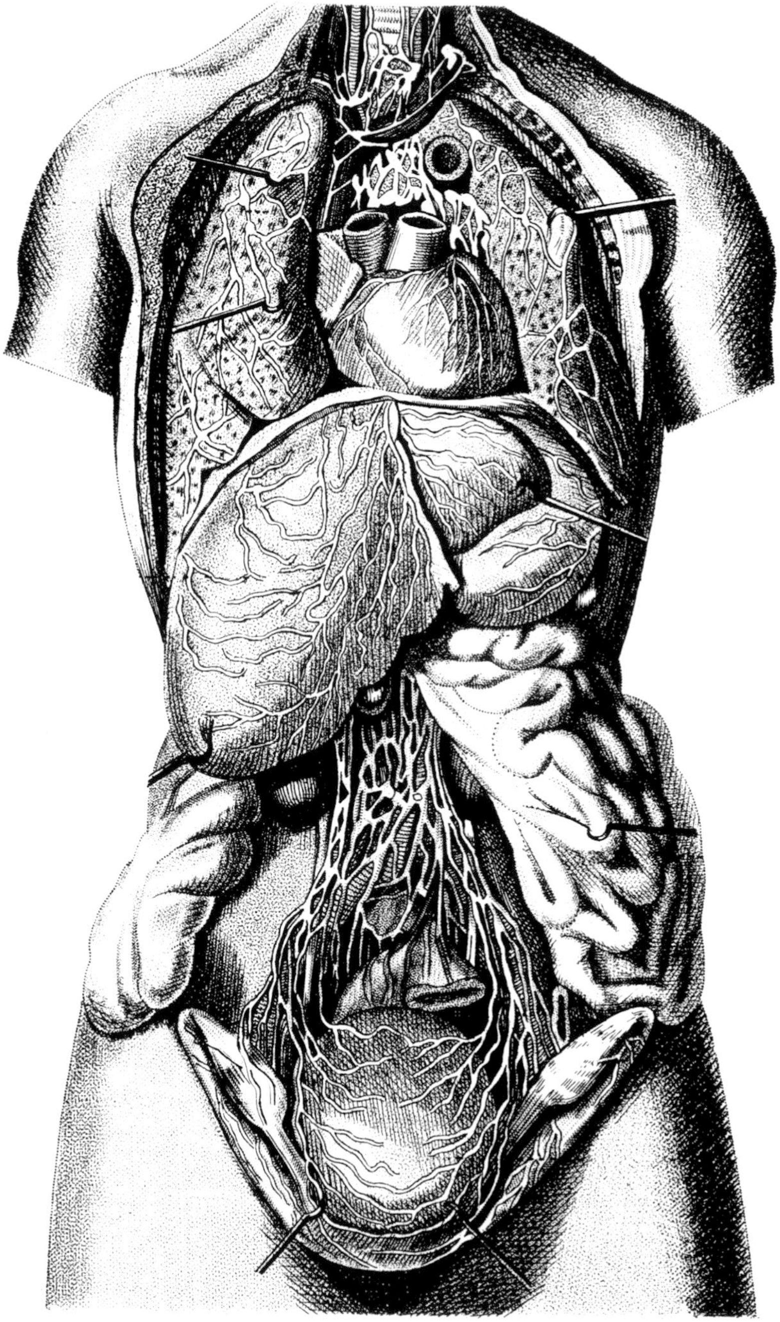

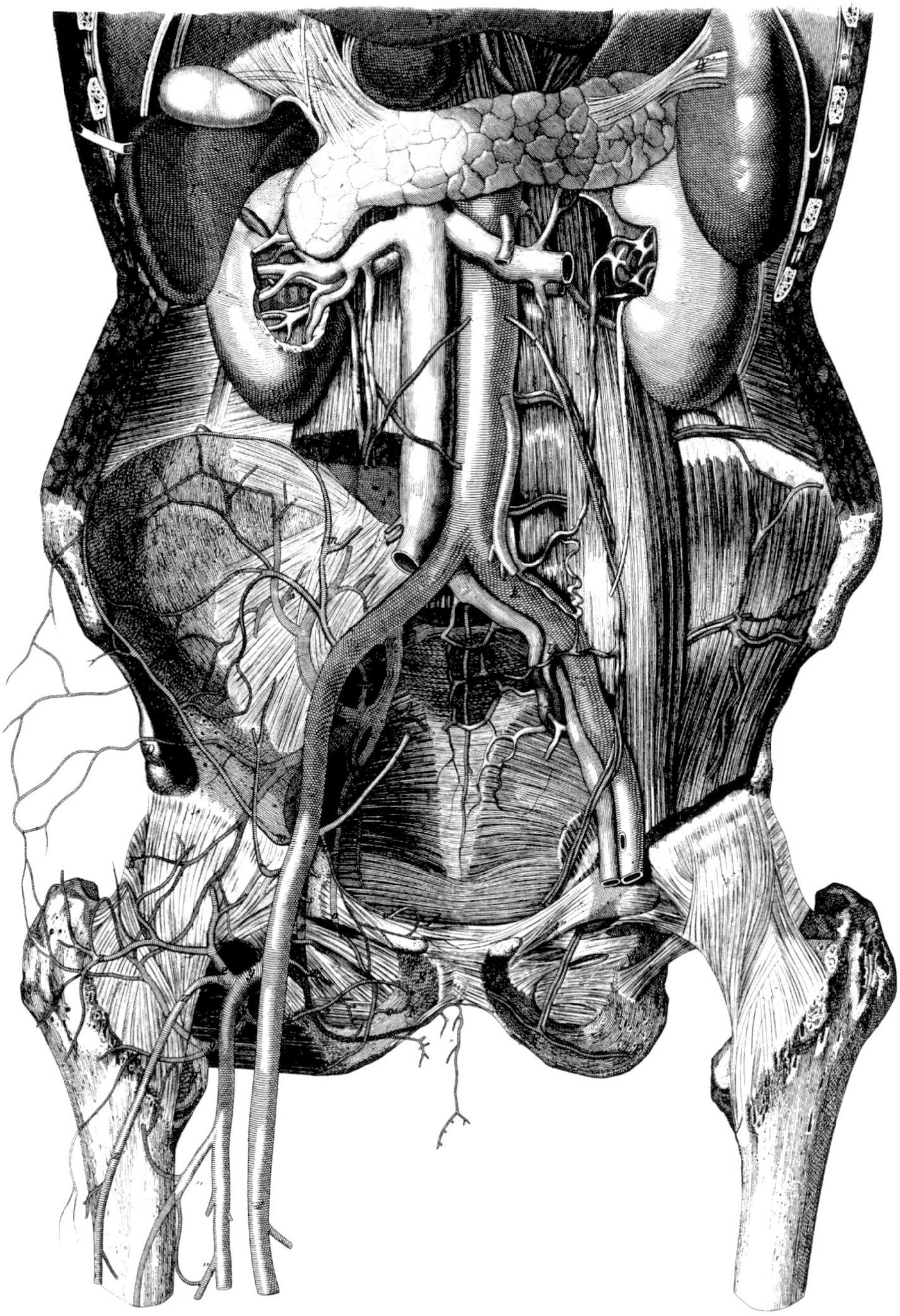

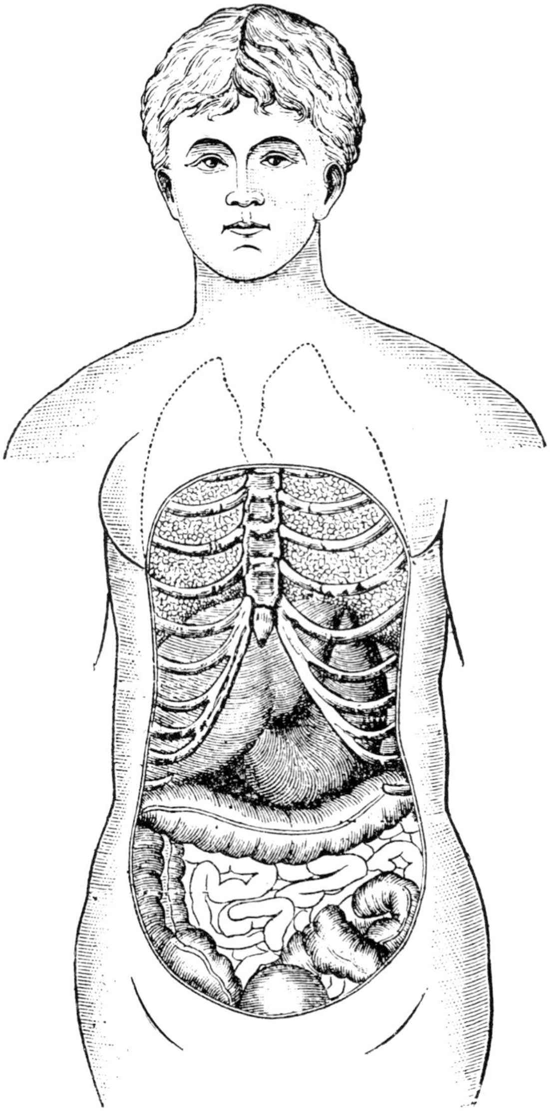

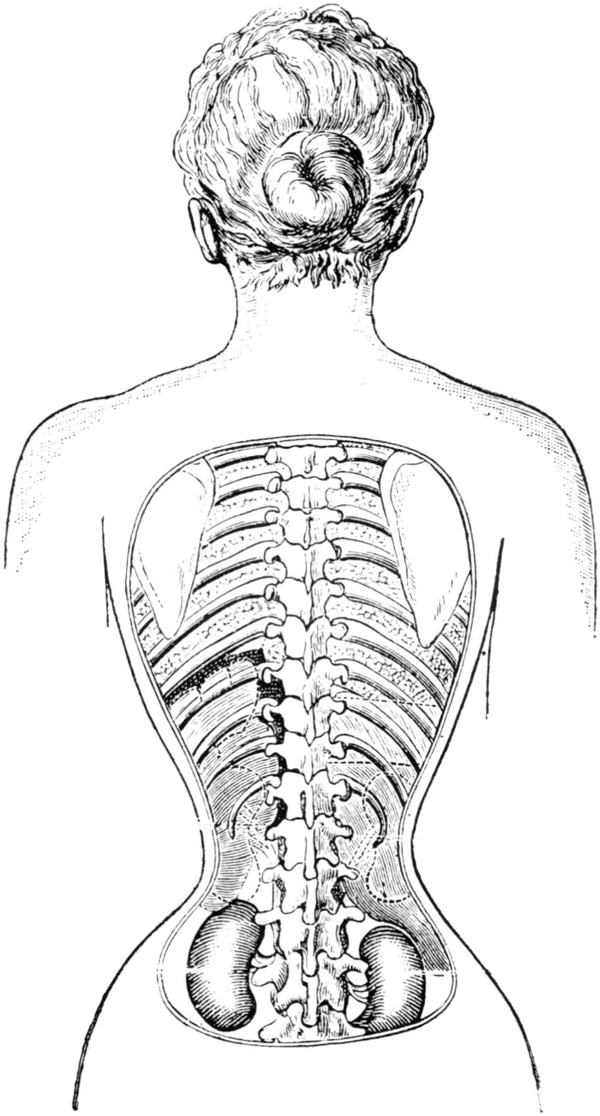

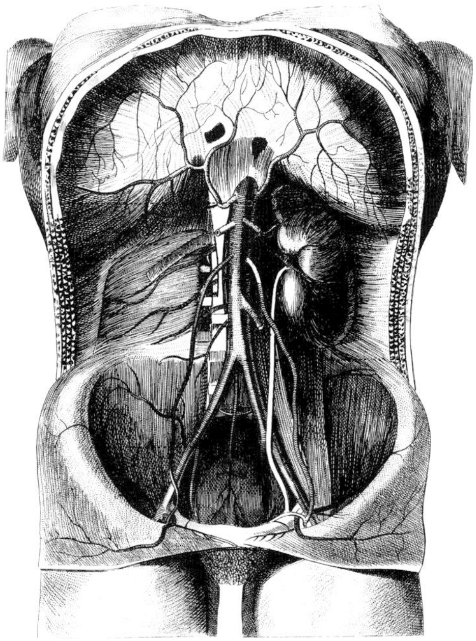

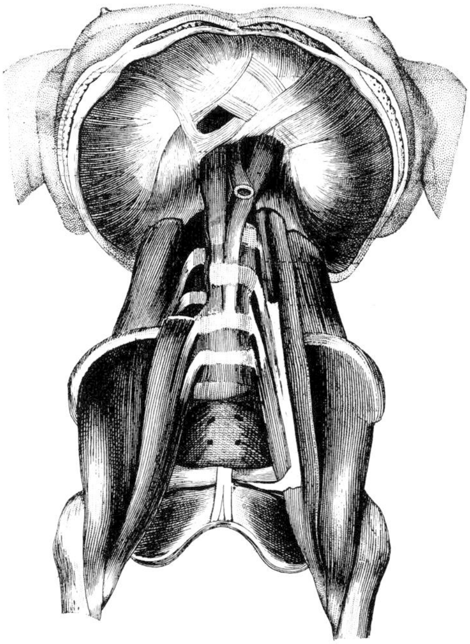

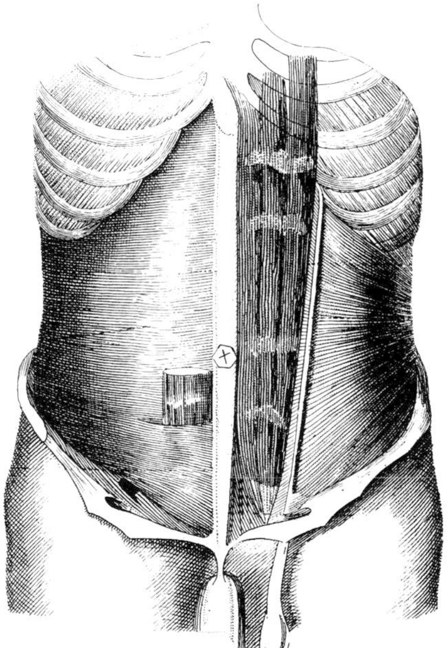

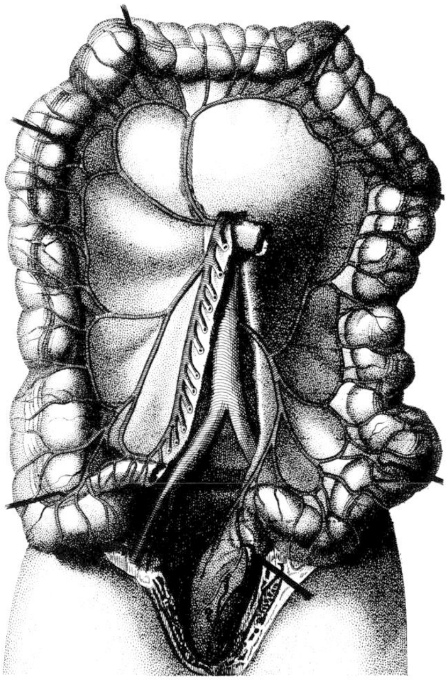

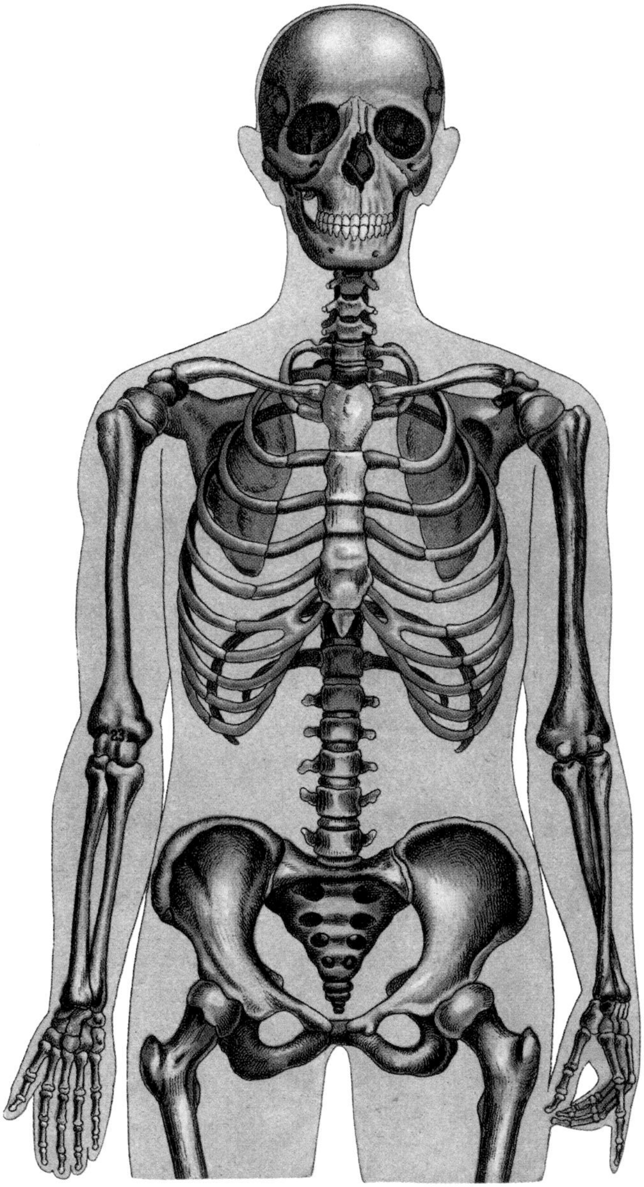

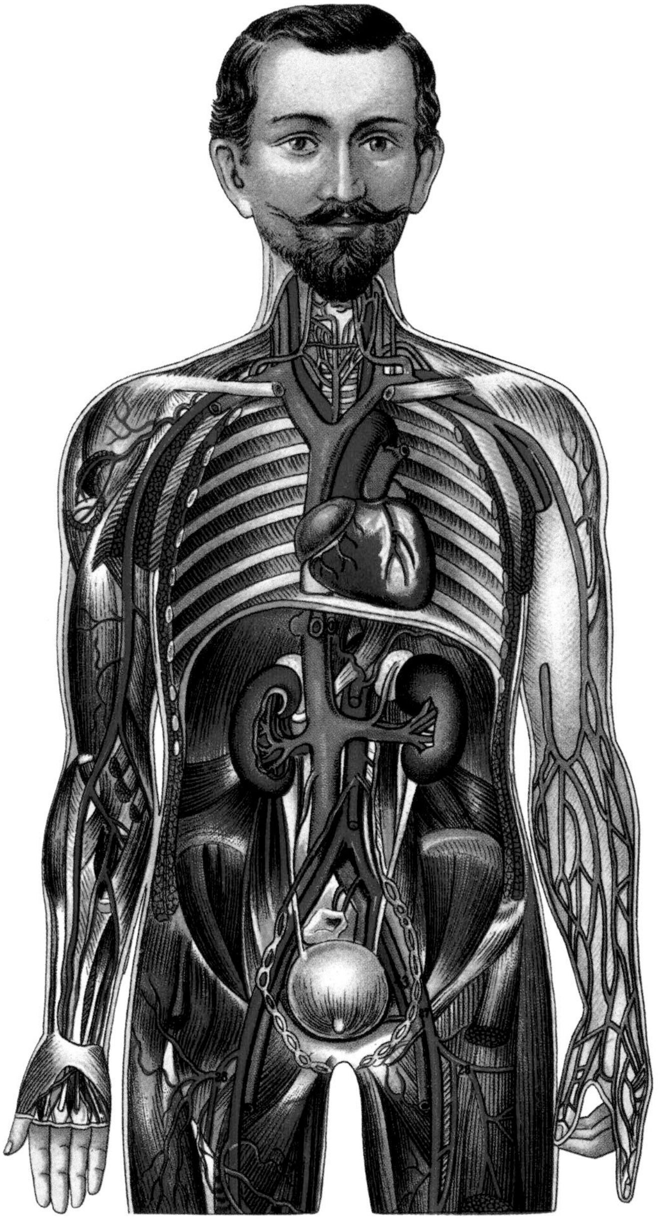

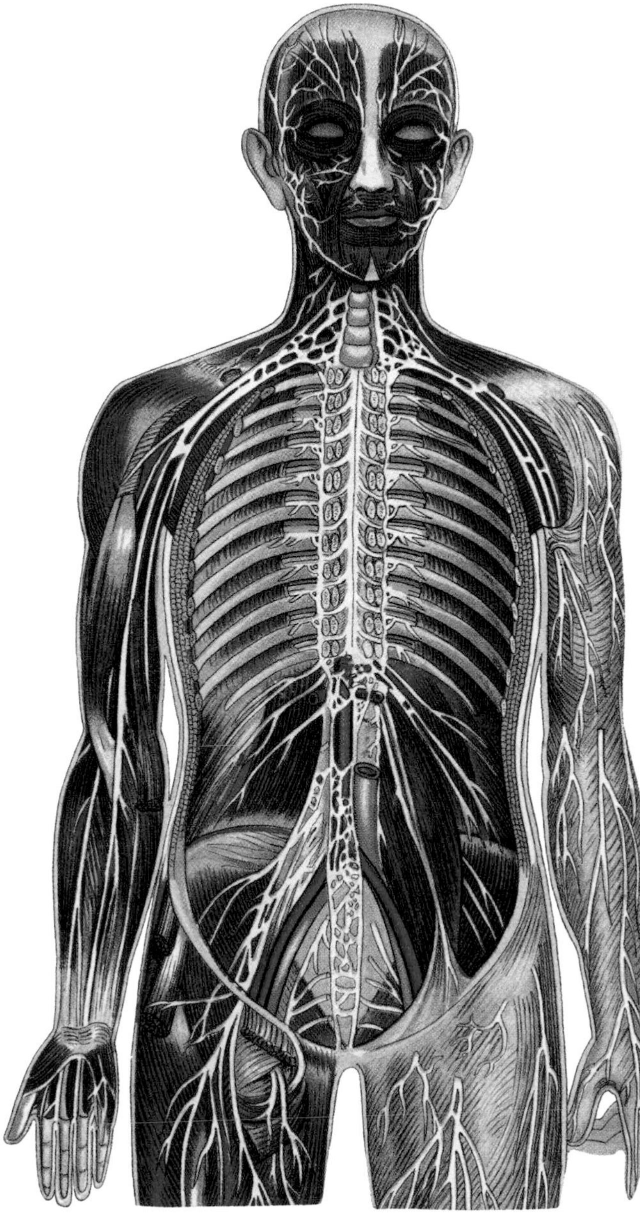

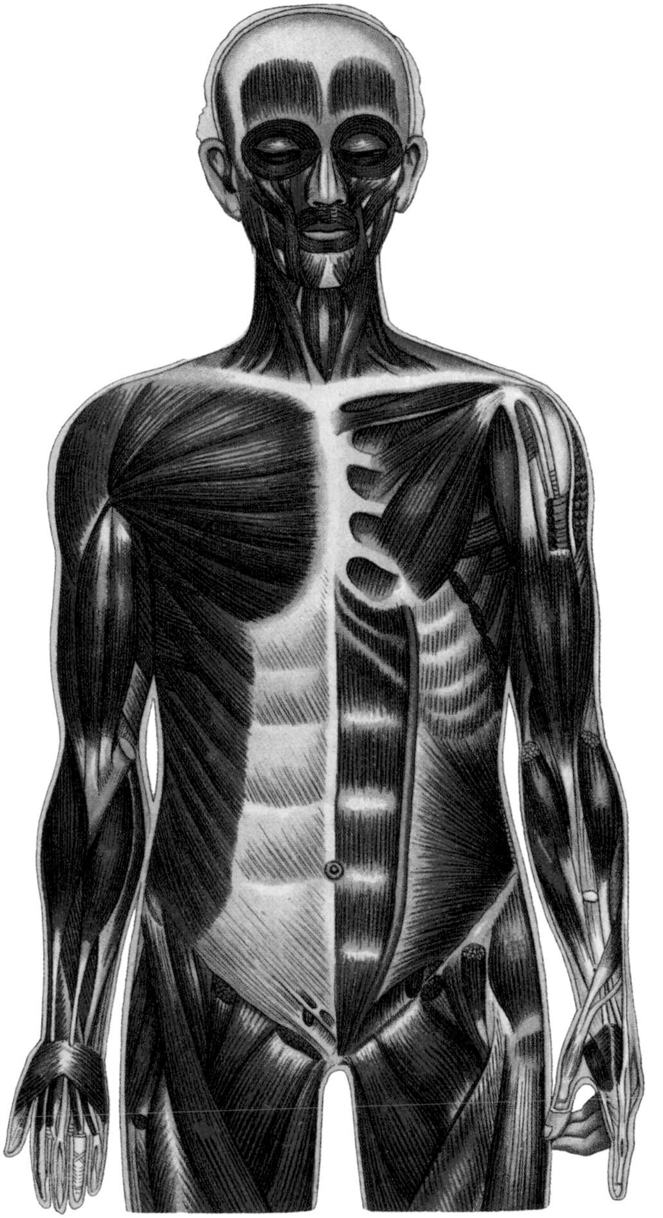

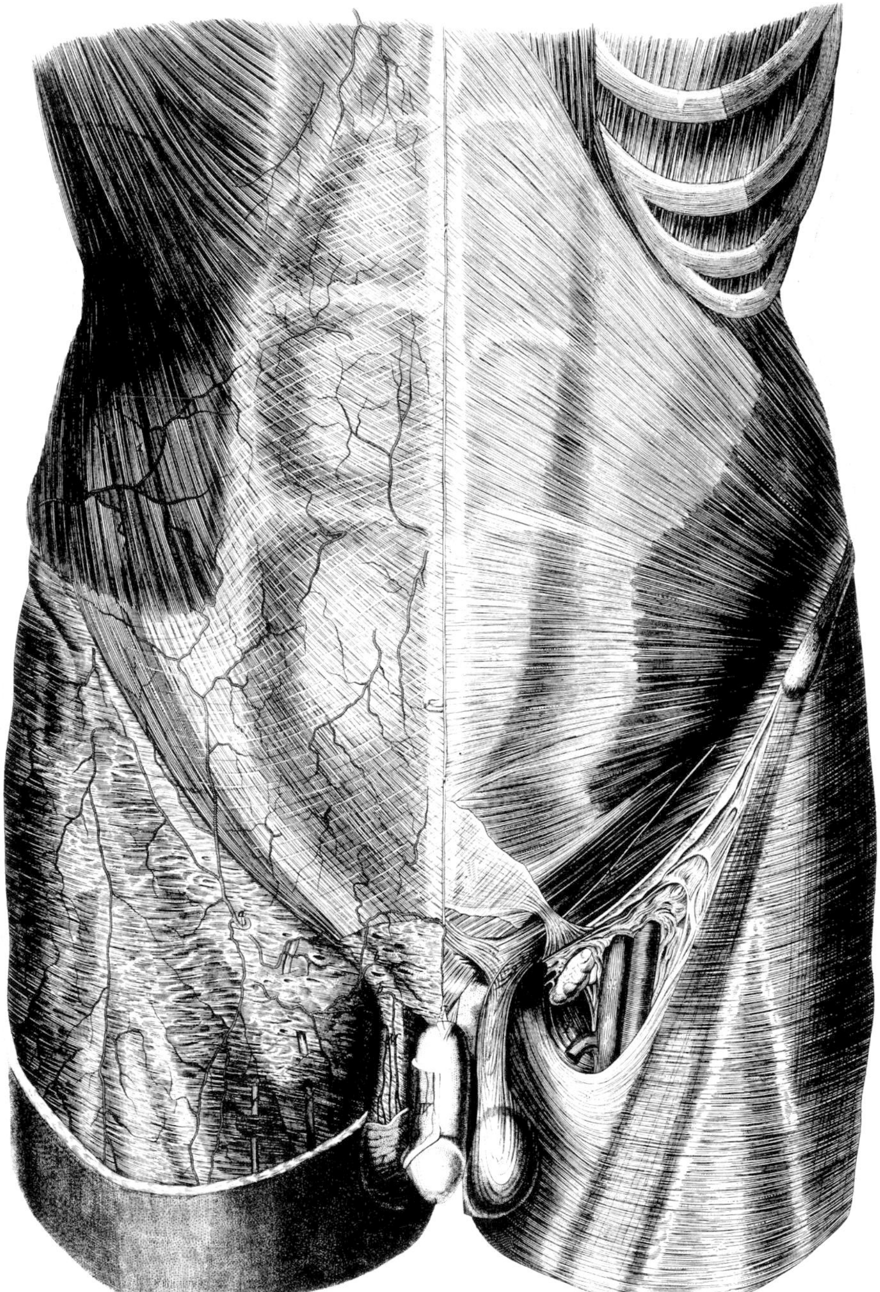

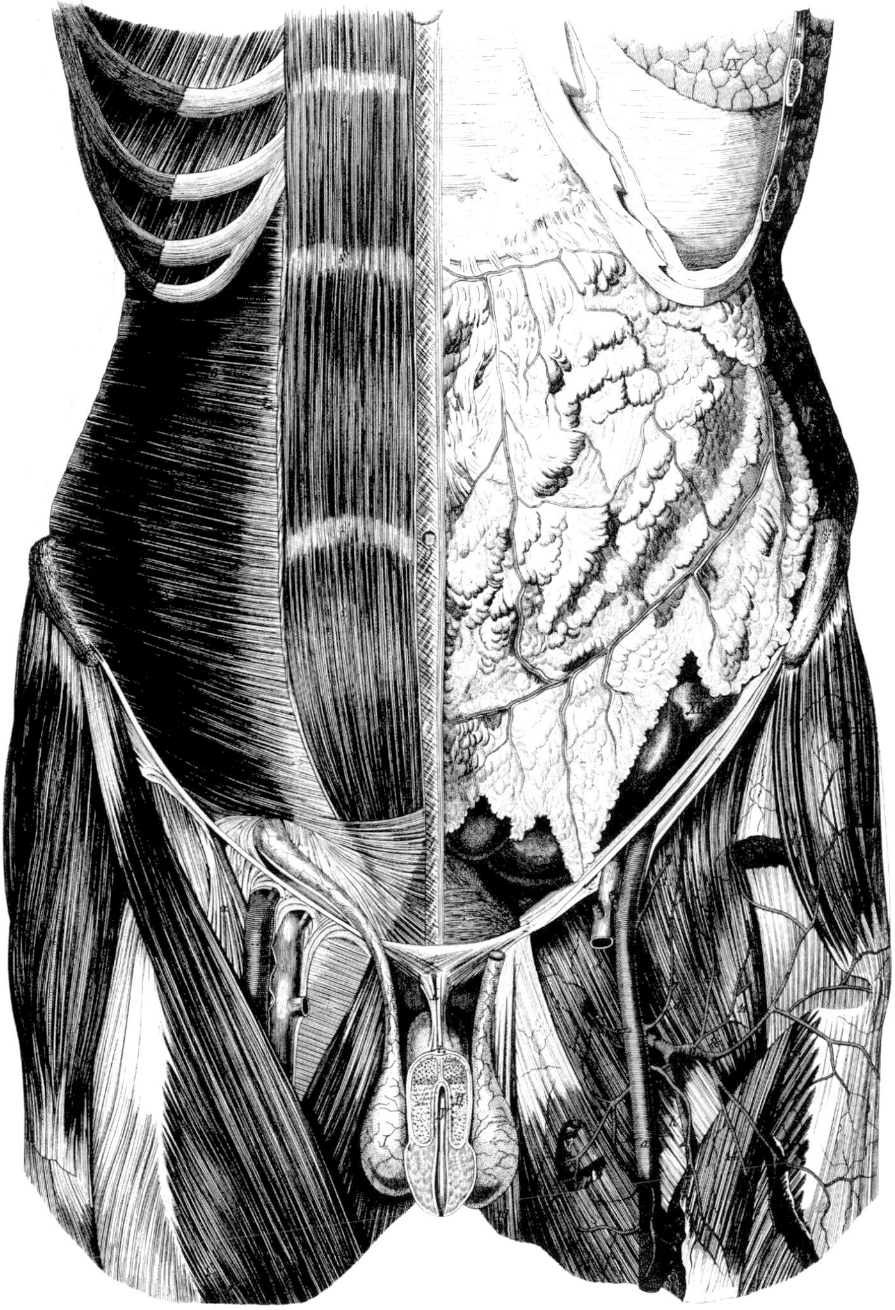

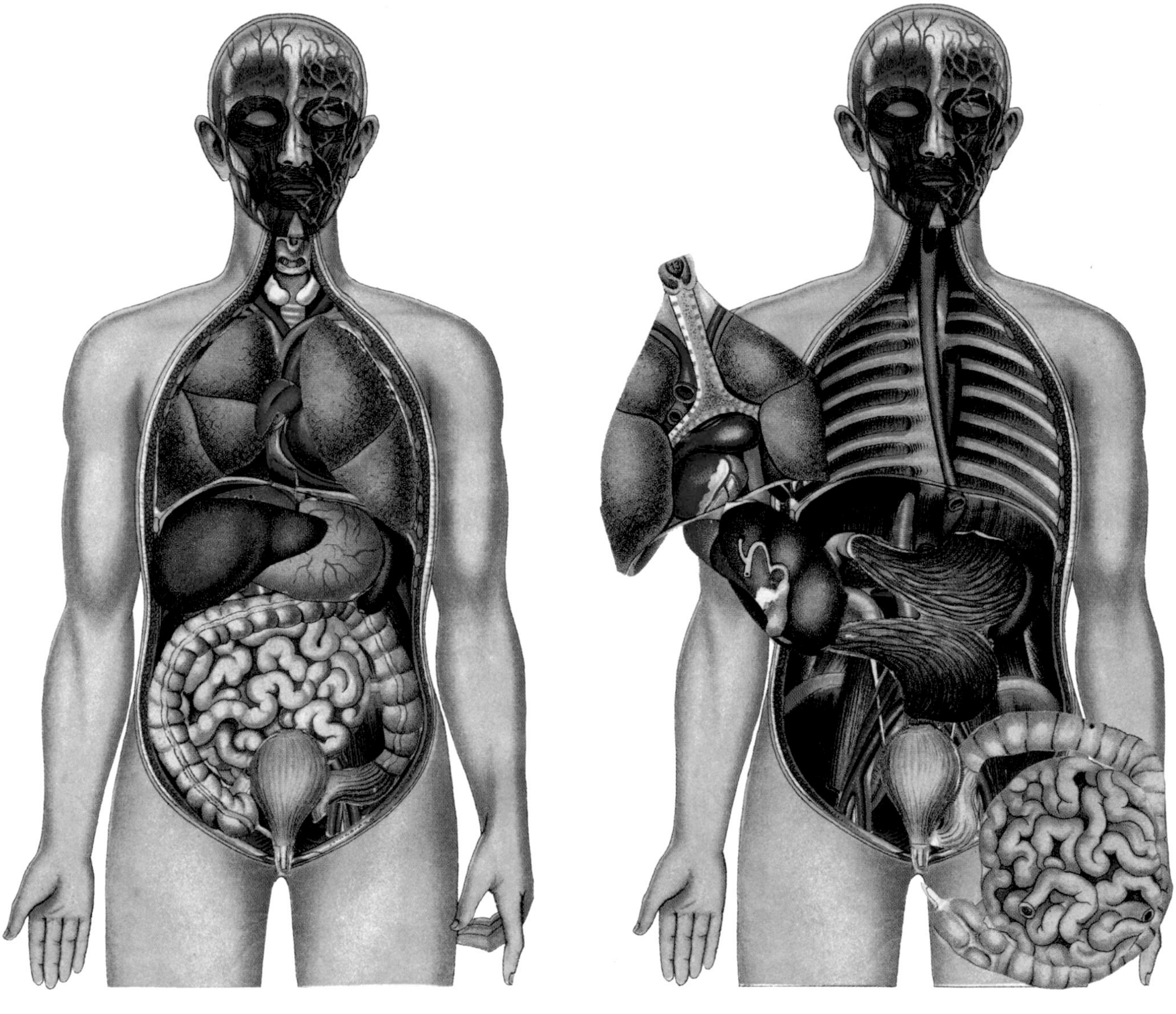

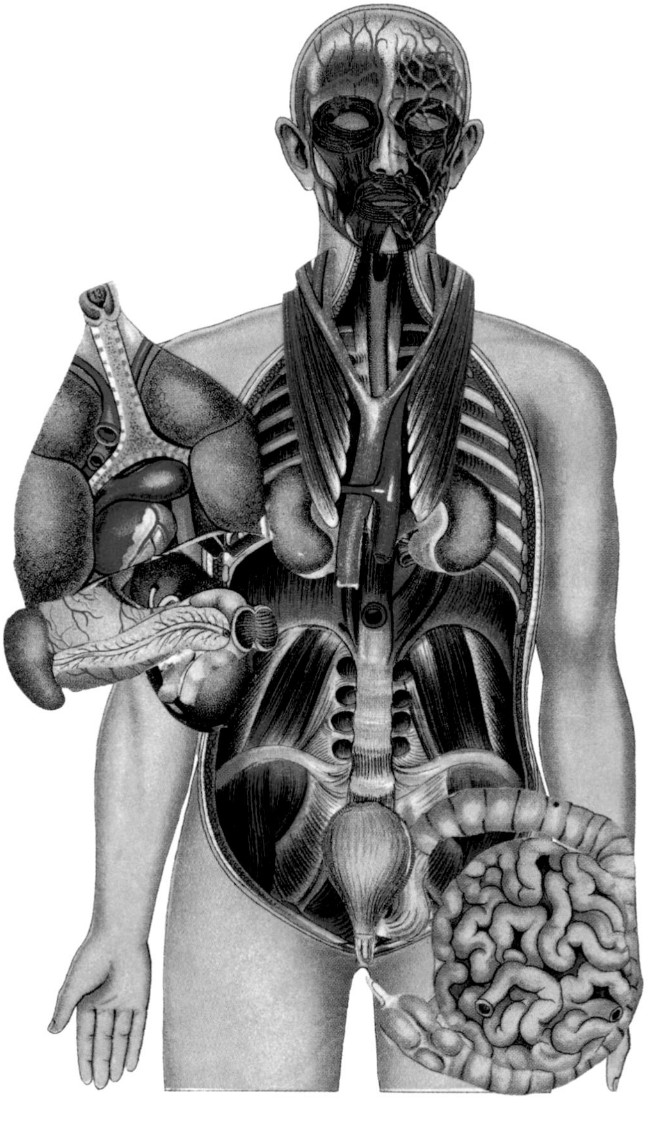

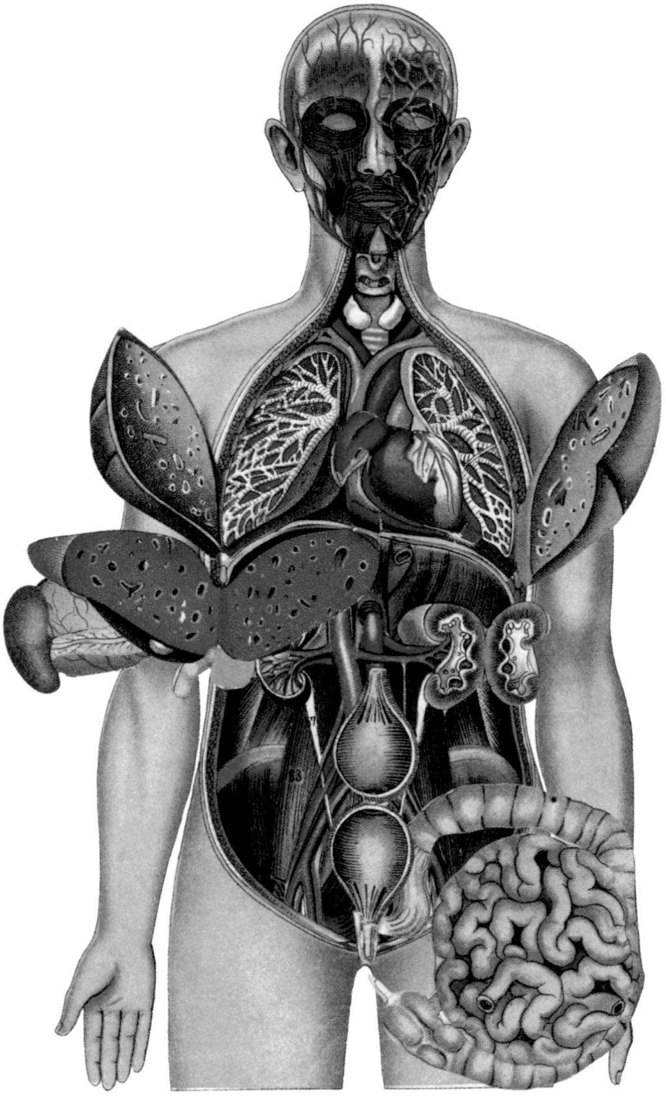

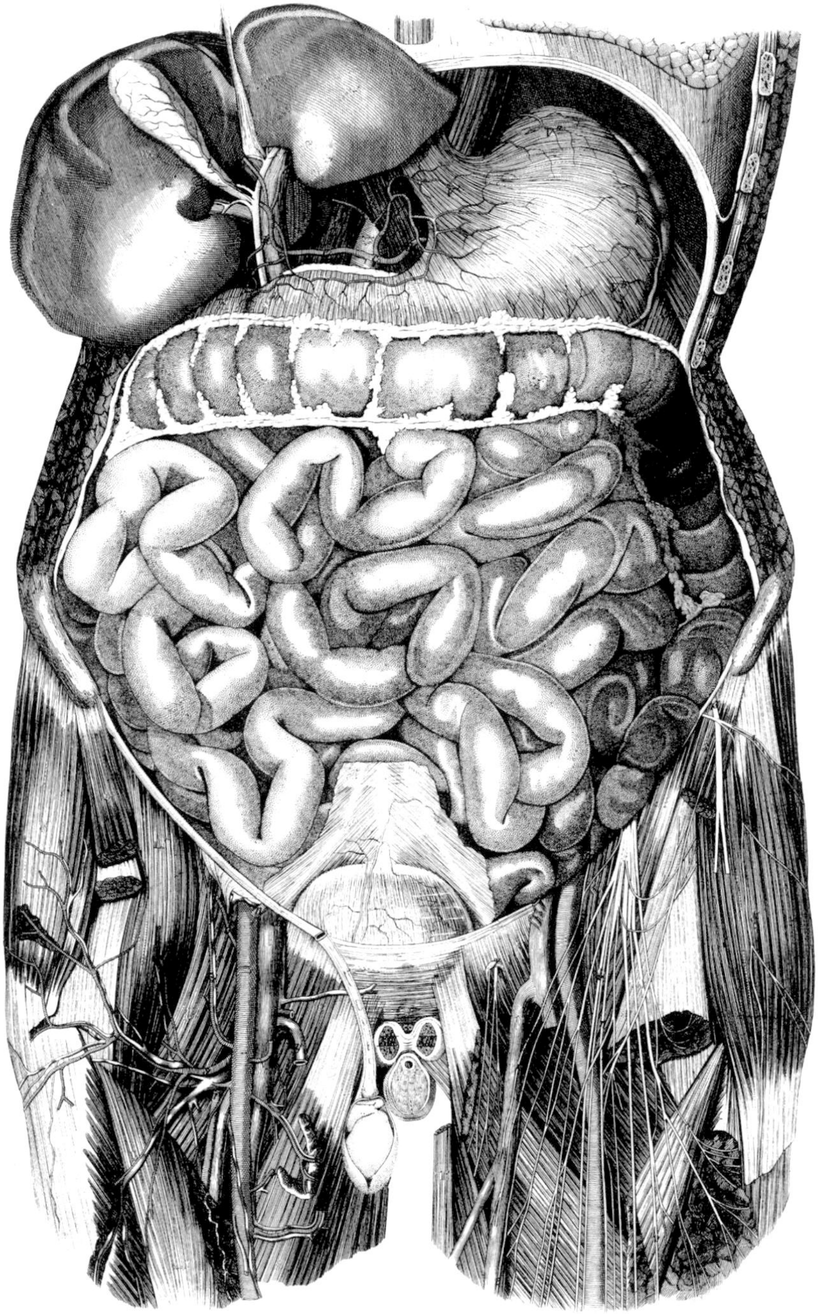

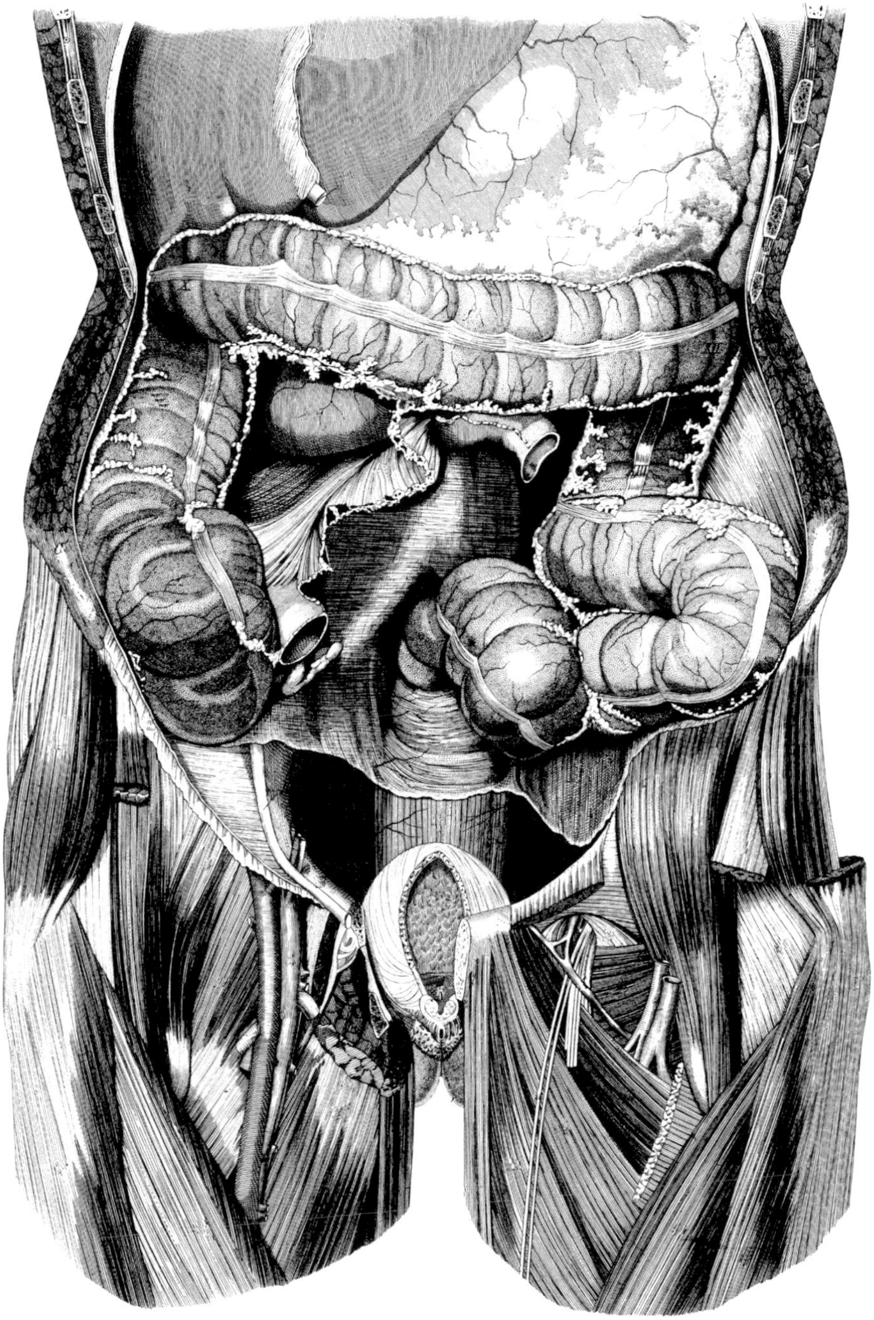

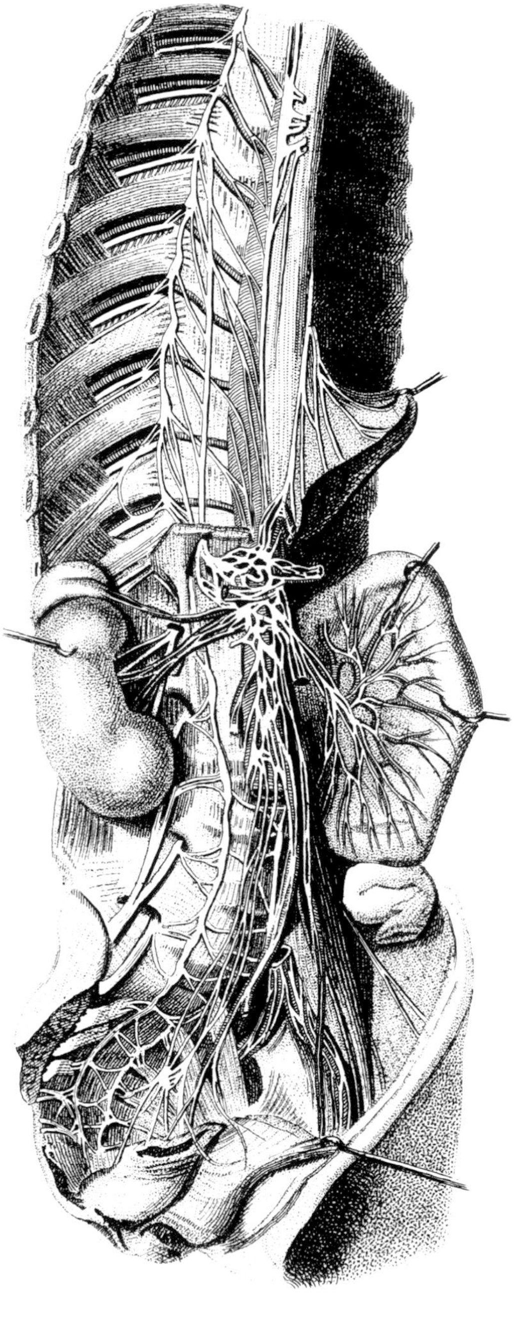

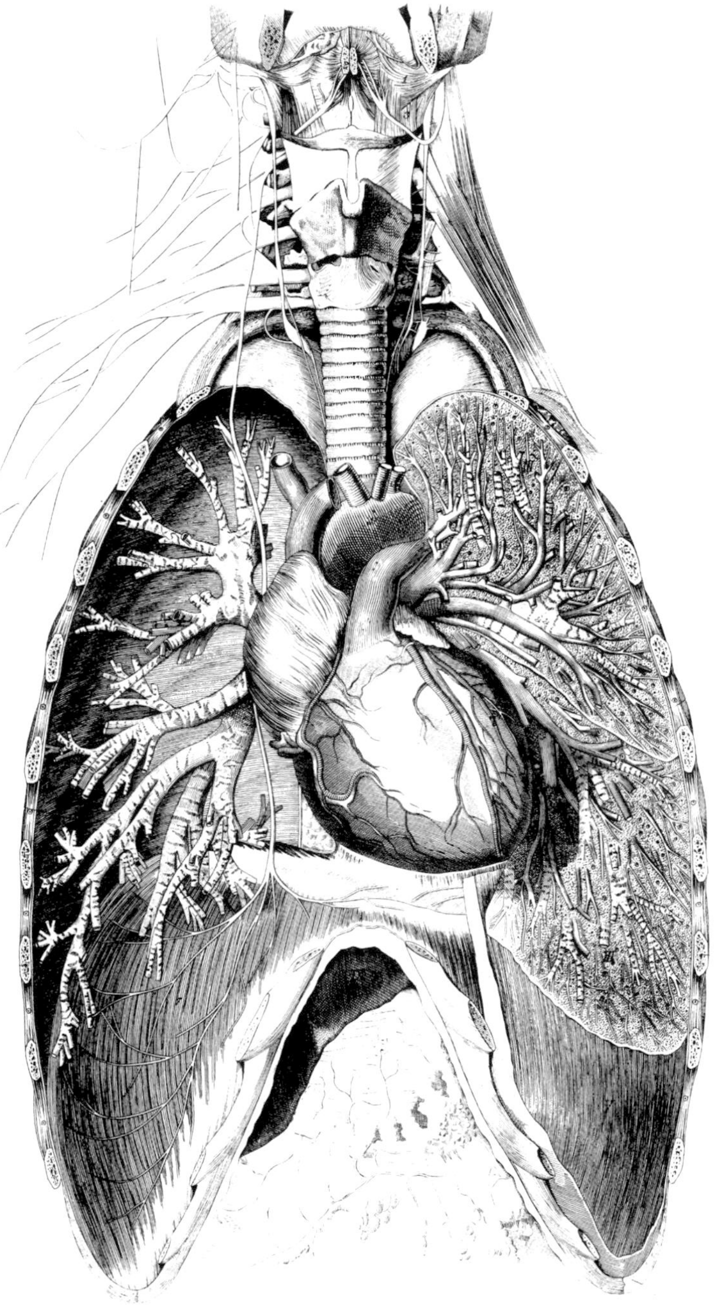

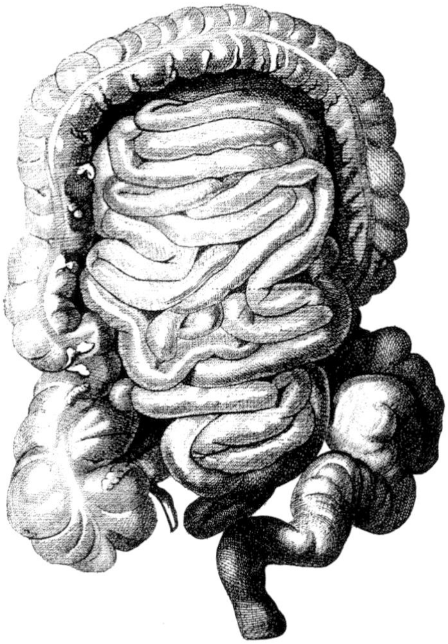
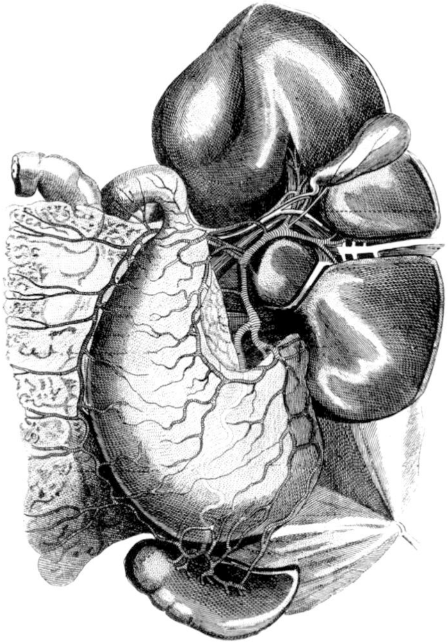
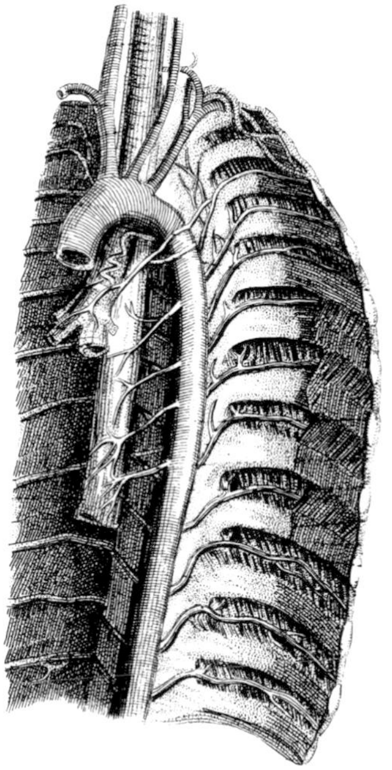
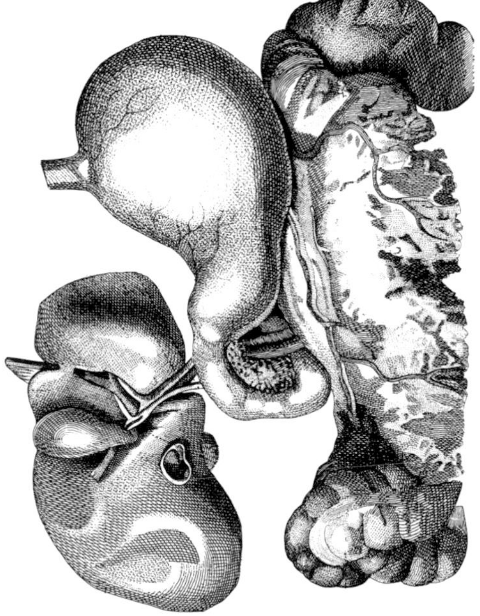

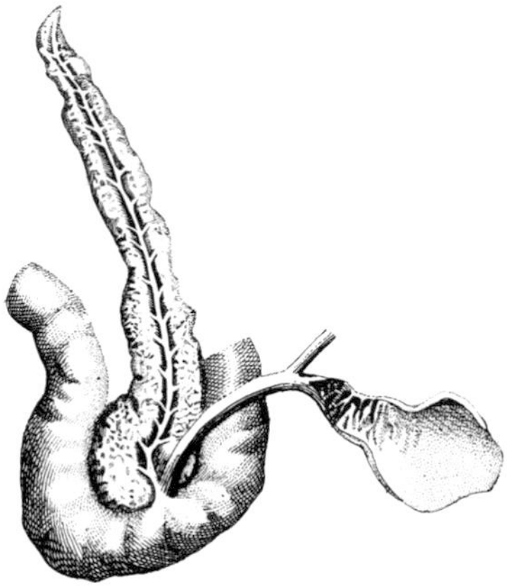
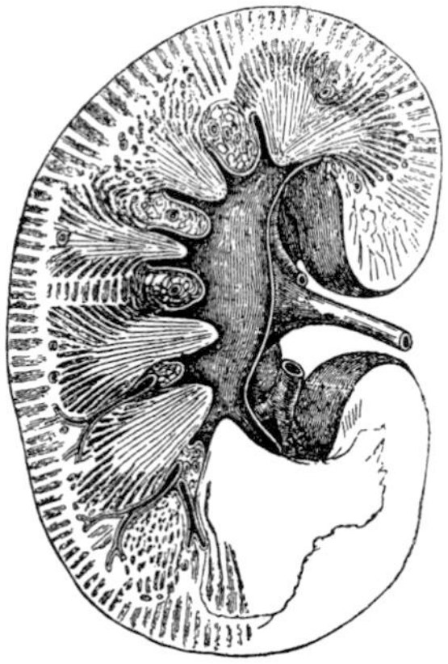
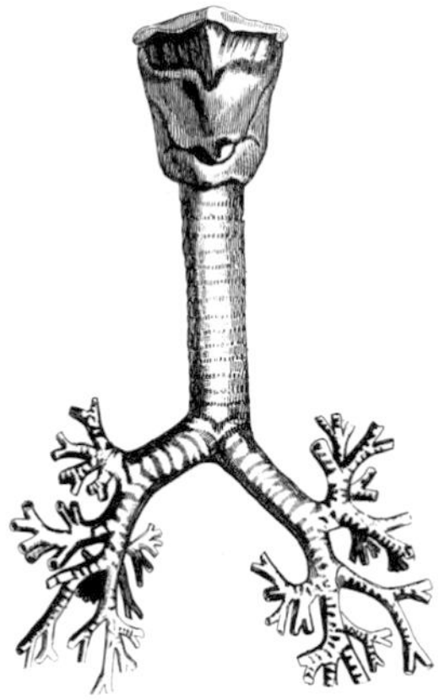
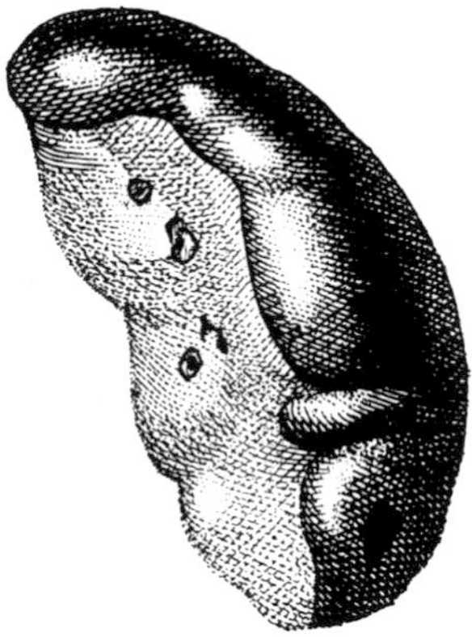
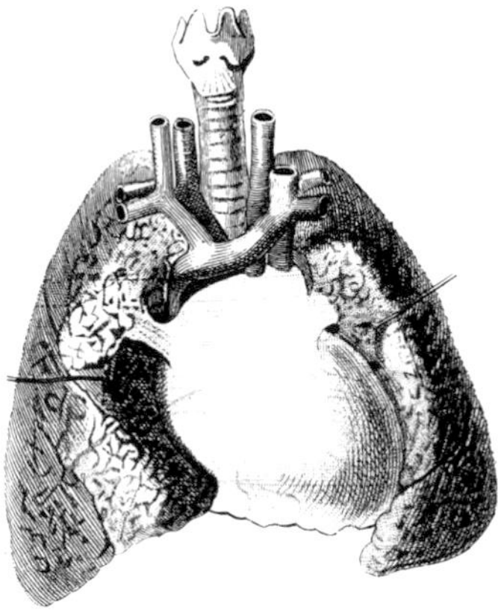
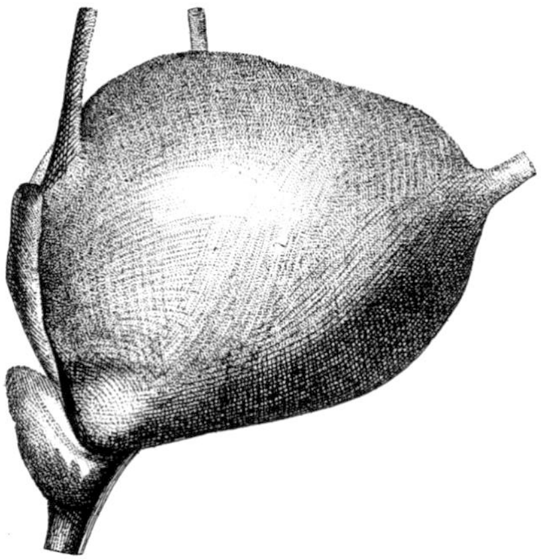
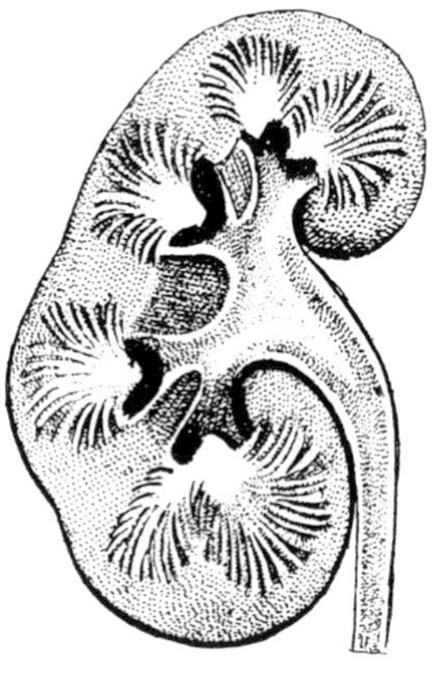
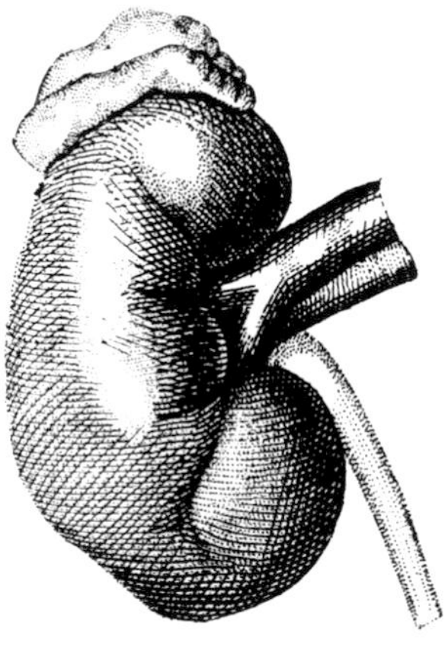
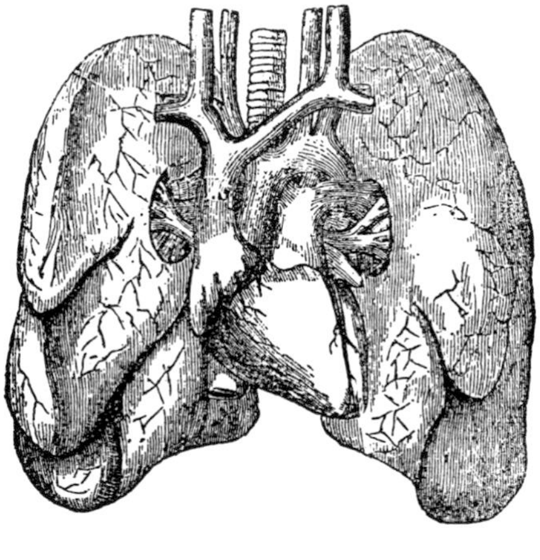

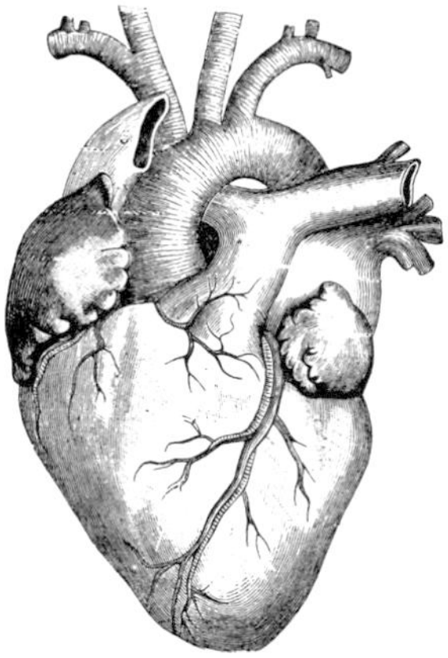
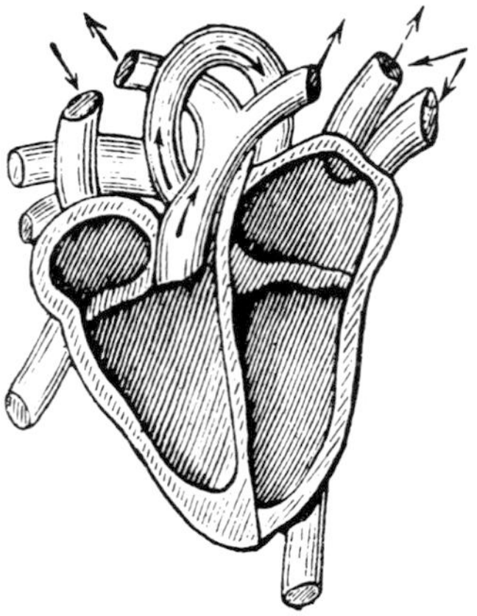
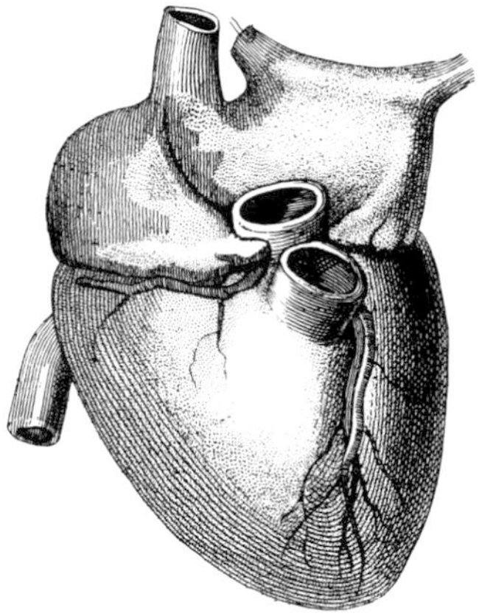
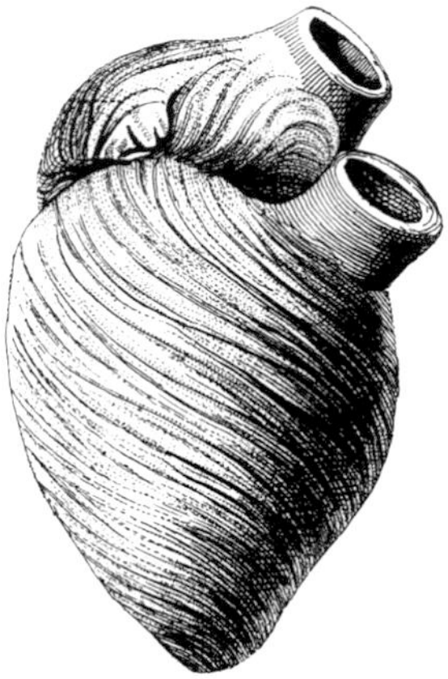
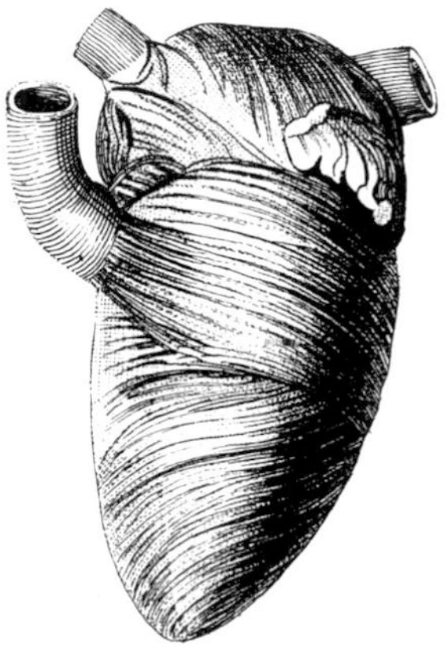
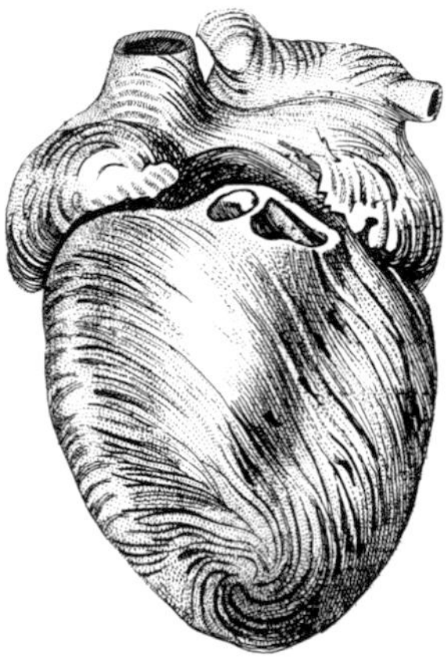
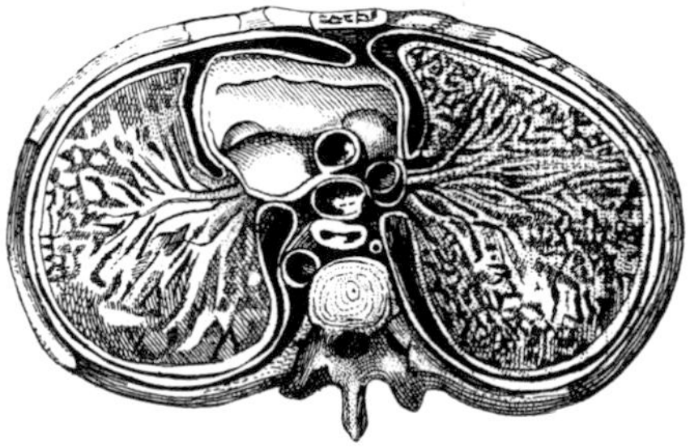
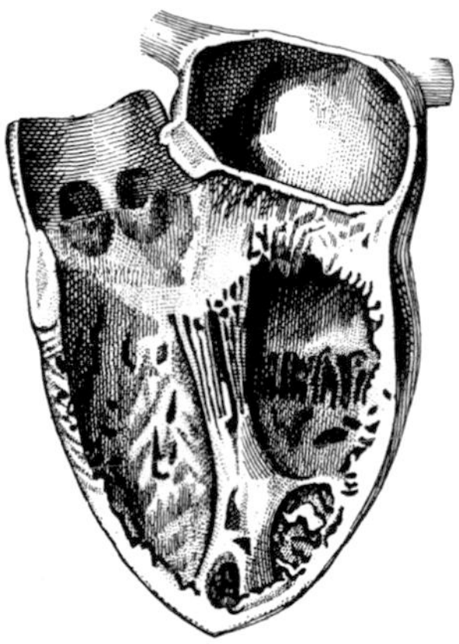
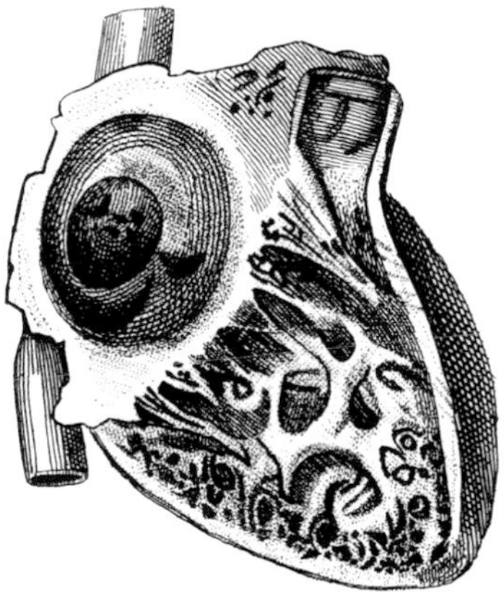

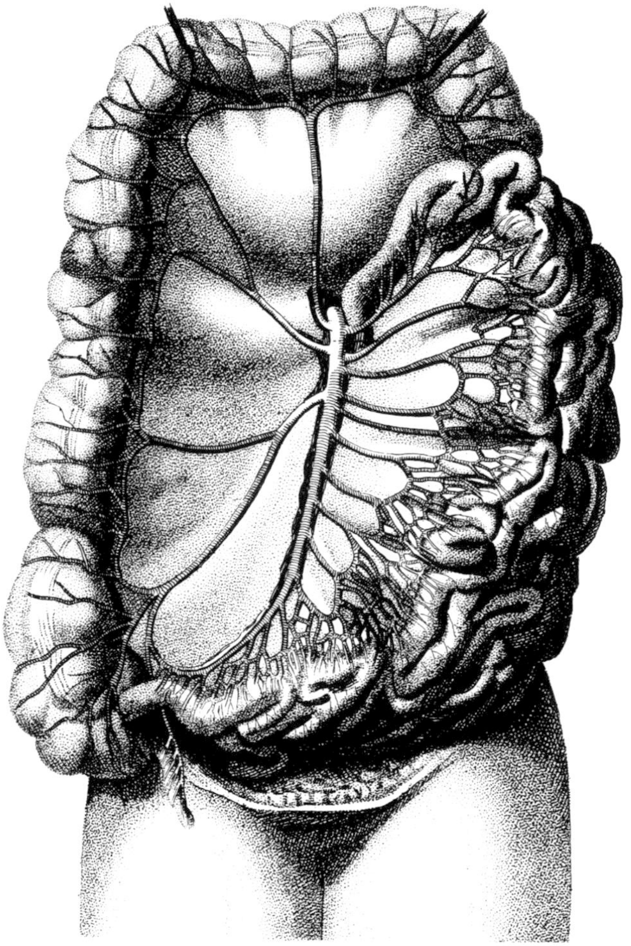

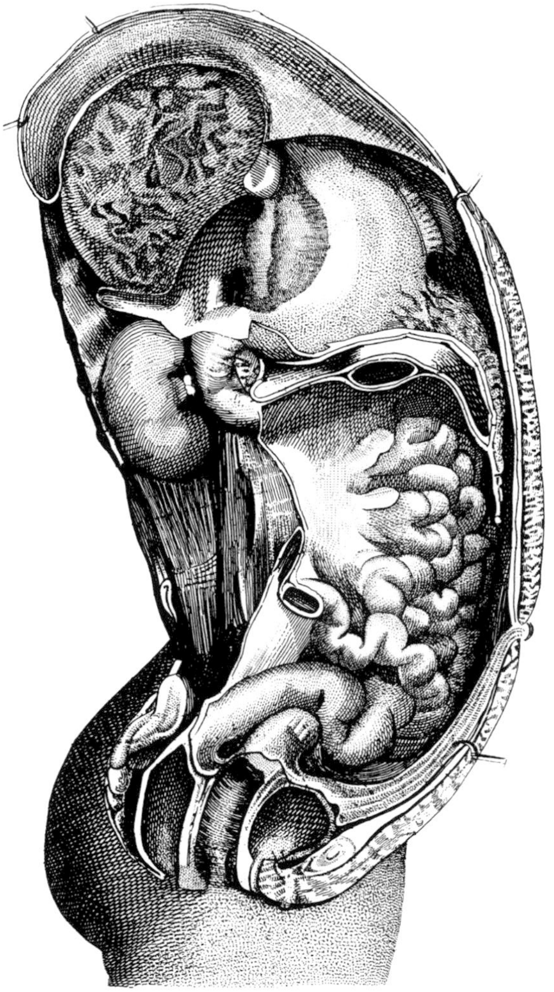

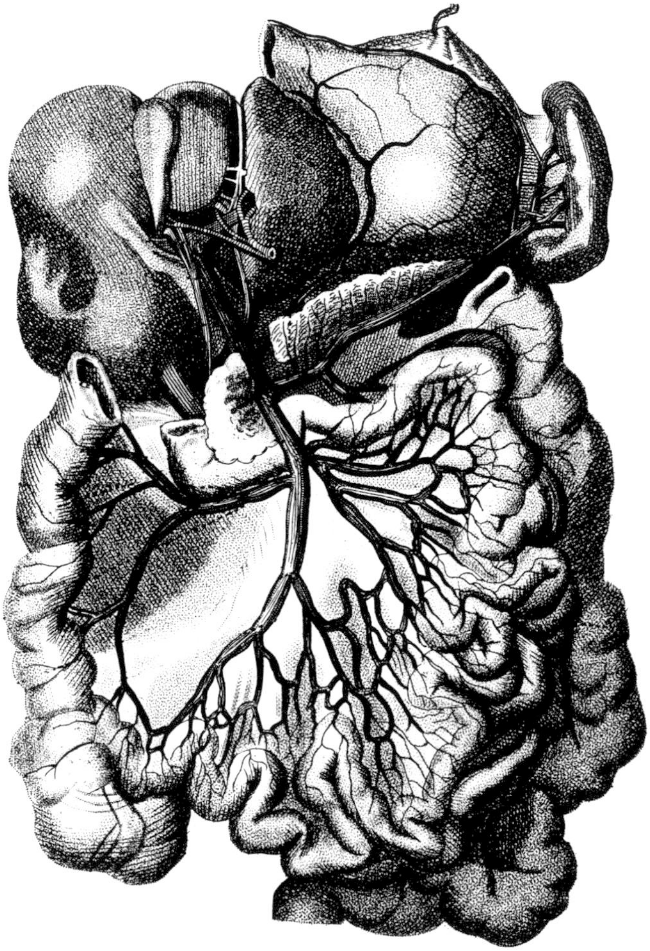

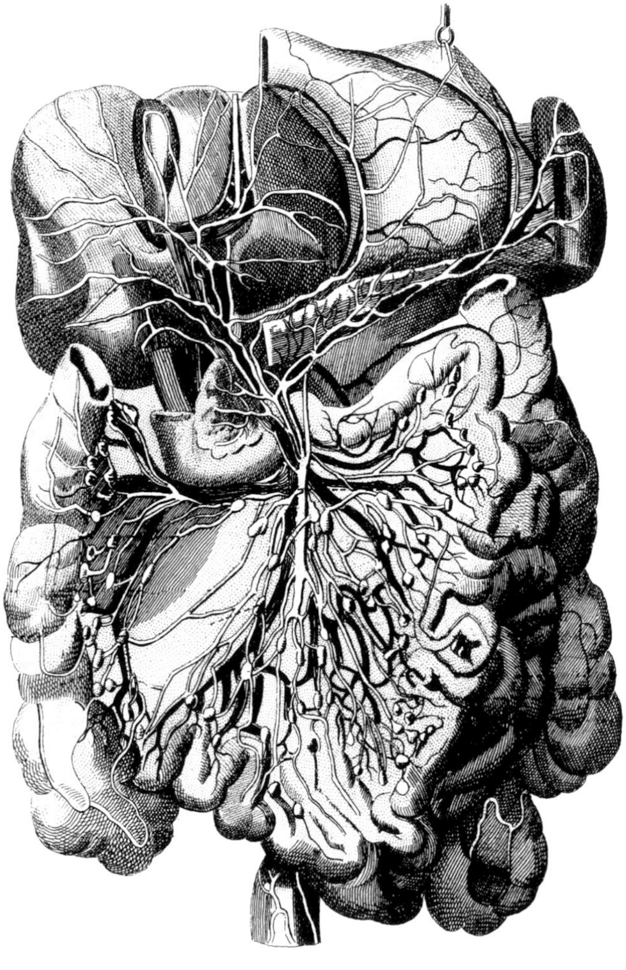

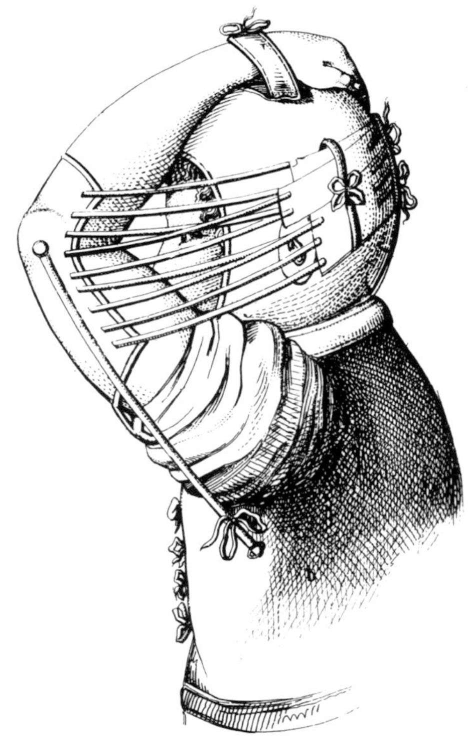

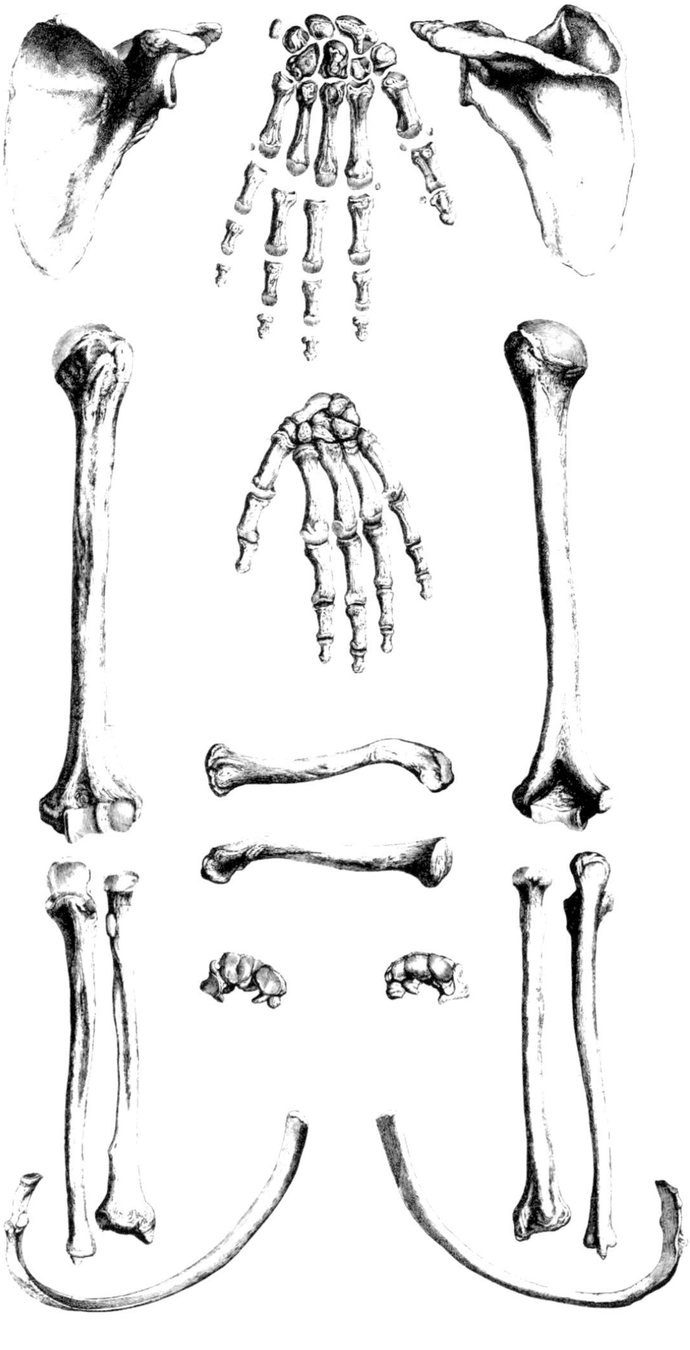

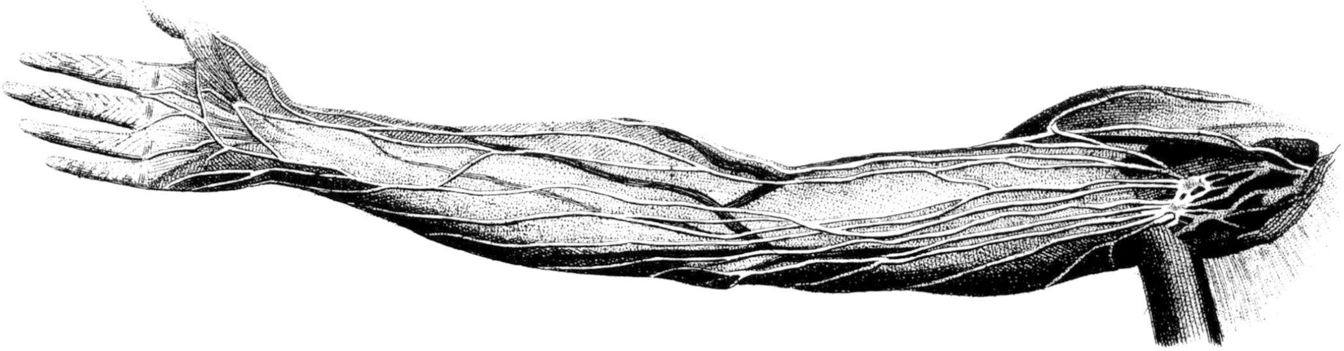

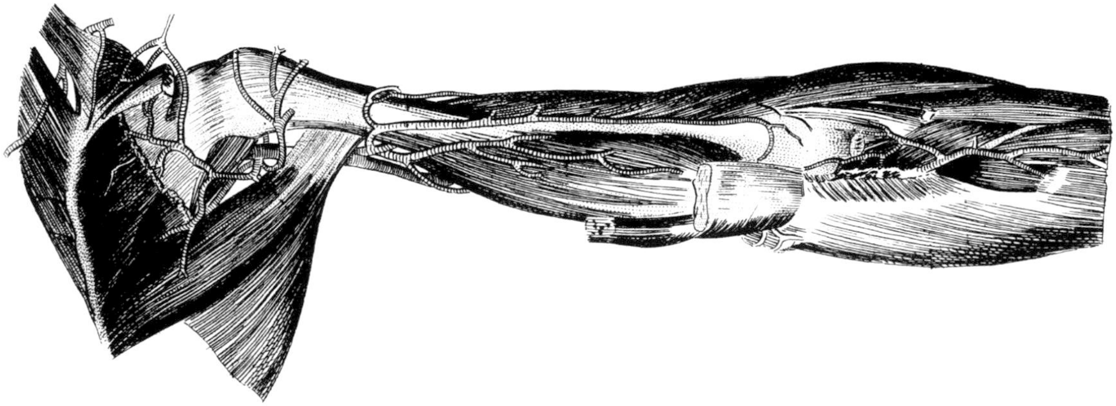

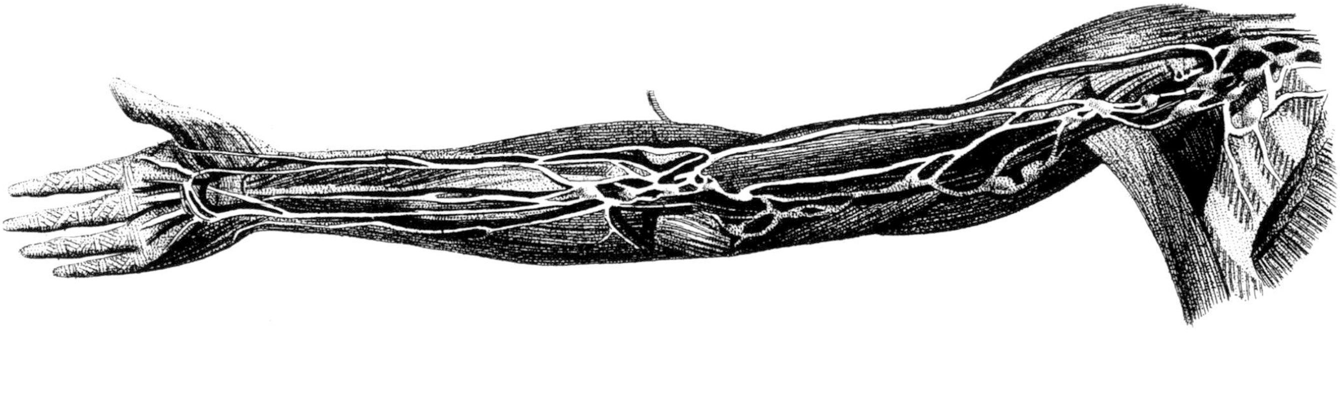

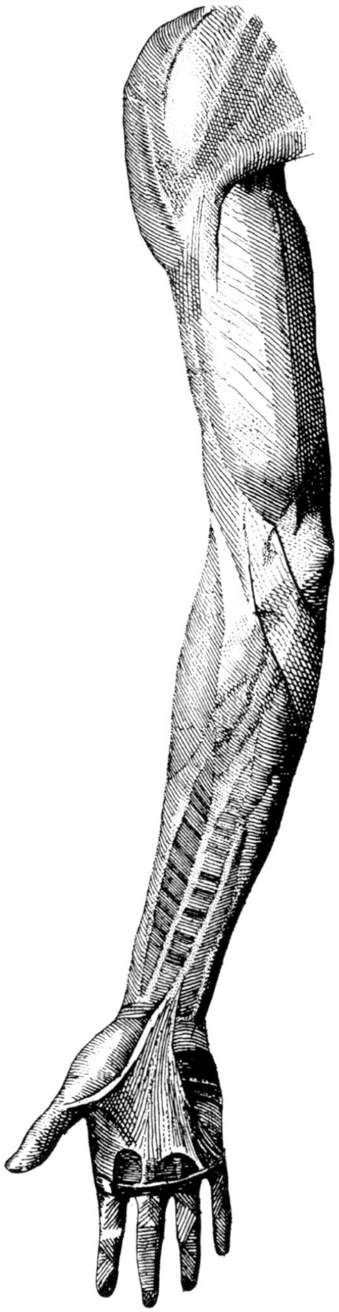
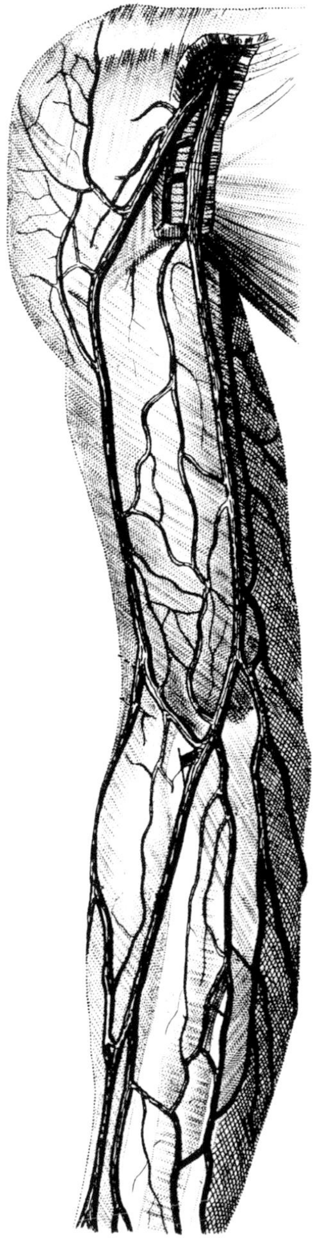
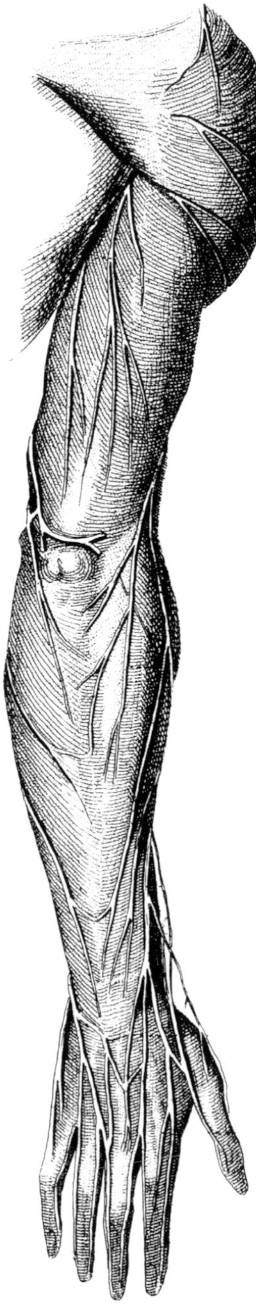

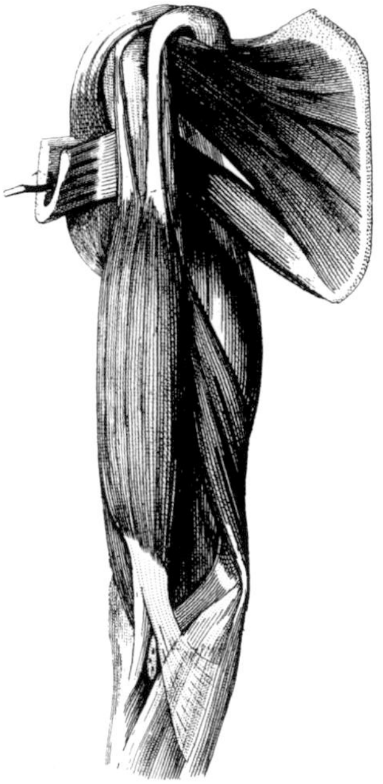
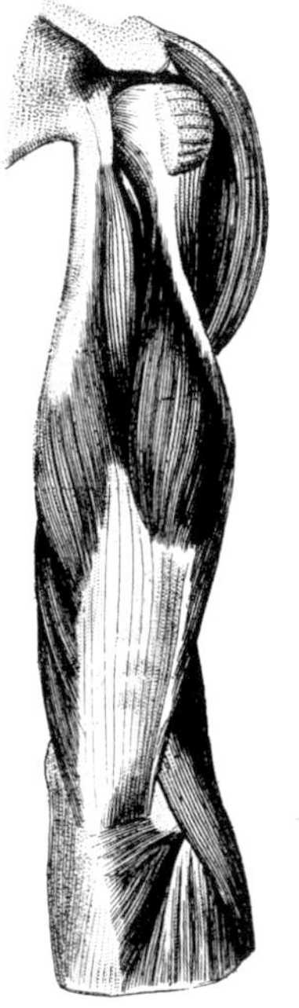
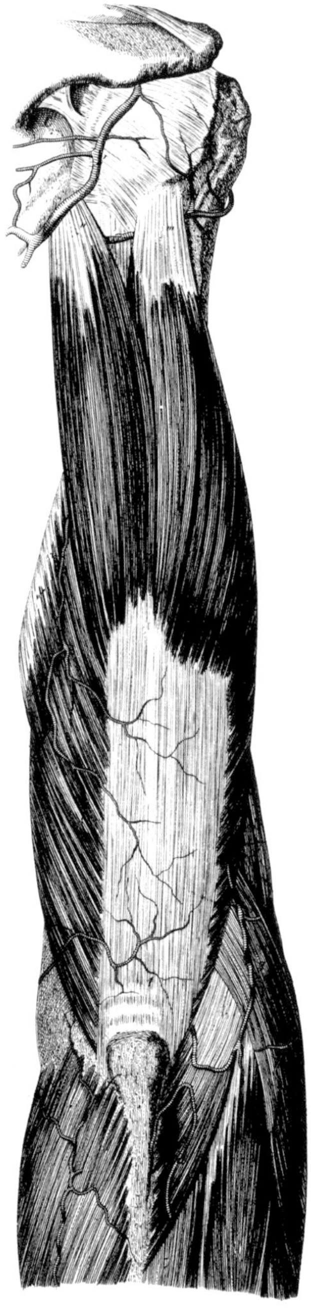
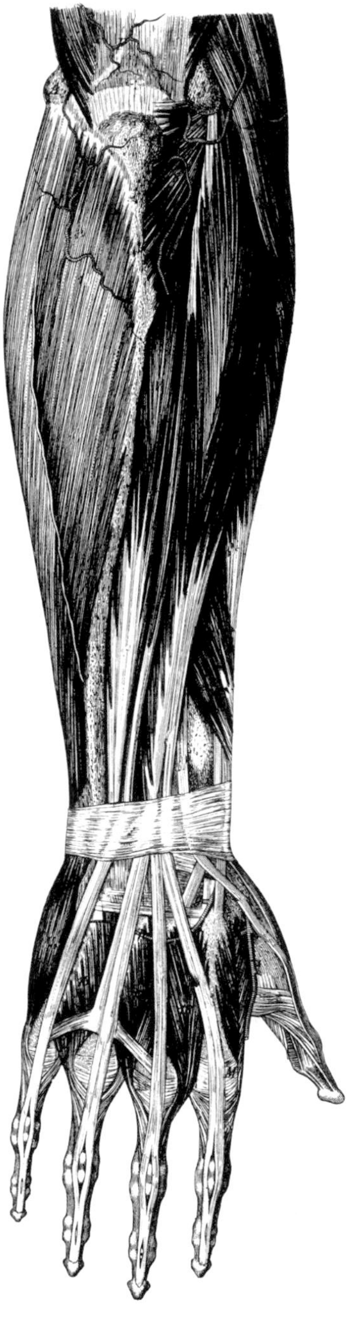

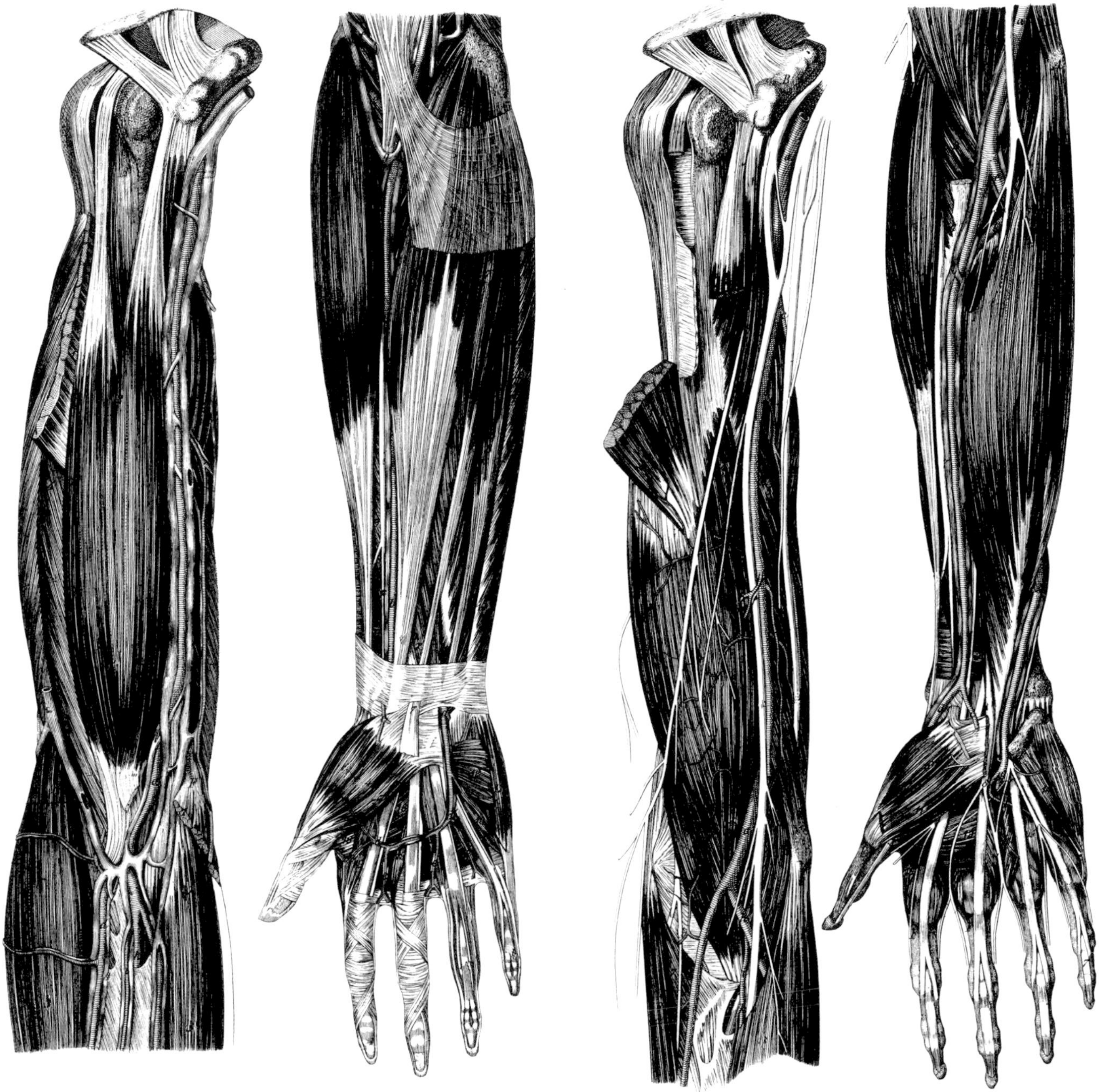

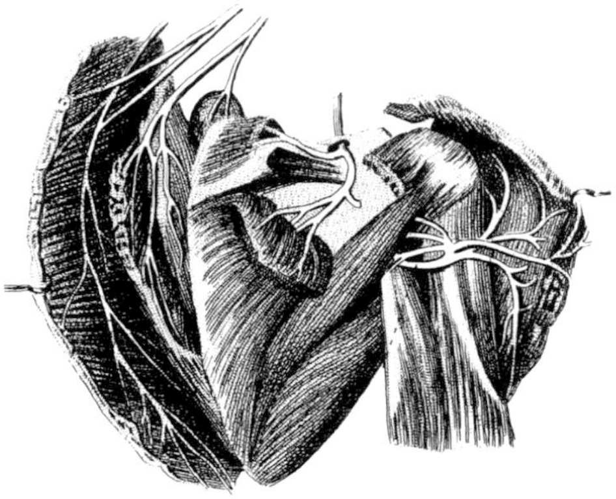
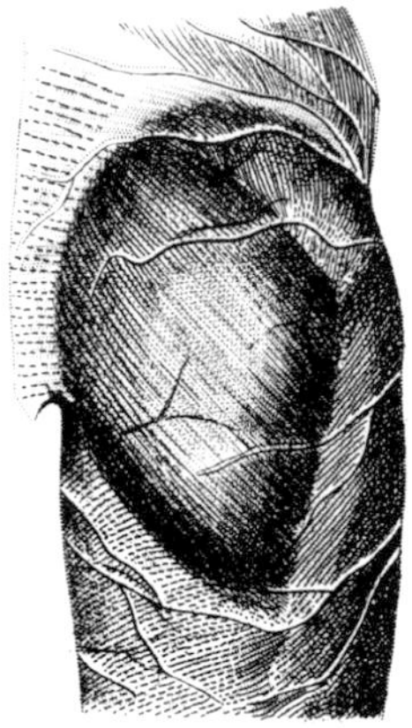
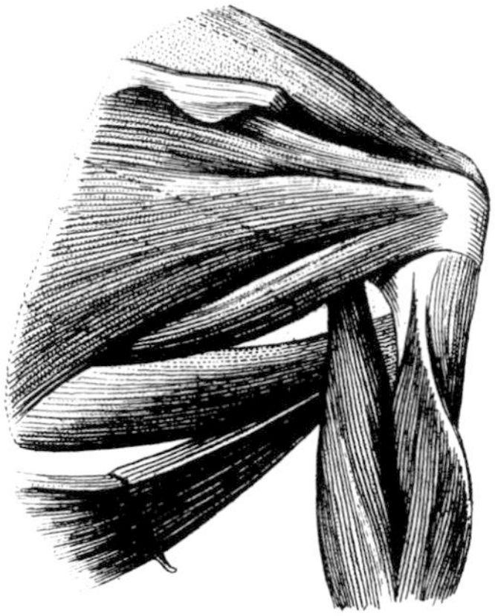
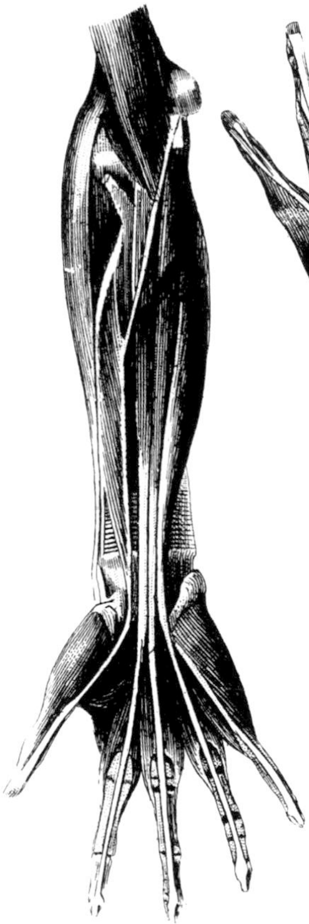
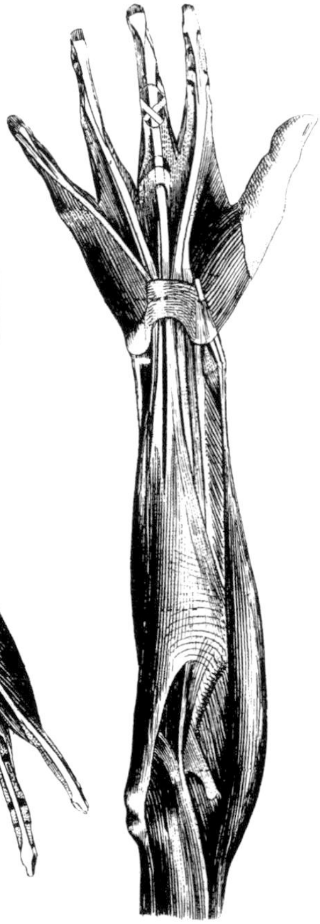
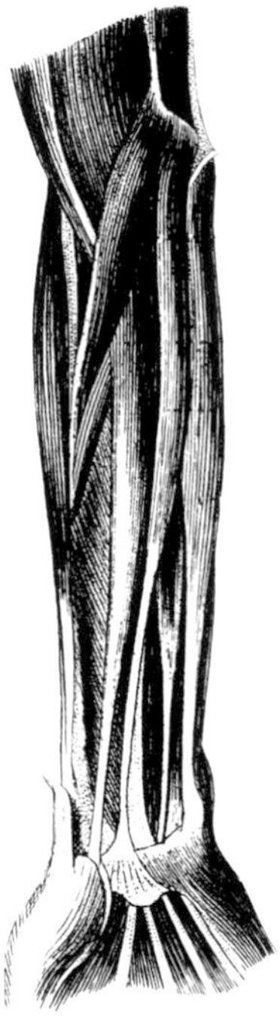
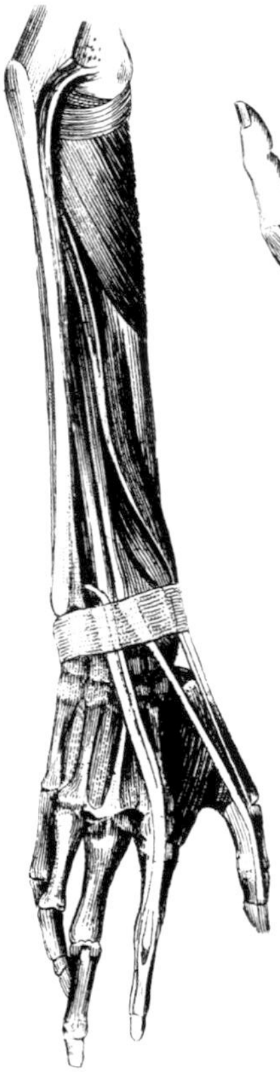
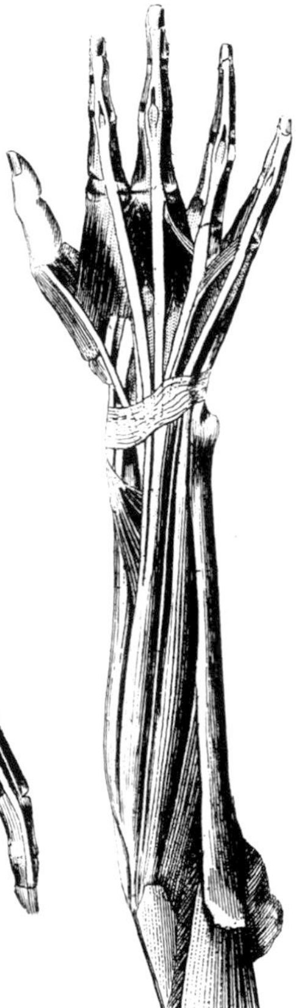

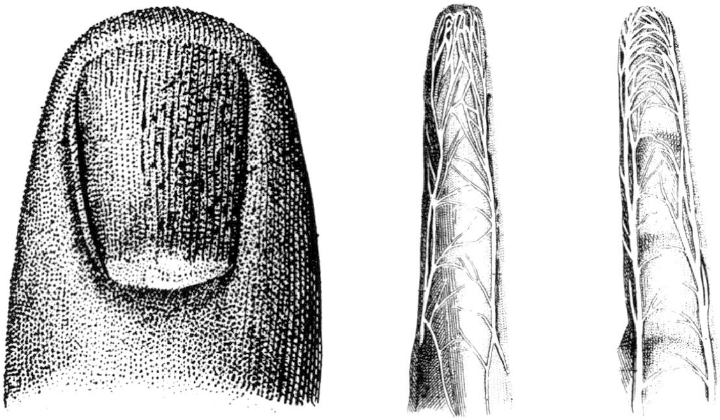

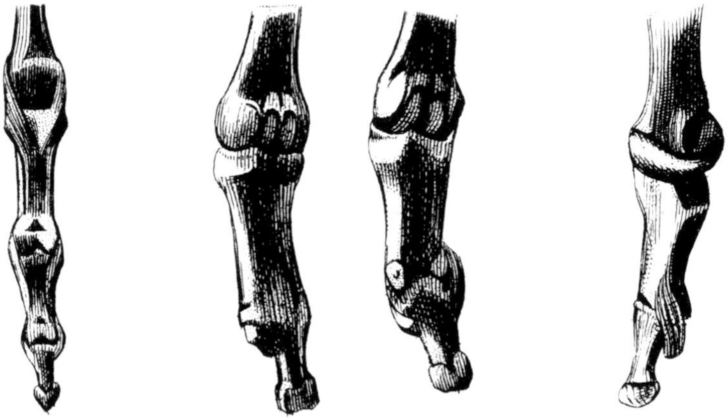

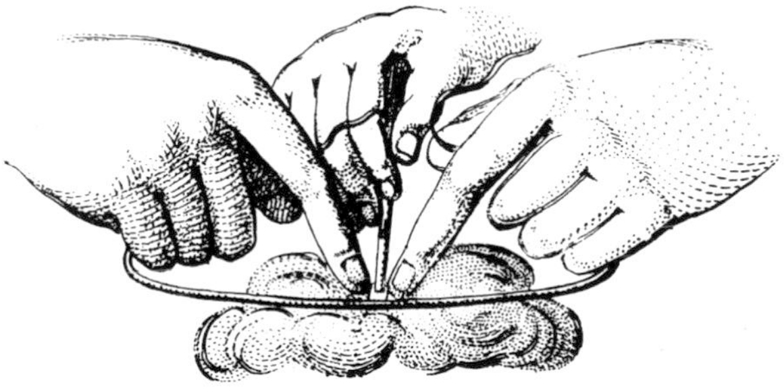

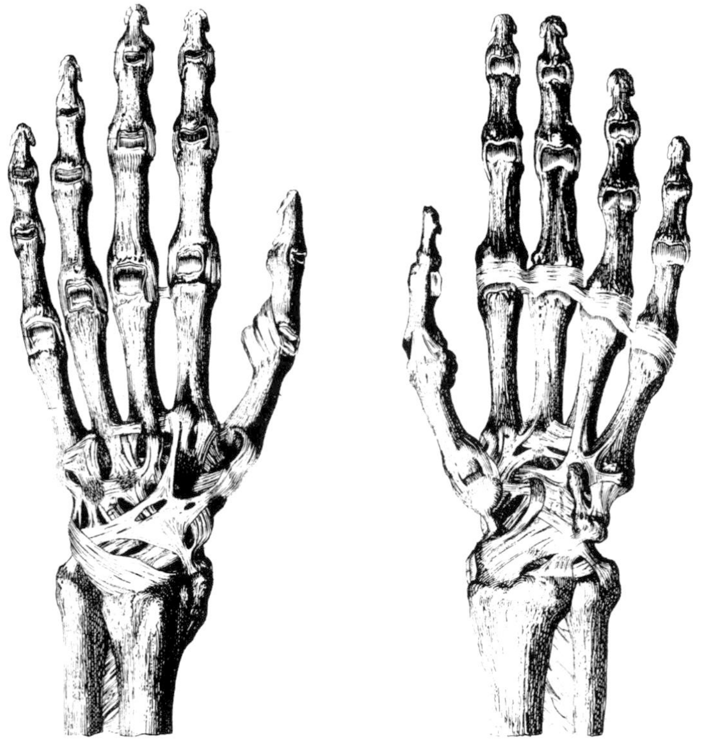

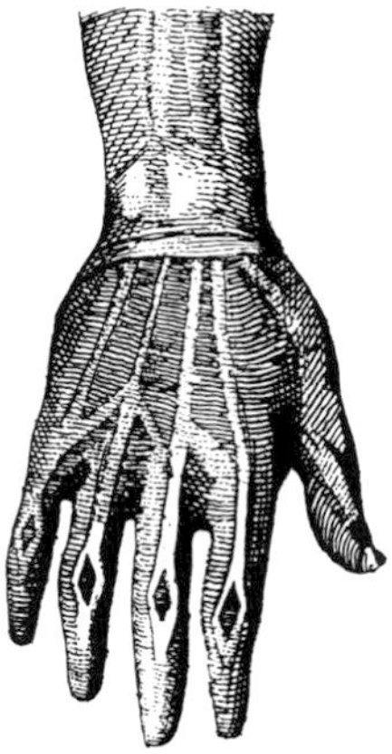
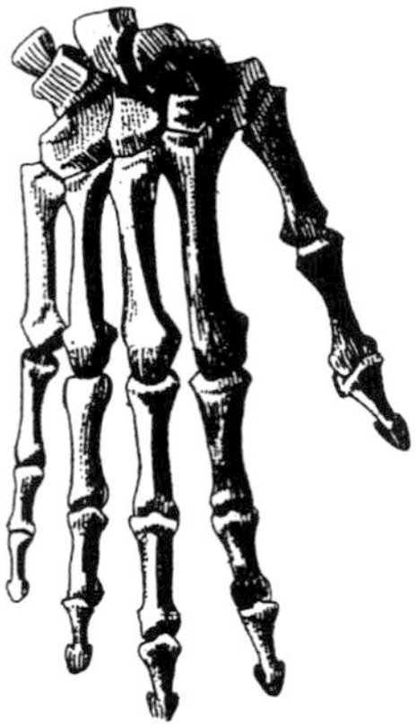
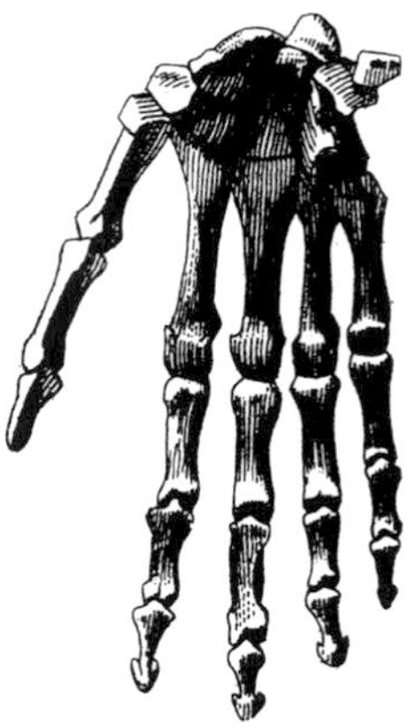
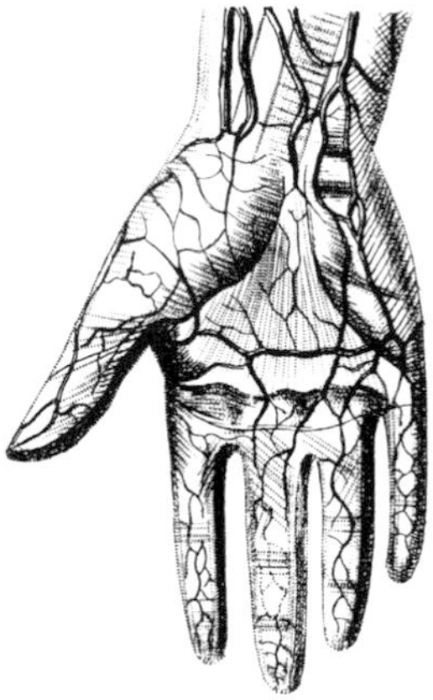
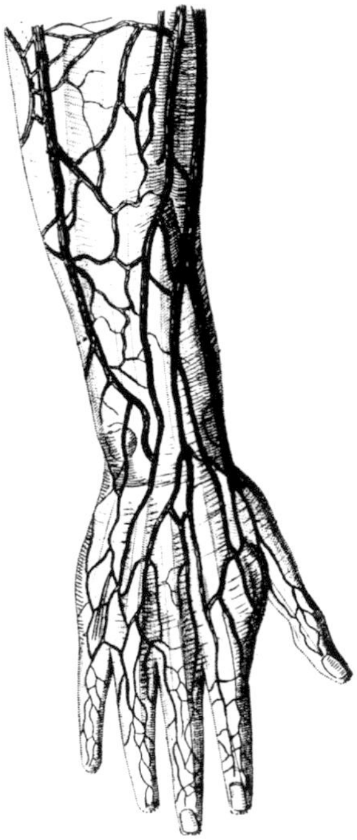
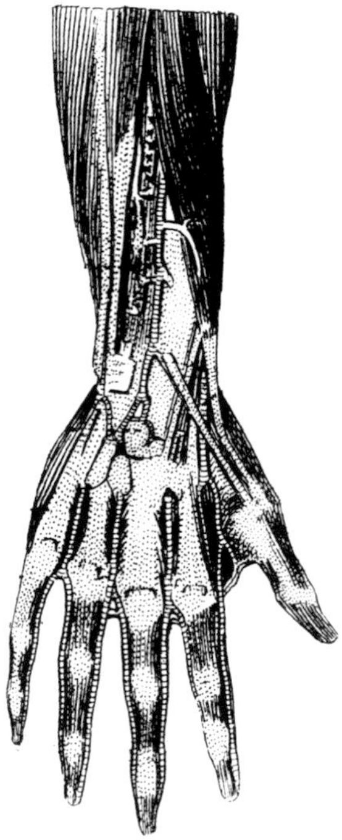
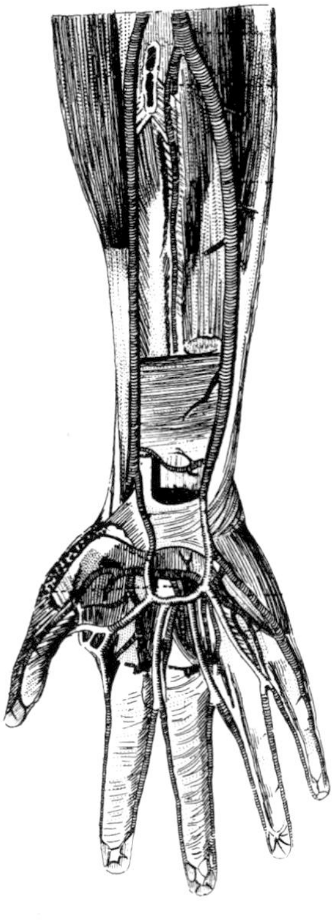

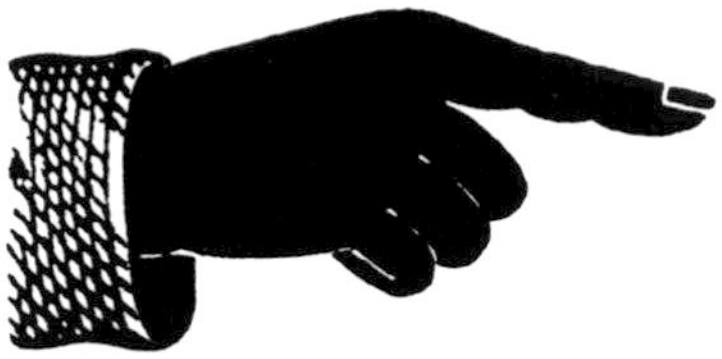
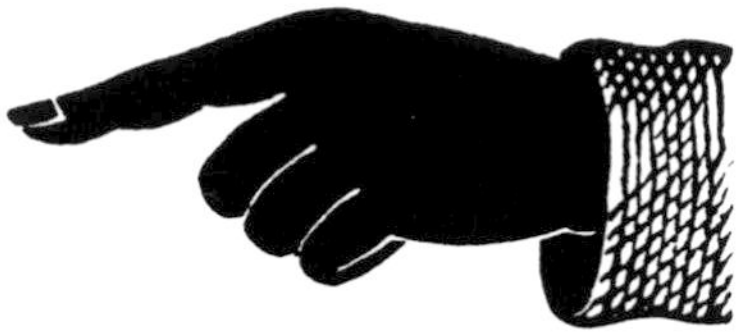
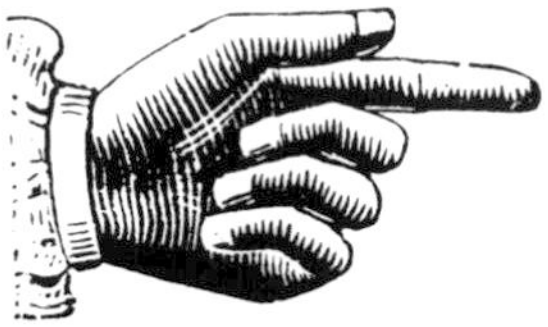
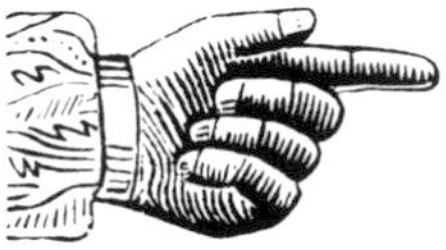
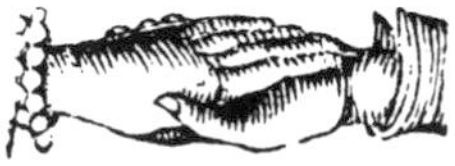
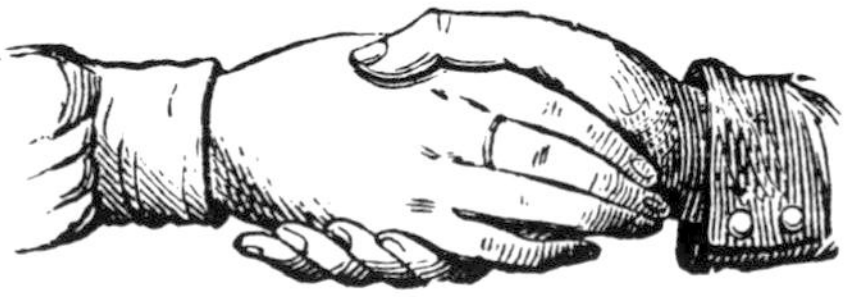
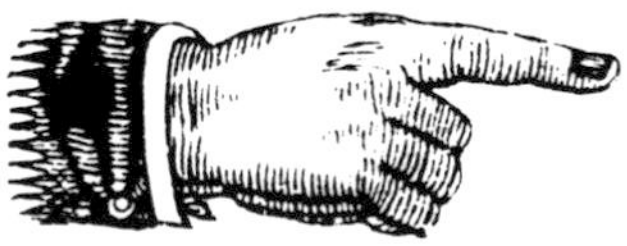
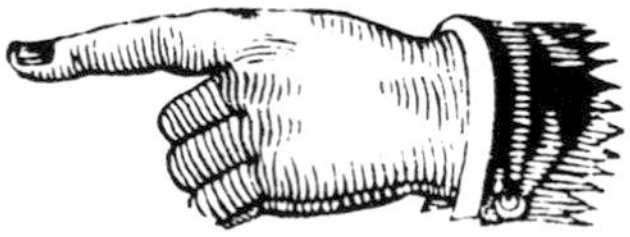
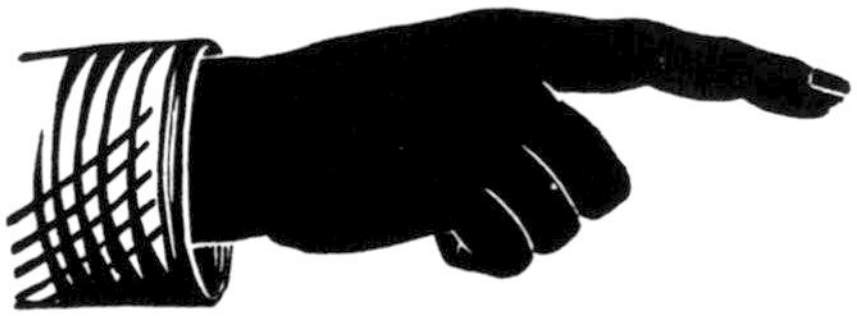

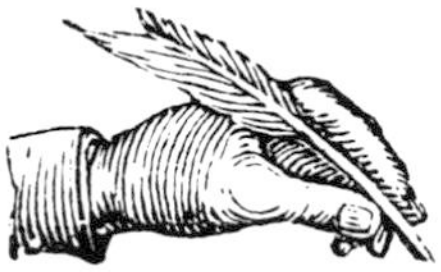
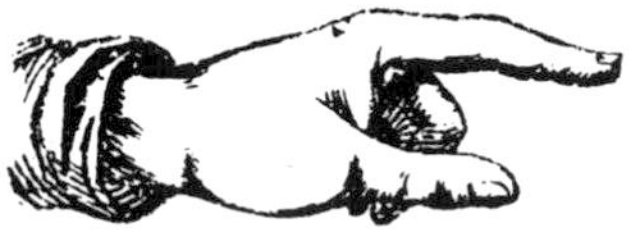
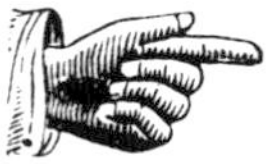
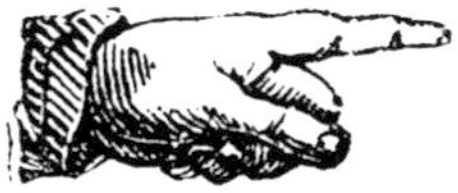
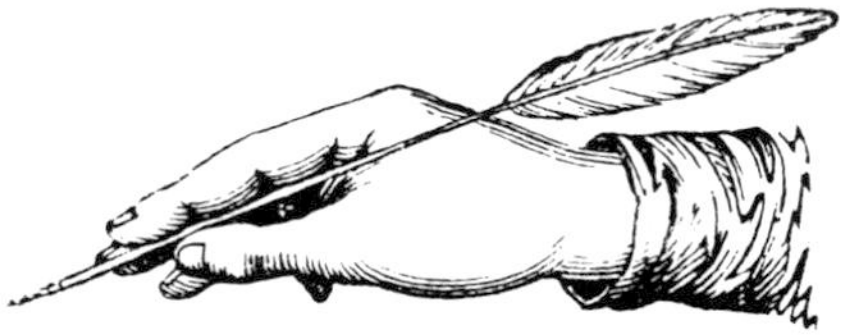
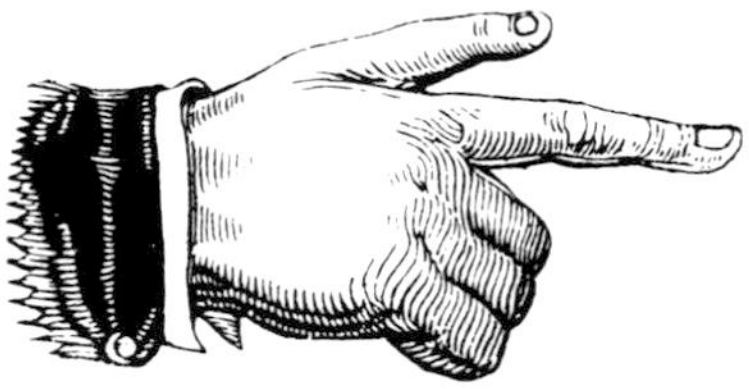
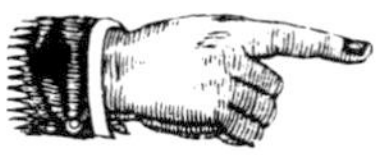
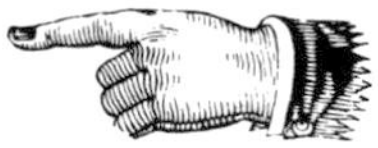
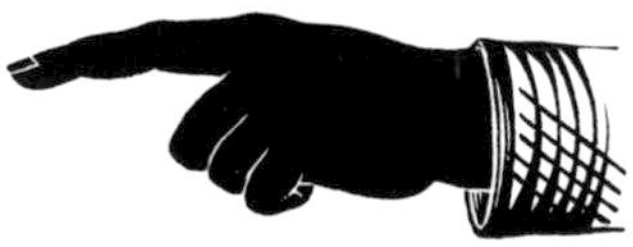
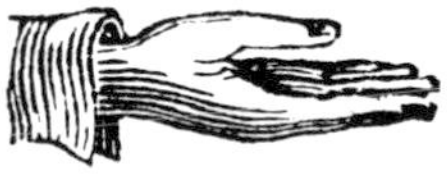

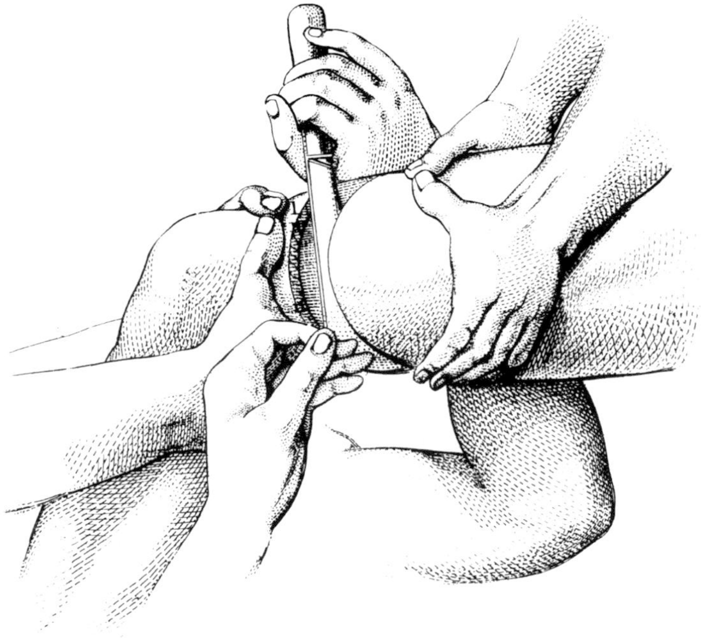

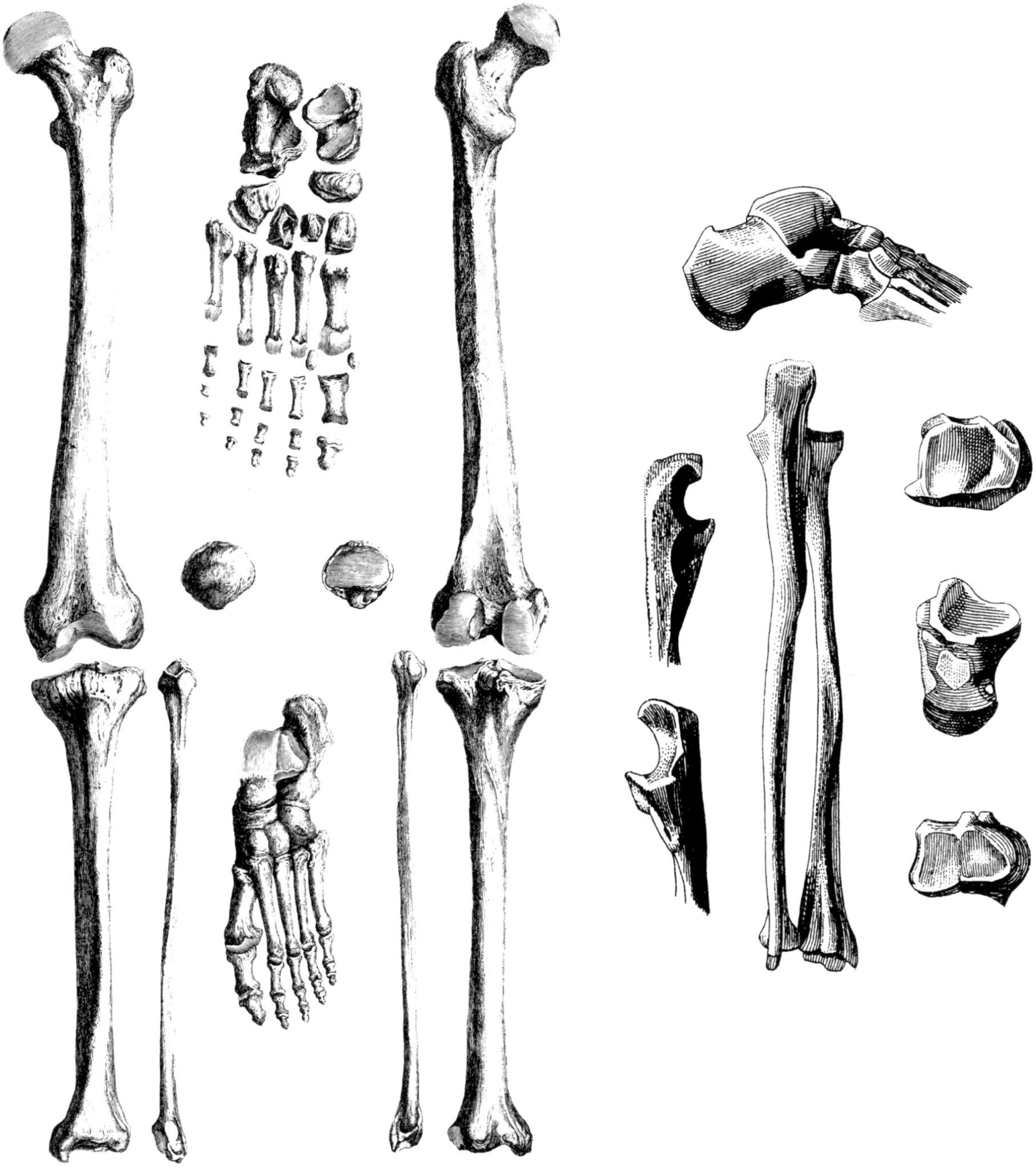

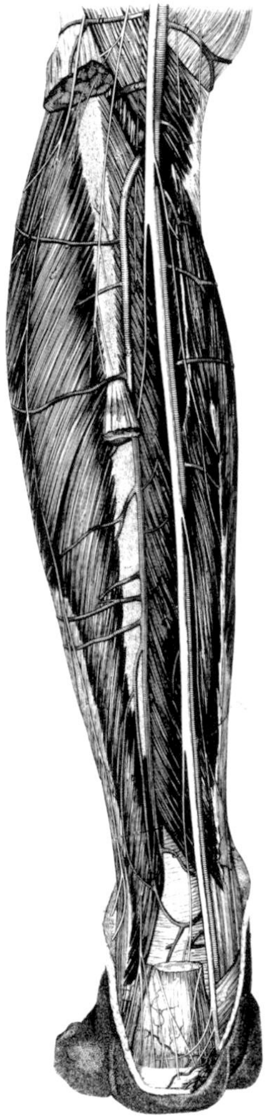
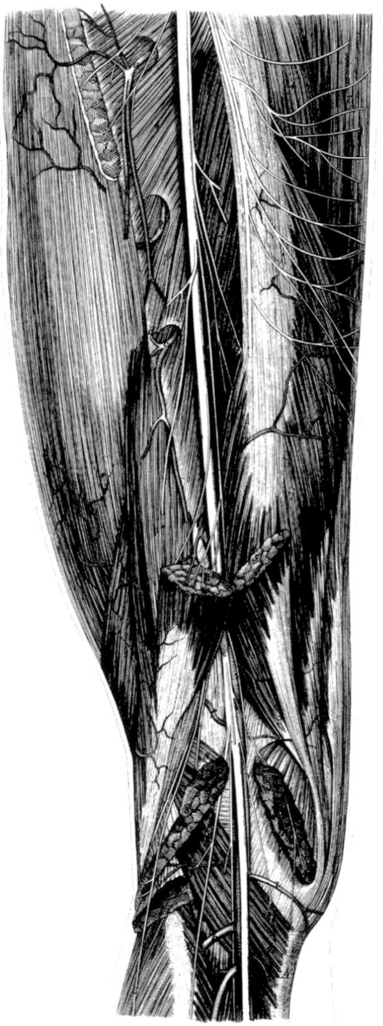
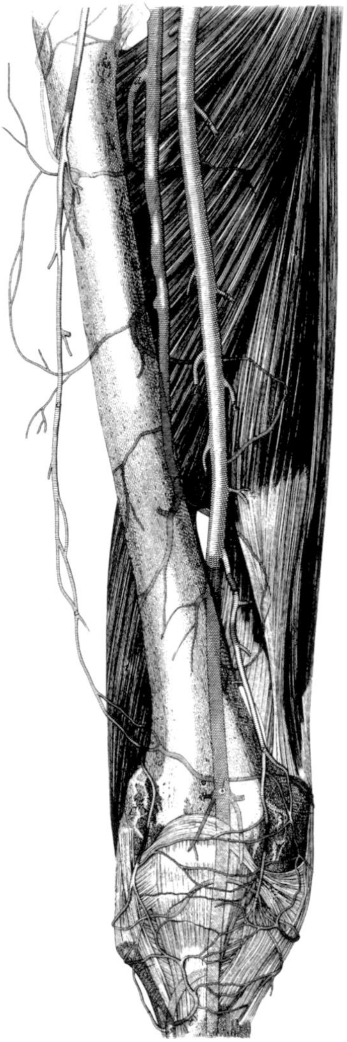
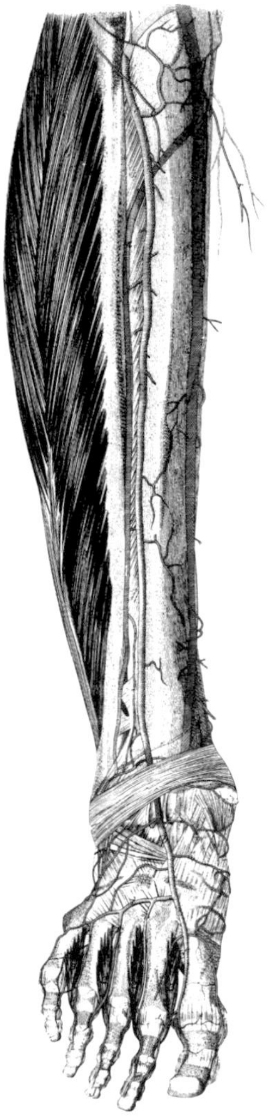

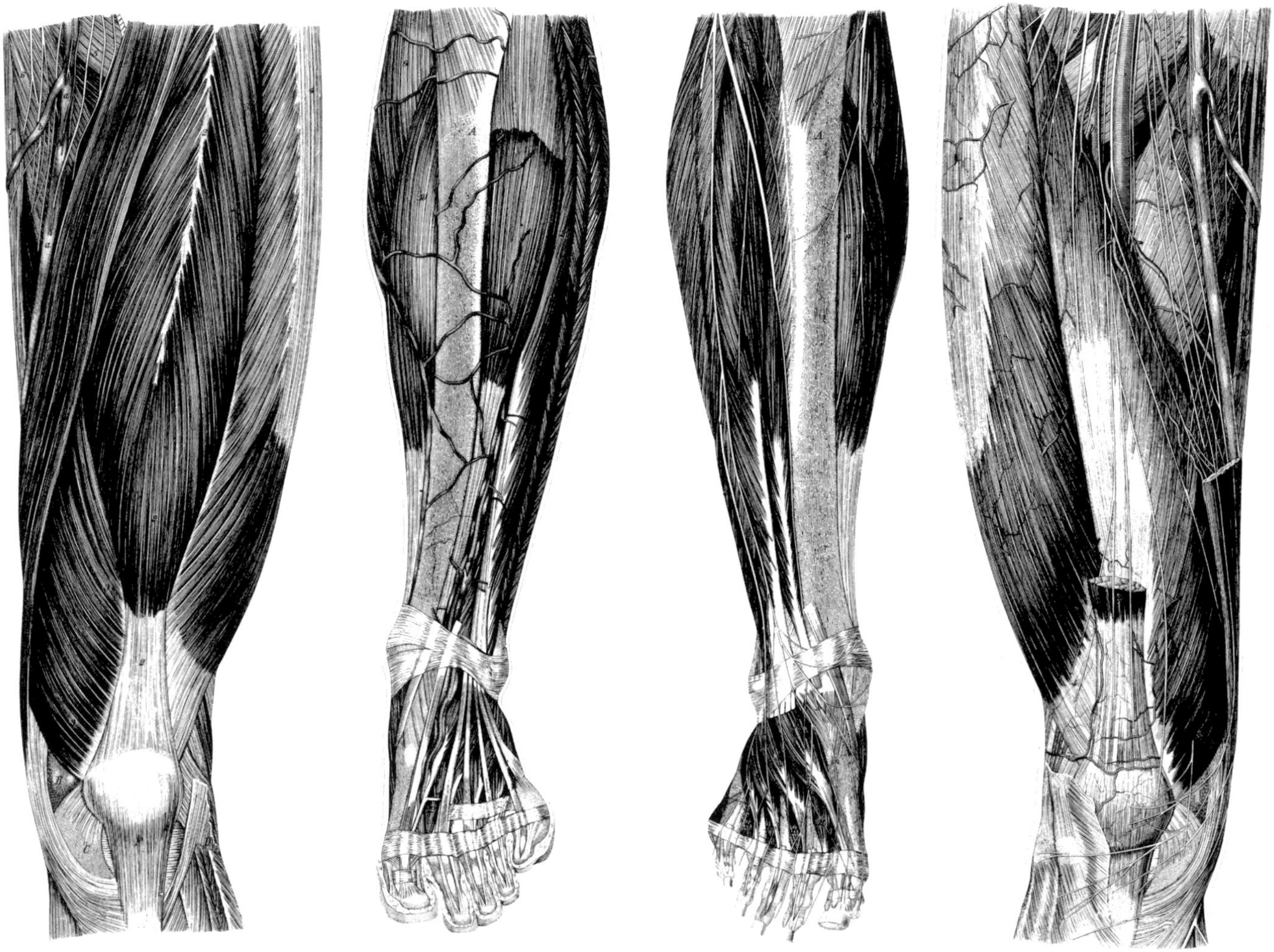

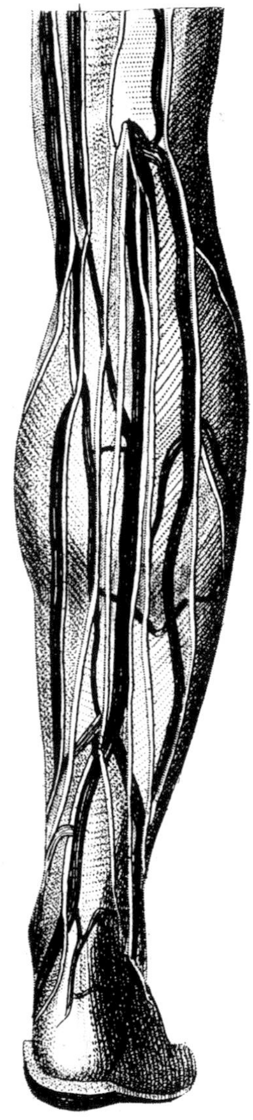
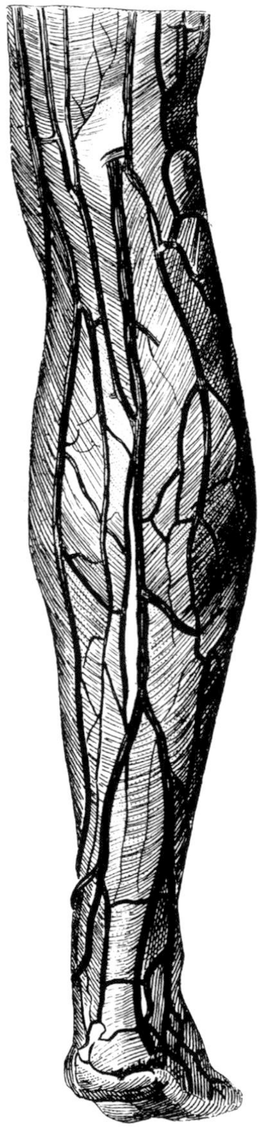
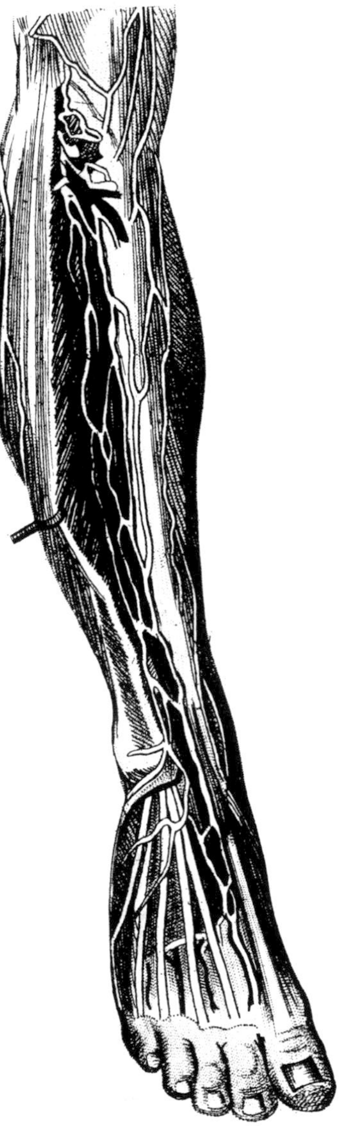

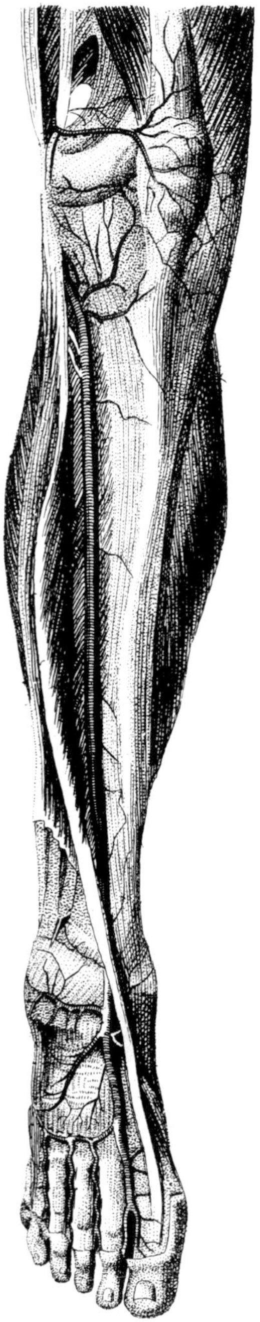

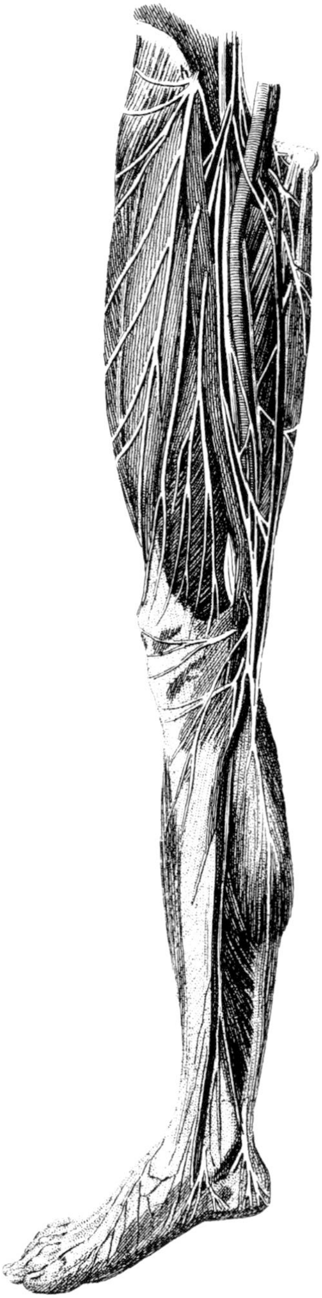

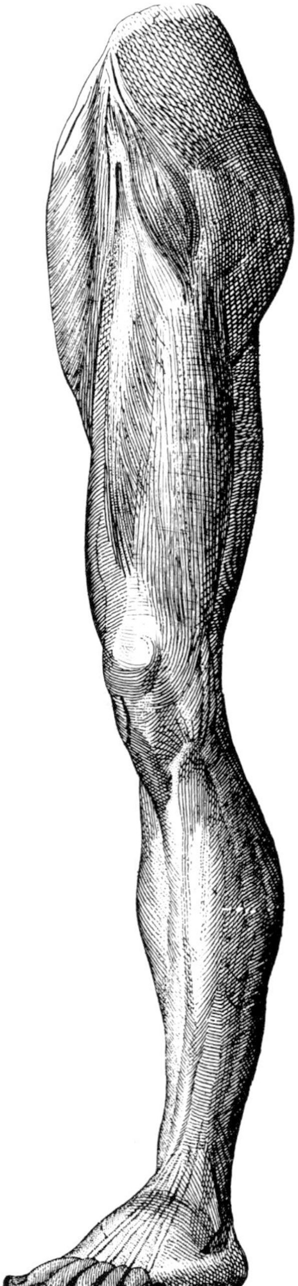

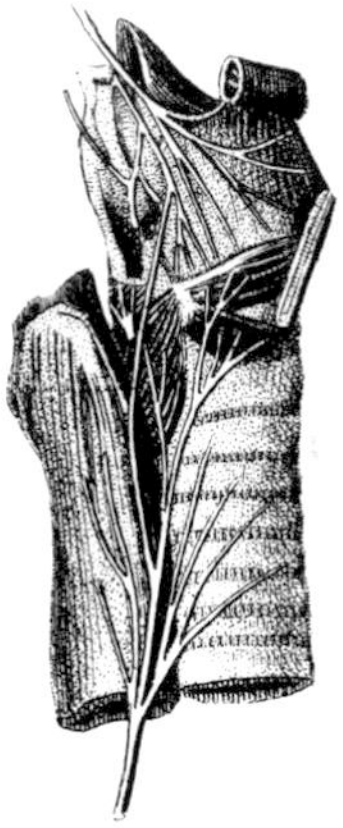
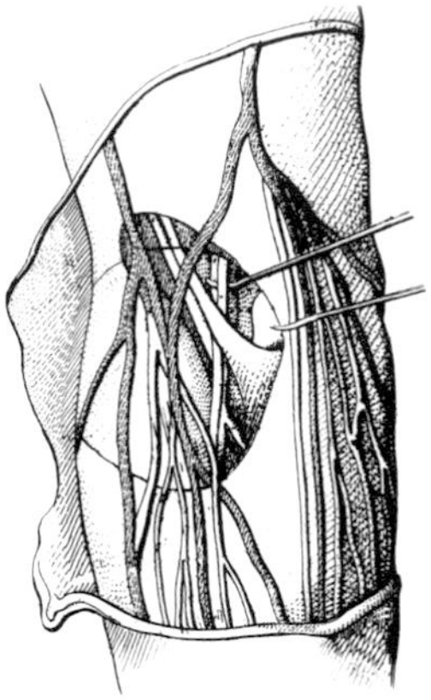
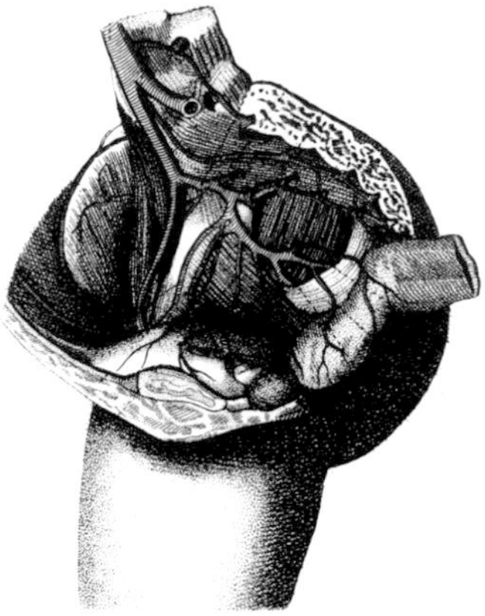
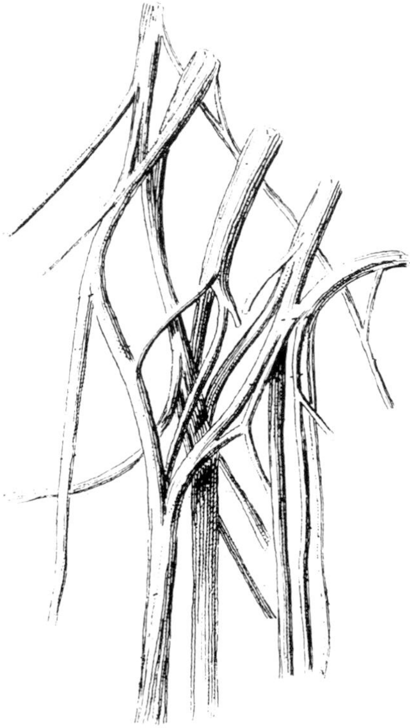
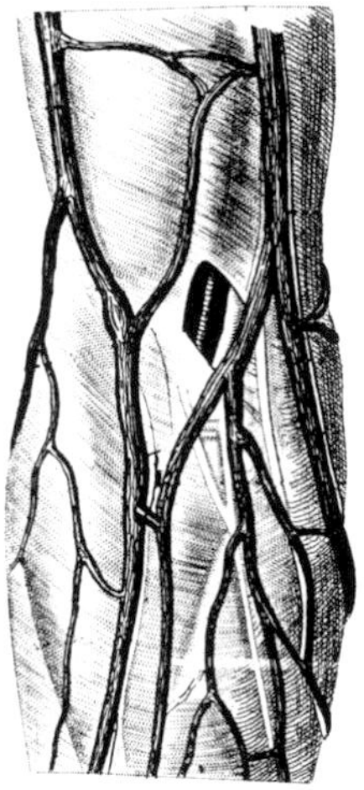
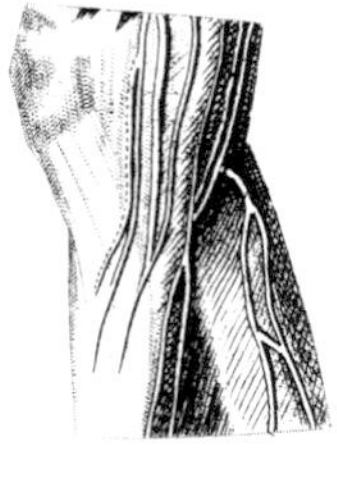
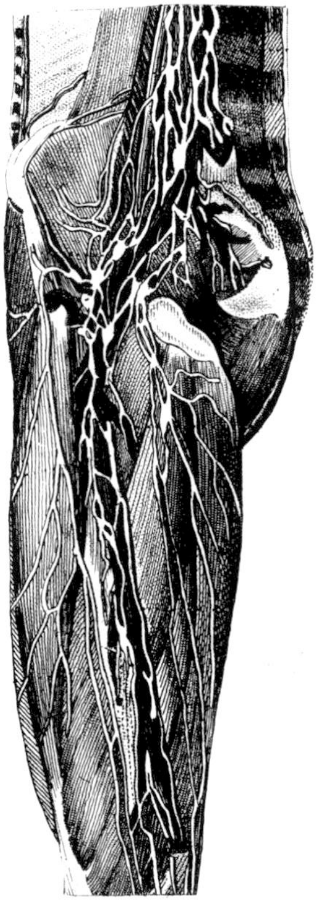

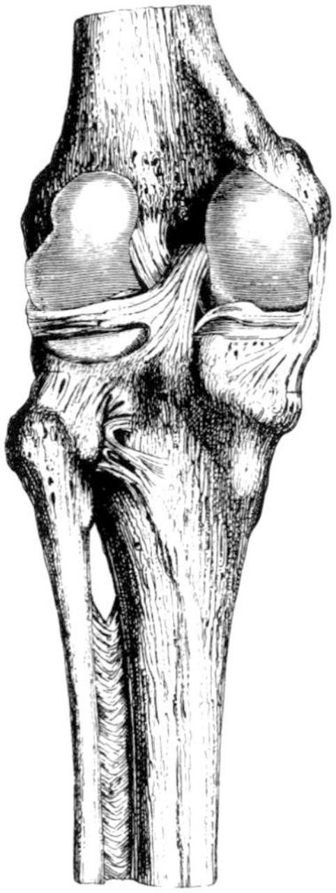

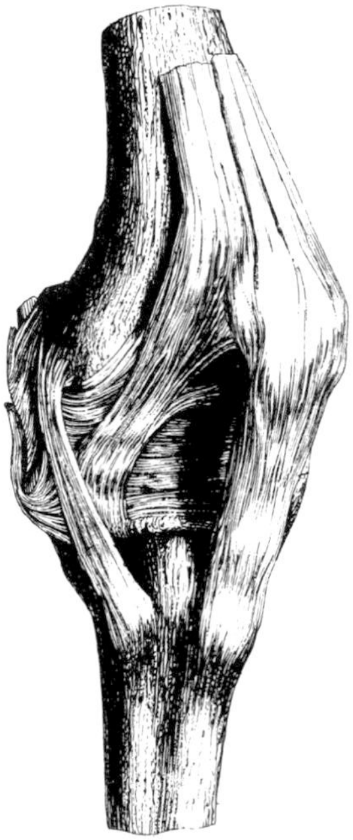

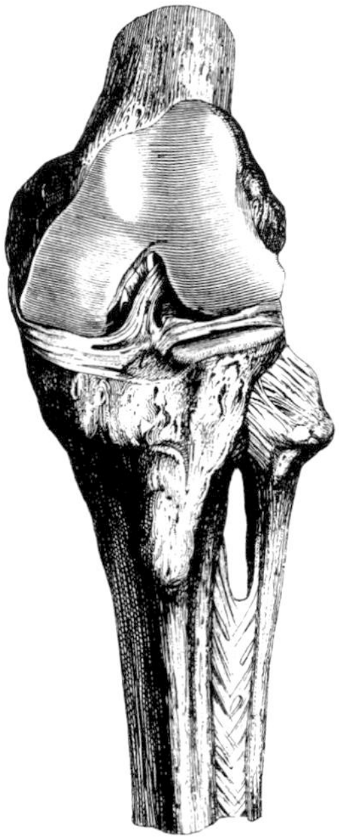

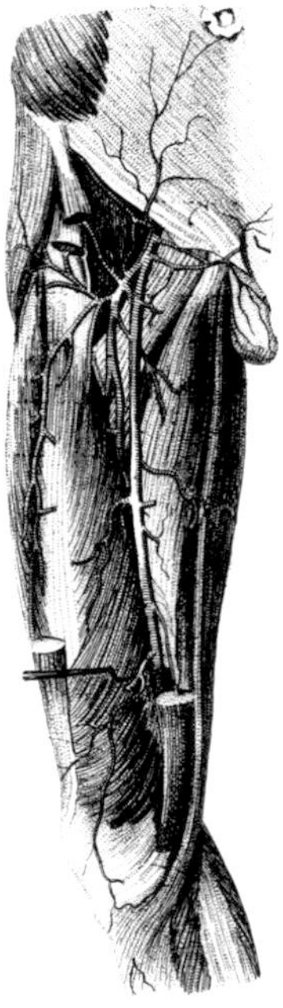

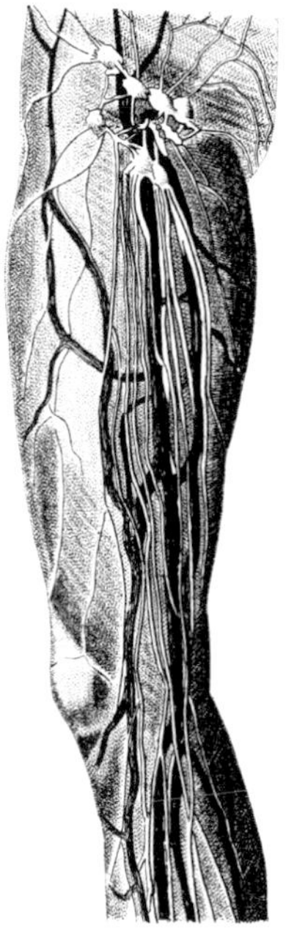

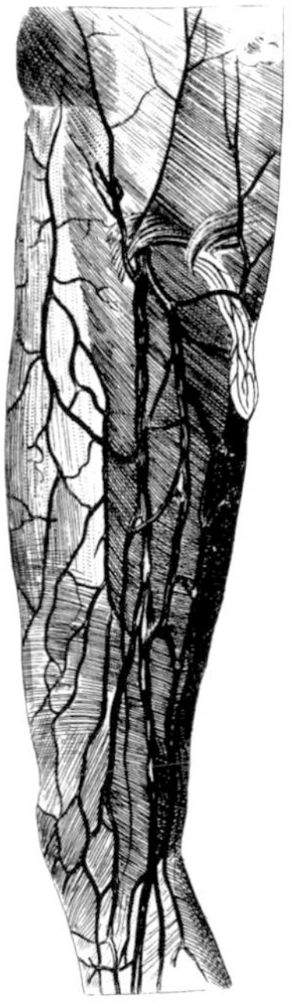

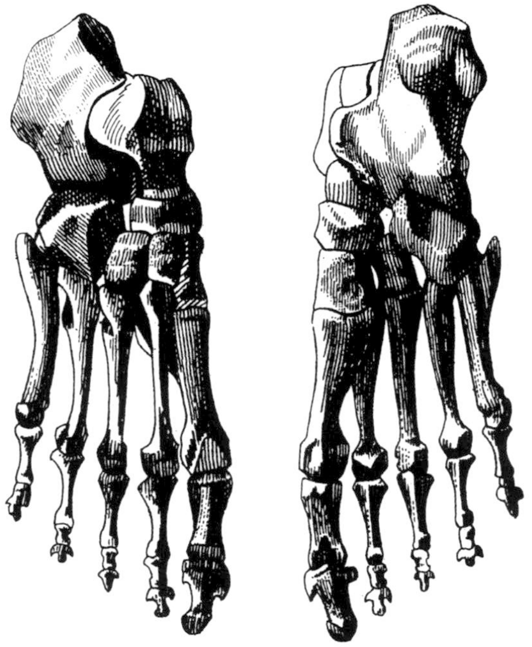

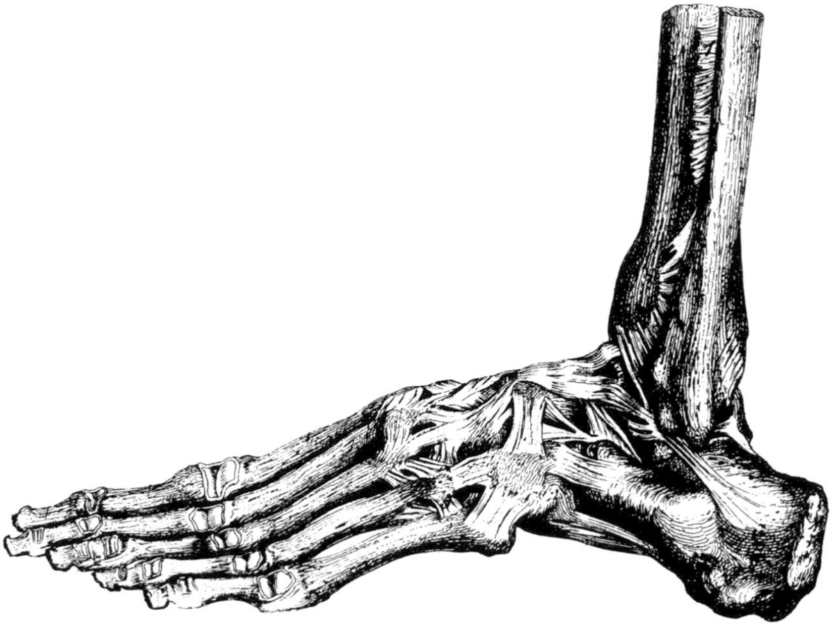

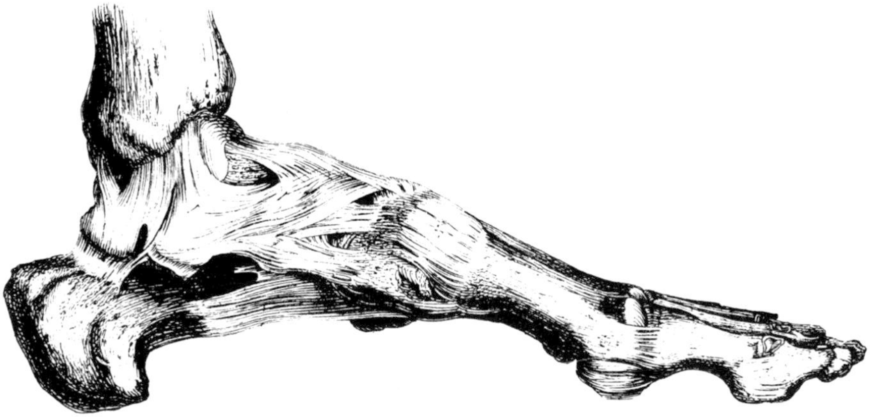

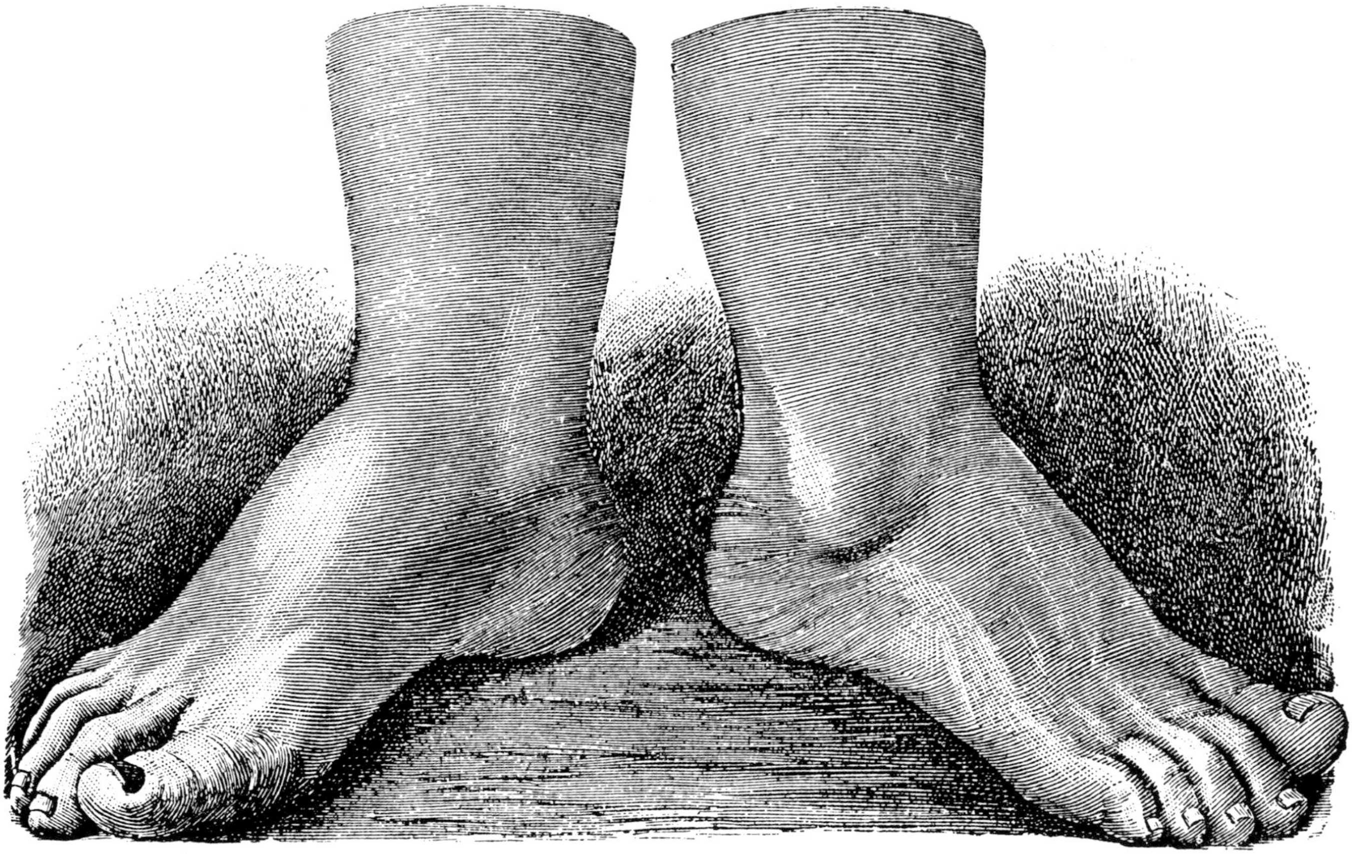

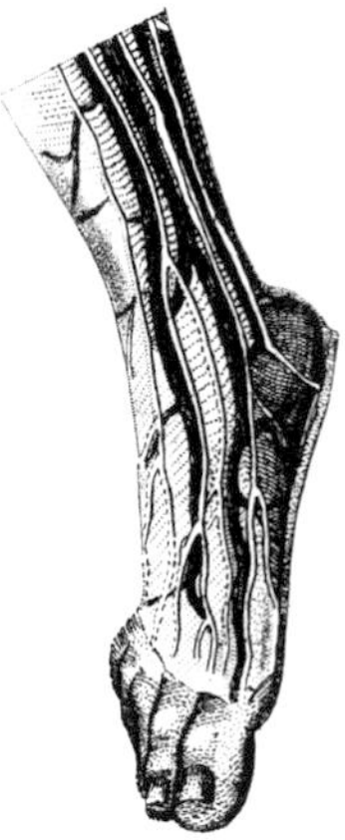

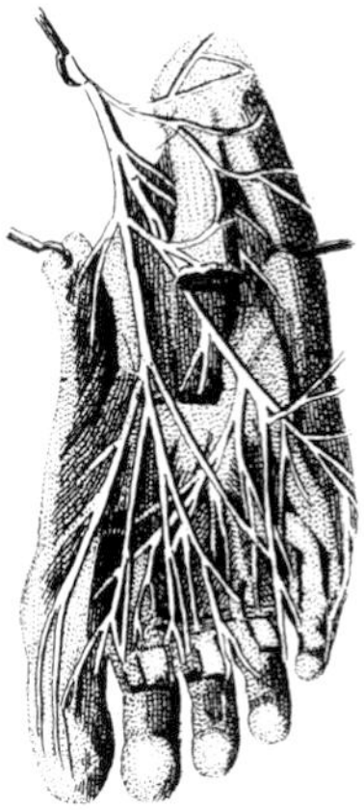

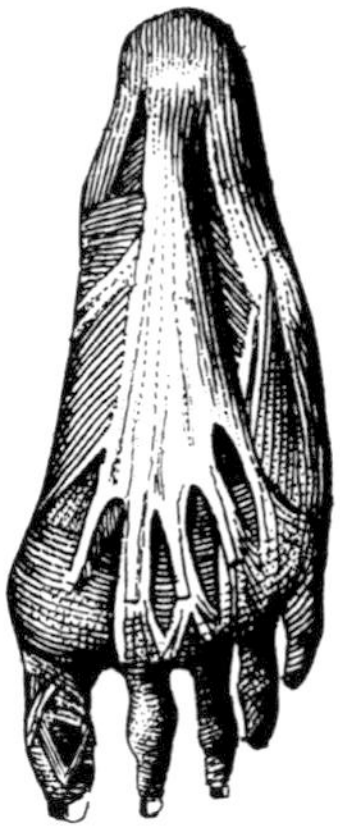

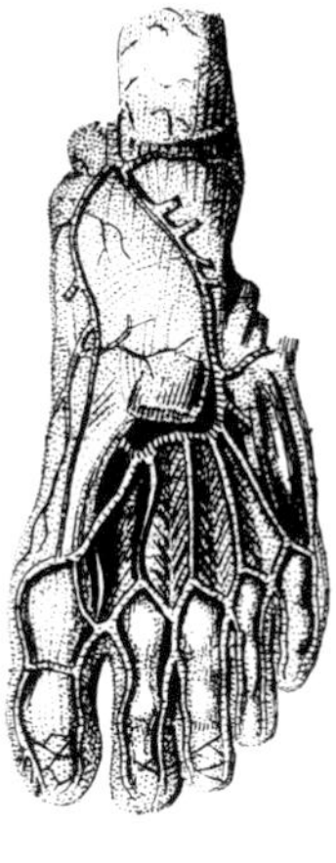

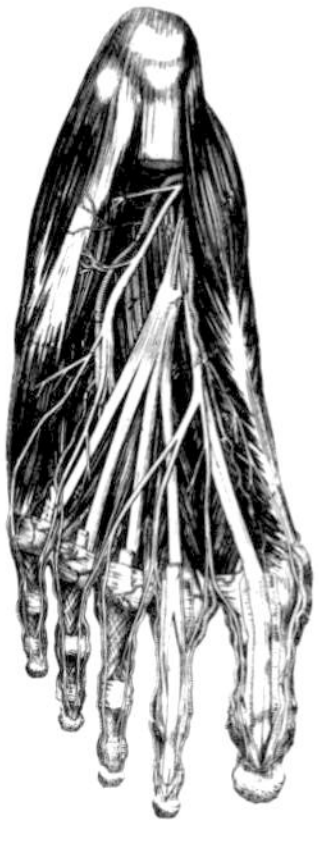

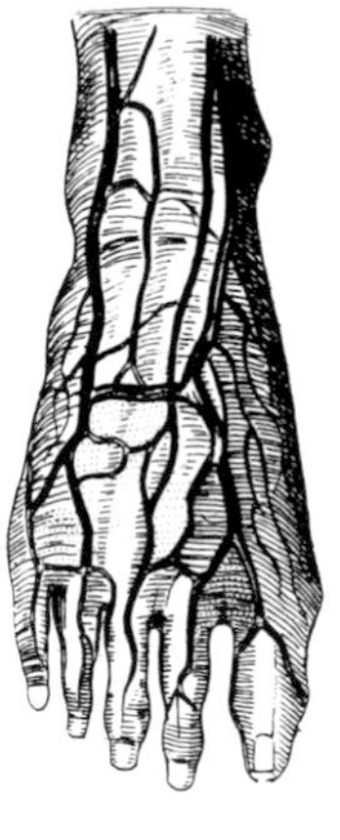

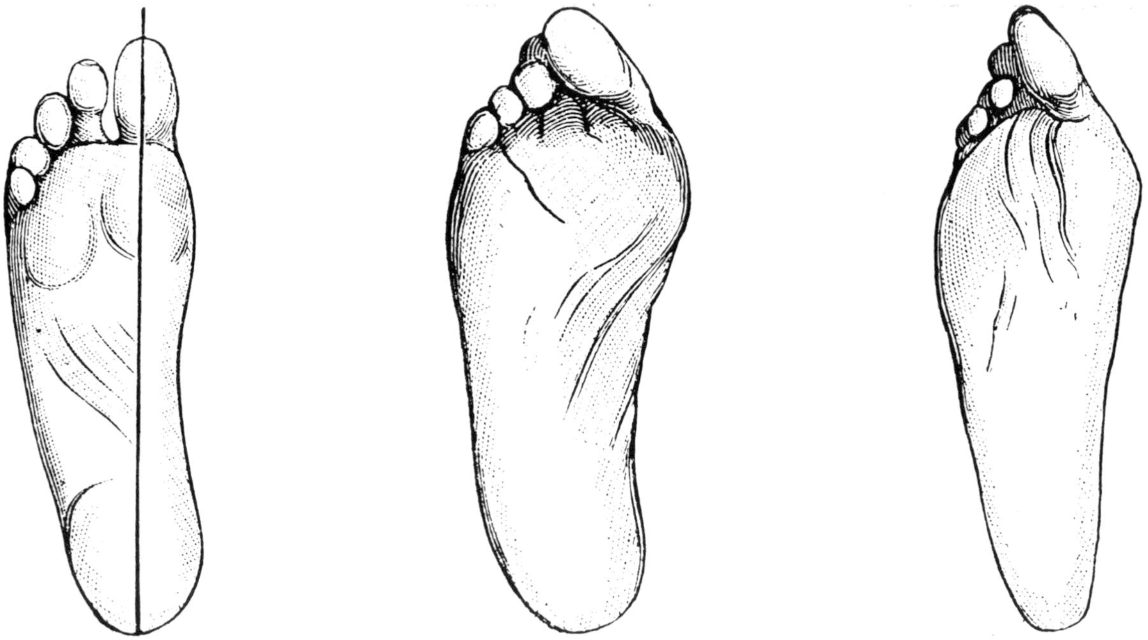

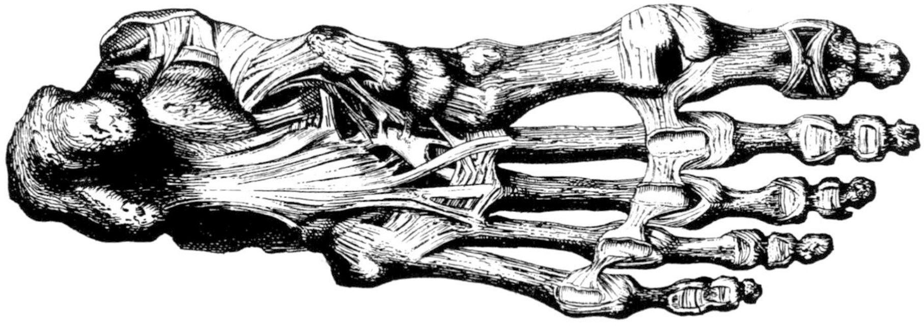